THE FOOD LOVERS'
LOW-FAT
COOKBOOK

Pear, Arugula, and Pecorino Salad, page 65

THE FOOD LOVERS' LOW-FAT COOKBOOK

Food & Wine BOOKS

American Express Publishing Corporation
New York

FOOD & WINE MAGAZINE
Editor in Chief: Dana Cowin
Food Editor: Tina Ujlaki

FOOD & WINE BOOKS
Editor in Chief: Judith Hill
Assistant Editors: Susan Lantzius and Laura Byrne Russell
Managing Editor: Terri Mauro
Copy Editor: Barbara A. Mateer
Wine Editor: Marguerite Thomas
Art Director: Nina Scerbo
Art Assistant: Leslie Andersen
Production Manager: Yvette Williams-Braxton

Vice President, Books and Information Services: John Stoops
Marketing Director: Mary V. Cooney
Marketing/Promotion Manager: Roni Stein
Operations Manager: Doreen Camardi
Business Manager: Joanne Ragazzo

Recipes Pictured on Cover: (Front) Asparagus and Pepper Salad with Ginger Dressing, page 79
(Back) *Top*: Calypso-Bean Soup, page 57, and Onion Parmesan Flatbread, page 58;
Fava-Bean Succotash with Crisp Phyllo Rounds, page 27
Center: Spring Pea Soup with Scallops and Sorrel, page 51; Seafood Stew with Roasted-Pepper Sauce, page 145
Bottom: Broccoli Rabe with Orecchiette, page 93; Fruit Soup with Champagne, page 249

AMERICAN EXPRESS PUBLISHING CORPORATION
©1997 American Express Publishing Corporation

LIBRARY OF CONGRESS CATALOGING-IN-PUBLICATION DATA
The food lovers' low-fat cookbook
p.   cm.
Includes index.
ISBN 0-916103-37-4
1. Cookery.   2. Low-fat diet—Recipes.   I. Food & wine (New York, N.Y.)
TX714.F663 1997
641.5'638—dc21   97-12286
                                           CIP

Published by American Express Publishing Corporation
1120 Avenue of the Americas, New York, New York 10036
Manufactured in the United States of America

CONTENTS

Spring Pea Soup with Scallops and Sorrel, page 51

INTRODUCTION

Rubbery low-fat cheese and fake sour cream may satisfy some people, but such counterfeits always send us scurrying for the Häagen-Dazs. Real food—in slimmed-down preparations—is what we need. And so here, at last, is a sensible low-fat book for people who love to cook.

The principles we've always followed have made "Low-Fat Cooking" one of FOOD & WINE's most popular columns: Stick to the same ingredients that all fine cooks use. Don't shun high-fat ingredients, just use them in smaller amounts. And if a substitution must be made, find another natural ingredient (such as applesauce or pureed potato) that will do the job. The results come very close to the flavor and texture of full-fat dishes. If you think they taste too good to be true, check the bottom of the page; each recipe comes with a nutritional analysis that includes total fat, saturated fat, cholesterol, and calories.

We hope you'll love our **Wild-Mushroom Linguine**, page 94, **Sea Bass with Citrus Couscous**, page 123, and **Caramelized-Apple French Toast**, page 231, as much as we do. **Baked Tortilla Crisps**, page 15—with five skinny salsa dips to choose from—are as good a snack as fried chips, maybe better. And don't forget dessert. With low-fat treats as luscious as **Lemon Cloud Cake with Poppy Seeds**, page 285, **Fudgy Chocolate Brownies**, page 299, or **Mocha Mousse**, page 309, you can forget all about that Häagen-Dazs.

Dana Cowin
FOOD & WINE Magazine

Judith Hill
FOOD & WINE Books

Fruit Soup with Champagne, page 249

LOW-FAT FOOD AND WINE

Those who enjoy wine know how it enhances the flavor of food. That's particularly important with low-fat food, because wine can help compensate for the pleasurable elements that are lost when rich ingredients are reduced or removed. The right wine can supply just that extra bit of magic to make a good dish truly exceptional.

Low-fat recipes often do a little flavor enhancement of their own, adding hot spices or tart citrus or a touch of sweetness to round out a dish. That can cause trouble for an unsuspecting wine. The very elements that make the low-fat recipes in this book taste so good can cause problems when the wrong wine is served. Those spices may increase the effect of the tannin in a wine; acidic ingredients can cause low-acid wines to taste flat; and even a small amount of honey or other sweetener can make bone-dry wines seem sour. That's why we've provided wine recommendations throughout the book that take into account the ingredients involved and suggest a harmonious pairing: aromatic white wines or young, fruity reds with hot, spicy food; high-acid wines to stand up to tart ingredients; wines with a matching note of sweetness, such as riesling, gewürztraminer, or chenin blanc, for slightly sweetened dishes.

In the end, though, the only really important rule for serving wine with low-fat food—or any other kind of food, for that matter—is to drink what you like. It will give a spark to even the simplest meal.

MARGUERITE THOMAS

chapter *1*

HORS D'OEUVRES &
FIRST COURSES

Fava-Bean Succotash with Crisp Phyllo Rounds, page 27

VEGETABLE-CHIP MEDLEY

You can buy vegetable chips at many supermarkets and health-food stores, but the oil they're fried in takes them out of the low-fat category. Our chips cook in a microwave, in small batches. They can also be baked in a 250° oven for about forty-five minutes. Whichever cooking method you choose, allow yourself plenty of time to make them.

MAKES ABOUT 6 CUPS

1 small sweet potato, peeled and cut into $1/16$-inch slices

2 medium unpeeled red potatoes, cut into $1/16$-inch slices

3 large radishes, cut into $1/16$-inch slices

1 small butternut squash, narrow end only, peeled and cut into $1/16$-inch slices

1 large thick carrot, cut into $1/16$-inch slices

1 small boniato (batata), peeled and cut into $1/16$-inch slices (optional)

1 small yuca (cassava), peeled and cut into $1/16$-inch slices (optional)

Salt

1 ripe plantain, peeled and cut into $1/16$-inch slices

1. Bring a pot of salted water to a boil. Add the sweet-potato slices. Return to a boil and boil for 1 minute. Remove the slices with a slotted spoon, put them on paper towels, and pat dry. Repeat with the remaining vegetables except the plantain, one vegetable at a time; pat dry. Keep each vegetable separate.

2. Coat a large microwave-safe plate with vegetable-oil cooking spray. Put some sweet-potato slices, without overlapping, on the plate and season with salt. Microwave on high for 5 minutes. Toss the slices and cook until crisp, about 2 minutes longer. Spread the chips on a platter to cool and then transfer them to a bowl. Repeat with the remaining boiled vegetables. Spray the plate before cooking each batch.

3. Put the plantain slices on the sprayed plate. Microwave until the slices are beginning to brown, about 6 minutes. Let cool. If necessary, microwave 1 to 2 minutes longer, until crisp.

—GRACE PARISI

MAKE IT AHEAD

Store the chips in an airtight container for up to a week. Recrisp in a 250° oven.

PER 1-CUP SERVING: CALORIES 131 kcal   TOTAL FAT .41 gm   SATURATED FAT .1 gm
CARBOHYDRATE 32 gm   PROTEIN 2.4 gm   CHOLESTEROL 0 mg

GRITZ CHEESE CRACKERS

Perfect for cocktail-hour canapés or for snacking at any time of day, these delicious little crackers get their flavor from Parmesan and cayenne and their snappy crunch from an unlikely ingredient: plain old grits.

MAKES ABOUT 50 CRACKERS

½ cup instant grits

½ cup flour

½ teaspoon baking soda

¼ teaspoon salt

⅛ teaspoon cayenne

4 teaspoons cold unsalted butter, cut into ¼-inch pieces

¼ cup grated Parmesan cheese

⅓ cup 1.5-percent buttermilk

1. Heat the oven to 350°. In a large bowl, whisk together the grits, flour, baking soda, salt, and cayenne. Cut or rub in the butter until the mixture is the texture of coarse meal.

2. Stir in the Parmesan. Pour in the buttermilk and stir to make a stiff dough. Turn the dough out onto a lightly floured surface and gently knead until smooth. Wrap in plastic and let sit for 15 minutes.

3. Cut the dough in half. Put one half on a lightly floured surface and cover the remaining dough with plastic. Roll out the dough to ¹⁄₁₆ inch thick. Using a 2-inch round biscuit cutter, stamp out the crackers and put them ½ inch apart on nonstick baking sheets.

4. Bake the crackers until golden and crisp, about 12 minutes. Transfer to racks to cool. Repeat with the remaining dough.

—GRACE PARISI

MAKE IT AHEAD

You can make the crackers ahead and keep them in an airtight container for up to two weeks.

PER 5-CRACKER SERVING: CALORIES 82 kcal **TOTAL FAT** 2.4 gm **SATURATED FAT** 1.4 gm **CARBOHYDRATE** 12.2 gm **PROTEIN** 2.6 gm **CHOLESTEROL** 6.2 mg

BAKED TORTILLA CRISPS

Baked chips have two advantages over fried: They're nearly fat free, and they're easy to make. The crisps are great with any of our low-fat salsas, pages 16 to 21.

10 SERVINGS

10 6-inch low-fat flour or corn tortillas
    Salt

1. Heat the oven to 350°. Cut each tortilla into six wedges and arrange the wedges in a single layer on two nonstick baking sheets. Sprinkle generously with salt.

2. Bake the tortilla wedges until crisp and golden, about 12 minutes for flour and 18 minutes for corn. Halfway through, switch the positions of the pans in the oven.

PER SERVING: CALORIES 70 kcal TOTAL FAT .5 gm SATURATED FAT 0 gm
CARBOHYDRATE 18 gm PROTEIN 2 gm CHOLESTEROL 0 mg

SPICY TORTILLA STRIPS

Instead of munching on potato chips, try this sweet, salty, spicy-hot snack of tortillas flavored with apple jelly, soy sauce, lime juice, and Tabasco sauce.

4 SERVINGS

3 tablespoons apple jelly
1 tablespoon lime juice
1 tablespoon soy sauce
1 teaspoon Asian sesame oil
½ teaspoon Tabasco sauce
4 6-inch low-fat flour tortillas, cut into ¼-inch-thick strips

1. Heat the oven to 350°. Coat a nonstick baking sheet with vegetable-oil cooking spray.

2. In a small stainless-steel saucepan, melt the jelly with the lime juice, soy sauce, oil, and Tabasco sauce over low heat. In a large bowl, toss the mixture with the tortilla strips. Spread the tortilla strips on the prepared baking sheet in a single layer.

3. Bake the tortilla strips, stirring occasionally, until they are golden, about 20 minutes. Let the tortilla strips cool on the baking sheet.

—GRACE PARISI

PER SERVING: CALORIES 141 kcal TOTAL FAT 2 gm SATURATED FAT .2 gm
CARBOHYDRATE 30 gm PROTEIN 3.2 gm CHOLESTEROL 0 mg

Two-Tomato Salsa with Poblanos

Fresh and sun-dried tomatoes team up for an original take on a favorite Mexican salsa. Four poblano chiles and a jalapeño make this salsa (pictured at the top left on page 18) a hot one. Served with tortilla chips, it's a perfect balance for those margaritas.

MAKES ABOUT 2 CUPS

1	pound poblano chiles (about 4)
1	jalapeño pepper
2	tomatoes, halved crosswise
12	reconstituted dry-packed or oil-packed sun-dried tomatoes, drained and chopped
1½	tablespoons chopped flat-leaf parsley
2½	tablespoons chopped cilantro
1	clove garlic, minced
2½	tablespoons minced red onion
2	teaspoons lime juice
	Salt

1. Roast the poblanos and the jalapeño over a gas flame or grill or broil them, turning with tongs until charred all over, about 10 minutes. When they are cool enough to handle, pull off the skin. Remove the stems, seeds, and ribs. Chop the poblanos fine and mince the jalapeño.

2. Set a strainer over a medium glass or stainless-steel bowl. Squeeze the tomatoes over the strainer to release the seeds. Press down on the seeds to release all the juice and reserve the juice. Chop the tomatoes and add them to the tomato juice.

3. Add the roasted poblanos and jalapeño, the sun-dried tomatoes, the parsley, cilantro, garlic, onion, and lime juice. Season with salt. Let sit at room temperature for about 3 hours before serving.

—Bob Chambers

Make It Ahead

You can make the salsa in advance and keep it for up to a day in the refrigerator.

Using Dry-Packed Sun-Dried Tomatoes

To reconstitute dry-packed tomatoes, put them in a small bowl, cover them with boiling water, and let sit until soft, about fifteen minutes. Drain.

PER ¼-CUP SERVING: CALORIES 107 kcal **TOTAL FAT** 7.7 gm **SATURATED FAT** 1 gm **CARBOHYDRATE** 9.7 gm **PROTEIN** 2 gm **CHOLESTEROL** 0 mg

ROASTED-TOMATO SALSA

After the tomatoes are roasted with garlic, a jalapeño, and a red bell pepper, the charred vegetables are tossed into a food processor with lime juice and a smoky chipotle chile. The result? A chunky, spicy Southwestern salsa (pictured at the top right on page 18).

MAKES ABOUT 2 ¹/₂ CUPS

1 pound plum tomatoes (about 4)

1 red bell pepper

2 cloves garlic, unpeeled

1 jalapeño pepper

2 shallots, chopped

1 chipotle chile *en adobo*,* chopped

¹/₂ teaspoon dried oregano

1 teaspoon lime juice

¹/₂ teaspoon cumin seeds

¹/₃ cup tomato juice, or more if needed

Salt

*Available at Latin American markets and specialty-food stores

1. Heat the broiler. Broil the tomatoes, bell pepper, garlic, and jalapeño about 8 inches from the heat, turning with tongs until charred all over, about 10 minutes. When the vegetables are cool enough to handle, pull the skin off the bell pepper and jalapeño and remove the stems, seeds, and ribs. Peel the garlic. Leave the charred skin on the tomatoes.

2. Put the vegetables in a food processor. Add the shallots, chipotle, oregano, and lime juice. Pulse until chopped coarse. Transfer to a medium glass or stainless-steel bowl.

3. In a small frying pan, toast the cumin seeds over moderately high heat, shaking the pan frequently, until fragrant, about 2 minutes. In a spice grinder, grind the seeds to a powder. Stir the ground cumin into the salsa and add the ¹/₃ cup tomato juice, or more as needed for desired consistency. Season with salt. Refrigerate for at least 4 hours before serving.

—BOB CHAMBERS

MAKE IT AHEAD

You can make the salsa in advance. It will keep for up to four days in the refrigerator.

PER ¹/₄-CUP SERVING: CALORIES 21 kcal   TOTAL FAT .2 gm   SATURATED FAT 0 gm   CARBOHYDRATE 4.7 gm   PROTEIN .7 gm   CHOLESTEROL 0 mg

Pepper and Corn Salsa

Red, yellow, and green bell peppers jazz up a unique summertime salsa seasoned with cumin and fennel seeds that have been toasted and then ground. You can buy preground spices and omit the dry-roasting step, but the flavor will be less intense. If you do choose to grind your own, a mortar and pestle, spice grinder, or even a coffee grinder will do the job nicely. The salsa is pictured opposite in the center with Baked Tortilla Crisps, page 15. Also pictured clockwise from the top are Two-Tomato Salsa with Poblanos, page 16; Roasted-Tomato Salsa, page 17; Mango Peach Salsa, page 21; and Pineapple Carrot Salsa, page 20.

MAKES ABOUT 2 1/2 CUPS

2　large red bell peppers

2　large yellow bell peppers

1　medium green bell pepper

3　jalapeño peppers

1　cup fresh (cut from about 2 ears) or frozen corn kernels

½　teaspoon fennel seeds

½　teaspoon cumin seeds

1　tablespoon lemon juice

3　tablespoons shredded fresh basil leaves
　　Salt and fresh-ground black pepper

1. Roast the bell peppers and jalapeños over a gas flame or grill or broil them, turning with tongs until charred all over, about 10 minutes. When the peppers are cool enough to handle, pull off the skin. Remove the stems, seeds, and ribs. Chop the bell peppers and jalapeños in a food processor. Scrape them into a medium glass or stainless-steel bowl.

2. In a large pot of boiling, salted water, cook the fresh corn, if using, for 1 minute. If using frozen corn, cook for just 30 seconds. Drain and let cool. Add the corn to the bell peppers and jalapeños.

3. In a small frying pan, toast the fennel and cumin seeds over moderately high heat, shaking the pan frequently, until fragrant, about 2 minutes. In a spice grinder, grind the seeds to a powder. Add the powder to the salsa along with the lemon juice and basil. Season with salt and pepper and let sit at room temperature for about 2 hours before serving.

—Bob Chambers

Make It Ahead

You can make the salsa ahead and keep it in the refrigerator for up to one day.

PER ¼-CUP SERVING: CALORIES 30 kcal　TOTAL FAT .3 gm　SATURATED FAT 0 gm　CARBOHYDRATE 6.6 gm　PROTEIN 1 gm　CHOLESTEROL 0 mg

PINEAPPLE CARROT SALSA

Many salsas use oil to balance the tartness of lemon or lime juice, but this one (pictured at the bottom left on page 18) cleverly uses the sweetness of raisins. Diced pineapple and grated carrots also contribute to the sweet-tangy taste here.

MAKES ABOUT 2½ CUPS

- ¼ cup pine nuts
- ¼ cup golden raisins
- ½ small pineapple, peeled, cored, and cut into ¼-inch dice (about 2 cups)
- ½ cup grated carrots
- ½ small red onion, chopped fine
- 2 tablespoons minced red bell pepper
- 1½ teaspoons chopped fresh tarragon
- 1 tablespoon chopped cilantro
- ½ jalapeño pepper, seeds and ribs removed, minced
- 1 tablespoon lemon juice
- Salt

1. In a small frying pan, toast the pine nuts over moderately low heat, stirring frequently, until golden brown, about 5 minutes. Or toast them in a 350° oven for about 8 minutes.

2. Put the raisins in a small bowl and add boiling water to cover. Let sit until soft, about 5 minutes. Drain.

3. In a medium glass or stainless-steel bowl, combine the raisins, pineapple, carrots, onion, bell pepper, tarragon, cilantro, jalapeño, and lemon juice. Add salt to taste. Let sit at room temperature for about 1 hour. Just before serving, stir in the pine nuts.

—BOB CHAMBERS

SALSA PARTNERS

Any of the skinny salsas in this chapter can serve as a dip for Baked Tortilla Crisps, page 15, but they are equally useful as a topping for meat or fish, salads or Mexican dishes. Our suggestions for serving:

• PINEAPPLE CARROT SALSA can top pork, chicken, or veal.

• MANGO PEACH SALSA, page 21, goes with poultry, salads, salmon, or snapper.

• PEPPER AND CORN SALSA, page 19, complements chicken and pork.

• ROASTED-TOMATO SALSA, page 17, is good served with burritos or tossed with pasta.

• TWO-TOMATO SALSA WITH POBLANOS, page 16, spices up tacos and burritos.

PER ¼-CUP SERVING: CALORIES 42 kcal TOTAL FAT 1.6 gm SATURATED FAT .2 gm CARBOHYDRATE 7.1 gm PROTEIN 1 gm CHOLESTEROL 0 mg

MANGO PEACH SALSA

Summer, when mangoes and peaches are at their best, is the perfect time for this zesty serrano-spiked fruit salsa (pictured at the bottom right on page 18).

MAKES ABOUT 2 1/2 CUPS

1	large mango, peeled and cut into 1/4-inch dice
1	large peach, peeled and cut into 1/4-inch dice
1/2	small red onion, chopped
2	plum tomatoes, seeded and diced
1/2	serrano chile, seeds and ribs removed, minced
1/4	teaspoon grated orange zest
2	tablespoons orange juice
1 1/2	teaspoons lime juice
1	tablespoon minced cilantro
2 1/4	teaspoons poppy seeds
	Pinch sugar (optional)
	Salt and fresh-ground black pepper

In a medium glass or stainless-steel bowl, combine the mango, peach, onion, tomatoes, serrano, orange zest, orange juice, lime juice, cilantro, poppy seeds, and the sugar, if using. Add salt and pepper to taste.

—BOB CHAMBERS

PER 1/4-CUP SERVING: CALORIES 37 kcal **TOTAL FAT** .4 gm **SATURATED FAT** .1 gm **CARBOHYDRATE** 8.7 gm **PROTEIN** .6 gm **CHOLESTEROL** 0 mg

Black-Bean and Chile Dip

Though bean dip is a natural accompaniment for the Baked Tortilla Crisps on page 15, this chile-packed version is also a great centerpiece for a tray of cool, crisp raw vegetables. Try it with bell peppers, celery, carrots, or jicama.

MAKES ABOUT 2½ CUPS

- 2 dried ancho chiles, broken into 2-inch pieces
- 3⅓ cups drained and rinsed canned black beans (from two 15-ounce cans)
- 2 cloves garlic
- 1 large jalapeño pepper, seeds and ribs removed, minced
- 3 tablespoons lime juice
- ¾ teaspoon ground cumin
- 1 teaspoon Worcestershire sauce
- 3 tablespoons chopped cilantro
- 2 scallions, white parts minced, tops sliced thin

1. Put the ancho chiles in a small bowl and pour enough boiling water over them to cover. Let soak until softened, about 20 minutes. Remove the chiles, reserving the soaking liquid. Stem and seed the chiles.

2. Put the chiles in a food processor. Add 2 cups of the beans, the garlic, jalapeño, lime juice, cumin, Worcestershire sauce, and 2 tablespoons of the reserved soaking liquid; puree. Put the puree in a medium bowl and stir in the remaining 1⅓ cups beans, the cilantro, and the minced scallions. Transfer to a serving bowl and sprinkle with the scallion tops.

—GRACE PARISI

MAKE IT AHEAD

You can make the dip in advance and keep it in the refrigerator for up to two days. Let sit at room temperature for about half an hour before serving.

PER ¼-CUP SERVING: CALORIES 73 kcal   TOTAL FAT 1 gm   SATURATED FAT .1 gm
CARBOHYDRATE 12 gm   PROTEIN 4.5 gm   CHOLESTEROL 0 mg

SMOKED-SALMON DIP WITH CRUDITÉS

Those two staples of the low-fat diet—cottage cheese and nonfat yogurt—are transformed into an elegant dip when they're pureed with smoked salmon and served with snow peas, fennel, and celery sticks.

8 SERVINGS

 5 ounces smoked salmon

⅔ cup 1-percent cottage cheese

¼ cup plain nonfat yogurt

 2 tablespoons lemon juice

 1 teaspoon Dijon mustard

    Fresh-ground black pepper

½ pound snow peas or sugar snap peas

 1 large fennel bulb, cored and cut into sticks

 4 ribs celery, cut into sticks

MAKE IT AHEAD

You can make the dip ahead and keep it in the refrigerator for up to two days.

---

1. In a food processor, chop the salmon. Add the cottage cheese, yogurt, lemon juice, and mustard. Puree, scraping the side of the bowl occasionally. Season with pepper. Transfer the dip to a bowl, cover, and refrigerate for at least 1 hour.

2. Bring a medium saucepan of salted water to a boil and add the snow peas. Return just to a boil and drain. Rinse with cold water and drain thoroughly.

3. Stir the dip and serve with the snow peas, fennel, and celery.

—MARTHA ROSE SHULMAN

PER SERVING: CALORIES 148 kcal   TOTAL FAT 2 gm   SATURATED FAT .6 gm   CARBOHYDRATE 16 gm   PROTEIN 16 gm   CHOLESTEROL 10 mg

EGGPLANT CAVIAR

Roasting eggplant makes for full flavor with minimal fat. The bread served with this dip is toasted au naturel to a crisp golden brown.

4 SERVINGS

- 1 large eggplant (about 2 pounds), halved lengthwise
- 1 tablespoon olive oil
- 1 small French baguette (about 6 ounces), sliced ¼ inch thick
- 1 red bell pepper, cut into ⅛-inch dice
- 1 small onion, minced
- 2 cloves garlic, minced
- 1 large tomato, peeled, seeded, and cut into ⅛-inch dice
- 3 tablespoons lemon juice
  Salt and fresh-ground black pepper
- 2 tablespoons minced fresh chives or scallion tops
- 1 tablespoon minced fresh basil

1. Heat the oven to 350°. Brush the cut side of the eggplant with 1 teaspoon of the oil. Put the eggplant, cut-side down, on a baking sheet and roast until tender, about 1 hour. Let cool.

2. Meanwhile, put the bread slices on another baking sheet and spray lightly with vegetable-oil cooking spray. Bake until crisp and golden, about 8 minutes.

3. In a nonstick frying pan, heat 1 teaspoon of the oil over moderate heat. Add the bell pepper, onion, and garlic and cook, stirring occasionally, until the vegetables are soft but not browned, about 6 minutes. Transfer to a bowl and let cool.

4. Using a spoon, scrape the eggplant flesh from the skin. Chop the eggplant and add it to the onion-and-pepper mixture. Stir in the tomato, the lemon juice, and the remaining 1 teaspoon oil. Season with salt and pepper and refrigerate until slightly chilled, about 20 minutes. Stir in the chives and basil. Serve with the toasts.

—HUBERT KELLER

MAKE IT AHEAD

You can make the dip in advance and keep it in the refrigerator for up to a day. Let it stand at room temperature for twenty minutes before serving.

PER SERVING: CALORIES 216 kcal   TOTAL FAT 5.5 gm   SATURATED FAT .7 gm   CARBOHYDRATE 38 gm   PROTEIN 6 gm   CHOLESTEROL 0 mg

SPINACH CROSTINI

If the two cloves of garlic in the spinach aren't enough for you, get an extra dose by rubbing the toasts with a peeled clove before assembling the hors d'oeuvres.

4 SERVINGS

1 tablespoon olive oil

2 cloves garlic, minced

Large pinch dried red-pepper flakes, or more to taste

1½ pounds spinach, stems removed and leaves washed (about 12 cups)

Salt

8 ½-inch slices Italian bread from a narrow loaf, or an equal quantity of halved or quartered slices from a larger loaf

1. In a medium saucepan, heat the oil over moderate heat. Add the garlic and red-pepper flakes; cook, stirring, for 30 seconds.

2. Add the spinach with the water that clings to the leaves and ½ teaspoon salt. Cover and cook, stirring occasionally, until the spinach is tender, about 5 minutes. The spinach should be moist but not too wet. If necessary, uncover the pan and continue cooking to dry slightly. Stir the spinach and season with salt to taste and, if you like, more red-pepper flakes.

3. Meanwhile, heat the broiler. Put the bread on a baking sheet and broil, turning once, until crisp and brown on the outside but still slightly soft in the center, about 3 minutes.

4. Mound the spinach on the toasts. Serve warm.

—MICHELE SCICOLONE

MAKE IT AHEAD

You can broil the toasts three to four hours ahead; keep them on the baking sheet. When you cook the spinach, reheat the toasts in a 250° oven until warmed through.

PER SERVING: CALORIES 158 kcal TOTAL FAT 5 gm SATURATED FAT .8 gm
CARBOHYDRATE 24 gm PROTEIN 6 gm CHOLESTEROL 0 mg

Fava-Bean Succotash with Crisp Phyllo Rounds

Delicate, flaky phyllo dough stays low in fat when you use vegetable-oil cooking spray instead of the traditional butter. Here, rounds of the dough are baked to a crisp and placed atop fava beans, corn, zucchini, and yellow squash.

4 SERVINGS

1⅓ pounds fava beans, shelled

¾ teaspoon unsalted butter

1 small red onion, chopped

2 cloves garlic, minced

1 small zucchini, cut into ¼-inch dice

1 small yellow summer squash, cut into ¼-inch dice

⅔ cup fresh (cut from about 1 ear) or frozen corn kernels

Salt and fresh-ground black pepper

3 sheets phyllo dough

¼ teaspoon chili powder

¾ teaspoon lemon juice

¾ teaspoon balsamic vinegar

¼ teaspoon Dijon mustard

1 cup frisée, torn into bite-size pieces

1. Bring a medium saucepan of salted water to a boil and add the fava beans. Bring back to a boil and cook for 1 minute. Drain. Rinse the beans with cold water, drain thoroughly, and peel.

2. In a medium saucepan, melt the butter over moderate heat. Add the onion and garlic and cook, stirring, for 1 minute. Stir in the favas, zucchini, summer squash, and corn. Season with salt and pepper. Cover and cook, stirring, until tender, about 15 minutes.

3. Heat the oven to 400°. Spray a baking sheet with vegetable-oil cooking spray. Put one phyllo sheet on a work surface, lightly spray with cooking spray, and sprinkle with ⅛ teaspoon of the chili powder. Lay the second sheet on top, spray lightly, and sprinkle with the remaining ⅛ teaspoon chili powder. Lay the third sheet on top. Using a 4-inch round cutter, stamp out four circles and transfer them to the prepared baking sheet. Bake until golden, about 7 minutes.

4. In a medium bowl, whisk the lemon juice with the vinegar and mustard. Season with salt and pepper. Add the frisée and toss.

5. To serve, reheat the succotash and mound on four plates. Put the phyllo rounds on the succotash; top with the frisée.

—Charles Wiley

PER SERVING: CALORIES 145 kcal   TOTAL FAT 3 gm   SATURATED FAT .7 gm
CARBOHYDRATE 24.8 gm   PROTEIN 6.4 gm   CHOLESTEROL 2 mg

RATATOUILLE TACO TOWERS

For a dish that's as striking to look at as it is delicious, flour tortillas are filled with Provençal vegetables, rolled up, baked, cut in half on the diagonal—and then set on end to tower over ratatouille and pesto.

4 SERVINGS

- 2 tablespoons olive oil
- 1 red onion, chopped fine
- 1 red bell pepper, chopped fine
- 1 yellow bell pepper, chopped fine
- 1 small zucchini, chopped fine
- ½ small eggplant, chopped fine
- 1 pound tomatoes (about 2), chopped fine
- 1 tablespoon plus ½ teaspoon minced garlic
- 3 tablespoons minced fresh basil
- 2 teaspoons minced fresh thyme
  Salt and fresh-ground black pepper
- 1 teaspoon pine nuts
- 4 6-inch flour tortillas

1. Heat the oven to 400°. In a large nonstick frying pan, heat 1 tablespoon of the oil over moderate heat. Add the onion and cook, stirring occasionally, until translucent, about 3 minutes. Add the bell peppers and cook until just tender, about 3 minutes. Add the zucchini and eggplant and cook until just tender, about 4 minutes. Stir in the tomatoes, the 1 tablespoon garlic, 2 tablespoons of the basil, and the thyme. Season with salt and pepper. Spread the mixture in a medium baking dish and roast until the vegetables are softened and beginning to brown, about 10 minutes. Transfer the ratatouille to a plate to cool. Reduce the oven temperature to 375°.

2. In a mortar, puree the remaining 1 tablespoon oil, 1 tablespoon basil, and ½ teaspoon garlic with the pine nuts. Season the pesto with salt and pepper.

3. Put the tortillas on a work surface. Spread half of the ratatouille on the tortillas, leaving a ½-inch border. Roll up the tortillas and secure each with a toothpick. Put the rolls on a baking sheet, seam-side down, and bake until crisp, golden, and heated through, about 10 minutes.

4. To serve, cut the ends off each roll and remove the toothpicks. Cut each roll diagonally in half. Stand two halves on end on each of four plates. Spoon the remaining ratatouille around the taco towers and put a spoonful of pesto on each plate.

—VINCENT GUERITHAULT

PER SERVING: CALORIES 227 kcal   TOTAL FAT 10 gm   SATURATED FAT 1.3 gm
CARBOHYDRATE 32 gm   PROTEIN 6 gm   CHOLESTEROL 0 mg

PICKLED-VEGETABLE EGGPLANT ROLLS

Plan to start this dish a day ahead—the carrot, bell peppers, and jicama need to sit in the pickling liquid overnight. They're then rolled up in thin slices of eggplant along with Swiss chard, grated cheese, and a cilantro puree. When the vegetable log is sliced, you get three pretty little rolls per plate.

4 SERVINGS

2 tablespoons plus 2 teaspoons white-wine vinegar

2 tablespoons plus 2 teaspoons water

1 small serrano chile, seeds and ribs removed, sliced thin

1 small clove garlic

2 teaspoons light-brown sugar

2 thyme sprigs

1 bay leaf

½ teaspoon mustard seeds

½ teaspoon fennel seeds

Salt

1 small carrot, cut into 2-by-⅛-inch matchstick strips

½ small red bell pepper, cut into 2-by-⅛-inch matchstick strips

½ small yellow bell pepper, cut into 2-by-⅛-inch matchstick strips

½ small jicama, peeled and cut into 2-by-⅛-inch matchstick strips

1 pound eggplant, cut lengthwise into 8 ⅛-inch slices

Fresh-ground black pepper

4 large Swiss-chard leaves

4 teaspoons Cilantro Puree, next page

4 teaspoons grated Monterey Jack, Parmesan, or Asiago cheese

1. In a small stainless-steel saucepan, bring the vinegar, water, serrano, garlic, brown sugar, thyme, bay leaf, mustard seeds, fennel seeds, and ¼ teaspoon salt to a boil over moderate heat.

2. In a medium stainless-steel bowl, combine the carrot, bell peppers, and jicama. Pour the hot pickling liquid over the vegetables and let cool. Cover and refrigerate overnight.

3. Heat the oven to 475°. Coat two baking sheets with vegetable-oil cooking spray. Put the eggplant slices on the baking sheets in a single layer and sprinkle with salt and pepper. Bake until the edges begin to brown, about 12 minutes. Brush the slices lightly with a pastry brush dipped in water so that they remain pliable. Let cool.

4. Meanwhile, in a saucepan of boiling, salted water, cook the Swiss-chard leaves until wilted, about 1 minute. Drain, rinse, and pat dry with paper towels. ➤

PER SERVING: CALORIES 91 kcal TOTAL FAT 1.7 gm SATURATED FAT .4 gm
CARBOHYDRATE 17.7 gm PROTEIN 3.8 gm CHOLESTEROL 2.5 mg

5. Put a 20-inch-long sheet of plastic wrap on a work surface, with a long side toward you. Arrange the eggplant slices in a row down the center of the plastic, slightly overlapping, to make a 7-by-16-inch rectangle. Lay the Swiss-chard leaves on the eggplant. About 1 inch from the side nearest you, arrange the vegetable matchsticks in a 1-inch-wide strip all along the Swiss chard. Spread the Cilantro Puree on the vegetables and top with the cheese.

6. Fold the nearest long side of the eggplant slices snugly over the vegetables and cheese. Roll, pulling up on the plastic, to make a 16-by-1½-inch roll.

7. Remove the plastic wrap from the stuffed eggplant roll. Using a thin sharp knife, cut the eggplant roll crosswise into twelve pieces. Stand three of the pieces on end on each of four plates.

—CHARLES WILEY

MAKE IT AHEAD

The rolls can be completed and cut as much as three hours in advance and kept, tightly wrapped in plastic, at room temperature.

CILANTRO PUREE

This tasty herb paste is also delicious on grilled vegetables or chicken sandwiches. It can be made up to four hours ahead; keep it refrigerated until serving.

MAKES ABOUT ¼ CUP

- 3 tablespoons cilantro leaves
- 1 clove garlic
- ⅓ jalapeño pepper, seeds and ribs removed
- 4 teaspoons dry bread crumbs
- 2 tablespoons dry white wine

Salt

Fresh-ground black pepper

In a mini-chopper or mortar, puree the cilantro, garlic, and jalapeño. Work in the bread crumbs. Gradually blend in the wine. Season with salt and pepper.

Shrimp Escabèche with Ginger-Grilled Pineapple

Traditionally, *escabèche* is made by pickling fried fish. This quick version features sautéed shrimp instead, in a cilantro marinade, with tangy grilled pineapple.

4 SERVINGS

- ¾ teaspoon olive oil
- 8 large shrimp, shelled
  Salt and fresh-ground black pepper
- 1 small onion, chopped fine
- ¼ teaspoon minced garlic
- 6 tablespoons orange juice (from about 1 orange)
- 2½ tablespoons lime juice
- 1½ tablespoons minced scallion
- 1½ tablespoons chopped cilantro
- 2½ teaspoons minced fresh ginger
- 2 teaspoons Asian sesame oil
- 1 pineapple, peeled, quartered lengthwise, and cored
- 1 teaspoon sesame seeds

1. In a large nonstick frying pan, heat the olive oil over high heat. Season the shrimp with salt and pepper. Cook for 1 minute. Add the onion and garlic and cook, stirring occasionally, until the shrimp are done, about 2 minutes longer. Stir in the orange juice, 1 tablespoon of the lime juice, the scallion, and cilantro. Remove and let cool.

2. In a medium stainless-steel bowl, combine the remaining 1½ tablespoons lime juice with the ginger, sesame oil, and ¼ teaspoon each salt and pepper. Brush the pineapple with the mixture and let stand at room temperature for 30 minutes.

3. In a small frying pan, toast the sesame seeds over moderate heat, shaking the pan, until golden, about 5 minutes. Let cool.

4. Light a grill or heat the broiler. Grill or broil the pineapple, turning once, until browned on both sides, about 4 minutes. Cut each pineapple quarter crosswise into four pieces and arrange on four plates. Top with the shrimp, drizzle with the orange-juice marinade, and sprinkle with the sesame seeds.

—Allen Susser

PER SERVING: **CALORIES** 165 kcal **TOTAL FAT** 4.7 gm **SATURATED FAT** .6 gm **CARBOHYDRATE** 28 gm **PROTEIN** 5.5 gm **CHOLESTEROL** 30.4 mg

SHRIMP COCKTAIL
WITH BLOODY-MARY SORBET

Any juice made with greens (such as parsley, spinach, celery, or chard) from a juice bar or health-food store will work in this recipe. On the West Coast, look for the widely available bottled Hansen's mixed-greens juice. In a pinch, you can use V8 juice, but you'll lose the color contrast with the tomato sorbet.

4 SERVINGS

- 2 tablespoons sugar
- 3 tablespoons water
- 3 plum tomatoes, peeled, seeded, and chopped
- ⅓ cup tomato juice
- 1 tablespoon tomato paste
- 2 teaspoons lemon juice
  Tabasco sauce
- 1½ tablespoons minced fresh chives
  Salt and fresh-ground black pepper
- 12 medium shrimp, shelled, tails left on
- ¼ cup savory-greens juice
- 4 teaspoons dry vermouth
- 1½ tablespoons sour cream
- 4 ribs celery with leafy tops
- 1 tablespoon cilantro leaves

1. In a small saucepan, combine the sugar and water and cook over moderate heat until the sugar dissolves. Let cool.

2. In a blender, puree the tomatoes with the tomato juice, tomato paste, lemon juice, and the sugar syrup. Add the Tabasco sauce and chives and season with salt and pepper. Transfer to an ice-cream maker and freeze according to the manufacturer's instructions.

3. In a medium saucepan of boiling water, cook the shrimp until just done, about 2 minutes. Drain and let cool.

4. Scoop the sorbet into four glasses. Pour 1 tablespoon of the greens juice and 1 teaspoon of the vermouth into each glass and top each with 1 teaspoon of the sour cream, a celery rib, a few cilantro leaves, and 3 shrimp.

—HANS RÖCKENWAGNER

PER SERVING: CALORIES 114 kcal TOTAL FAT 2 gm SATURATED FAT .9 gm
CARBOHYDRATE 12 gm PROTEIN 10.6 gm CHOLESTEROL 73 mg

CLAMS IN SHERRY AND BLACK-BEAN SAUCE

Like many traditional Vietnamese dishes, this one is low in fat. Serve the clams with a French baguette; the bread is ideal for sopping up the briny broth.

4 SERVINGS

1 tablespoon cooking oil

1 large shallot, minced

1 large clove garlic, minced

¼ cup medium-dry sherry

1 teaspoon sugar

¼ teaspoon fresh-ground black pepper

1 teaspoon fermented black-bean and chili sauce*

¼ cup water

3 dozen littleneck clams, scrubbed

2 large scallions including green tops, sliced thin

*Available at Asian markets and some specialty-food stores

1. In a large stainless-steel pot, heat the oil over high heat. Add the shallot and cook, stirring, for 10 seconds. Add the garlic; cook, stirring, for 10 seconds. Add the sherry, sugar, and pepper and boil for 1 minute. Stir in the black-bean sauce and water; bring to a boil.

2. Discard any clams that have broken shells or do not clamp shut when tapped.

Add the clams to the sauce in the pot. Cover and bring to a boil. Cook, shaking the pot occasionally, just until the clams open, about 3 minutes. Remove the open clams. Continue to cook, uncovering the pot as necessary to remove the clams as soon as their shells open. Discard any that do not open.

3. Divide the clams among four shallow bowls. Pour the cooking liquid over the clams and sprinkle with the scallions.

—MARCIA KIESEL

FERMENTED BLACK-BEAN AND CHILI SAUCE

You'll find fermented black-bean and chili sauce is available under a variety of names—soy chili sauce, black-bean chili sauce, and soybean paste with chili. Just be sure the ingredient list includes fermented black beans (also called fermented soybeans) and chiles.

PER SERVING: CALORIES 161 kcal   TOTAL FAT 4.7 gm   SATURATED FAT .6 gm
CARBOHYDRATE 7 gm   PROTEIN 17.6 gm   CHOLESTEROL 46 mg

RICE-PAPER ROLLS WITH SMOKED SALMON

Rice-paper spring-roll wrappers are perfect for low-fat cooking: You can roll up all sorts of things inside them, and they contribute no fat to the final tally. The thin, brittle sheets become pliable when moistened. They are available from Asian markets in a variety of shapes and sizes.

4 SERVINGS

- 4 teaspoons sesame seeds
- 2 teaspoons soy sauce
- 2 teaspoons white-wine vinegar
- 2 teaspoons slivered fresh ginger
- ¼ teaspoon minced fresh hot pepper, or more to taste
- ¼ teaspoon Asian sesame oil
- ⅛ teaspoon sugar
- ⅛ teaspoon salt
- 2⅔ cups shredded green cabbage
- ⅓ cup thin-sliced red bell pepper
- ⅓ cup thin-sliced onion
- 4 8-inch rice-paper rounds
- 2½ ounces sliced smoked salmon, cut into thin strips

1. In a small frying pan, toast the sesame seeds over moderate heat, shaking the pan, until golden, about 5 minutes. Let cool.

2. In a small glass or stainless-steel bowl, combine the soy sauce, vinegar, ginger, hot pepper, sesame oil, sugar, and salt. In a large bowl, toss the cabbage with the bell pepper and onion. Add the dressing and toasted sesame seeds and toss.

3. Fill a medium bowl with water. Dip each rice-paper round into the water and then shake off any excess water. Arrange the rounds on a work surface. Let soften for about 2 minutes and then pat dry with paper towels.

4. Measure ¼ cup of the cabbage salad and, if very wet, squeeze lightly. Put the cabbage on the lower third of a rice-paper round and top with a quarter of the salmon strips. Fold the rice paper over the filling and roll up tightly, folding in the ends as you go. Repeat with the remaining rice-paper rounds and filling.

—MARCIA KIESEL

PER SERVING: CALORIES 62 kcal   TOTAL FAT 2.6 gm   SATURATED FAT .4 gm
CARBOHYDRATE 5.5 gm   PROTEIN 4.7 gm   CHOLESTEROL 4 mg

chapter *2*

SOUPS

Spring Pea Soup with Scallops and Sorrel, page 51

FRESH TOMATO SOUP WITH GUACAMOLE

Avocados are famously high in fat, but that doesn't mean guacamole has to disappear from your diet. It makes a great garnish for spicy soups, and the small amount used allows you to savor the flavor worry free.

4 SERVINGS

½ teaspoon cumin seeds

2 pounds tomatoes (about 4), peeled, seeded, and chopped

1 onion, chopped coarse

3 tablespoons minced jalapeño pepper

1 tablespoon rice

2 cups water

½ teaspoon sugar, or more if needed
    Salt and fresh-ground black pepper

½ small avocado, preferably Hass

1 scallion including green top, chopped

2 tablespoons chopped cilantro, plus whole leaves for serving

1 teaspoon lime juice

1. In a small heavy frying pan, toast the cumin seeds over moderately high heat, shaking the pan, until fragrant, about 1 minute. Grind the seeds in a mortar with a pestle or in a spice grinder.

2. In a medium stainless-steel pot, combine the tomatoes, onion, 1 tablespoon of the jalapeño, the rice, and ground cumin. Cover the pot and bring to a simmer over moderate heat. Reduce the heat and cook, stirring occasionally, until the rice is very soft, about 30 minutes.

3. In a blender or food processor, puree the tomato mixture until smooth. Return the puree to the pot and stir in the water. Add the sugar and season with salt and pepper. Bring the soup just to a simmer over moderate heat.

4. In a small bowl, mash the avocado with a fork. Stir in the scallion, chopped cilantro, lime juice, and remaining 2 tablespoons jalapeño. Season with salt and pepper.

5. Ladle the soup into four bowls and top with the guacamole. Scatter the cilantro leaves over all.

—MICHELE SCICOLONE

PER SERVING: CALORIES 110 kcal   TOTAL FAT 3.7 gm   SATURATED FAT .6 gm
CARBOHYDRATE 19 gm   PROTEIN 3 gm   CHOLESTEROL 0 mg

COOL LEEK SOUP

Don't discard the leek greens when preparing this; they go in the pot too. The leeks are pureed with shallots, garlic, and plenty of parsley for a bright green soup that's as nutritious as it is flavorful. Quickly cooling the puree keeps the color at its peak.

4 SERVINGS

2 teaspoons olive oil

4 medium leeks, white and all of the green, split lengthwise, cut crosswise into thin slices, and washed well

4 shallots, cut into thin slices

2 cloves garlic, minced

4 cups Vegetable Stock, page 61, or canned vegetable broth

⅔ cup flat-leaf parsley leaves

Salt and fresh-ground black pepper

1 tablespoon lemon juice

Sweet paprika

1. In a large pot, heat the oil over high heat. Add the leeks, shallots, and garlic and reduce the heat to low. Cook, covered, stirring occasionally, until the leeks are soft, about 10 minutes. Add the stock and bring to a boil. Stir in the parsley and remove the soup from the heat.

2. In a blender or food processor, puree the soup. Strain into a large bowl; press firmly with a spoon to get all the puree.

3. Set the bowl of soup in a larger bowl of ice water. Stir the soup constantly to cool it as quickly as possible. Season with salt and pepper.

4. Just before serving, add the lemon juice. Ladle the soup into four bowls and sprinkle with paprika.

—MARCIA KIESEL

MAKE IT AHEAD

After chilling the soup, cover it with plastic wrap and keep refrigerated for up to two days. Add the lemon juice just before serving.

PER SERVING: CALORIES 359 kcal TOTAL FAT 5 gm SATURATED FAT .6 gm
CARBOHYDRATE 76 gm PROTEIN 8.6 gm CHOLESTEROL 0 mg

FIVE-LILY CHOWDER

No, you won't find any flowers floating in this robust chowder. The name refers to the onions, leeks, chives, shallots, and garlic—all members of the lily family. These five potent ingredients are added to the soup in stages to provide contrasting textures.

4 SERVINGS

3½ cups Chicken Stock, page 61, or canned chicken broth

1½ teaspoons olive oil

1½ pounds onions, chopped

2 shallots, cut into thin slices

2 leeks, white part only, halved lengthwise, sliced thin, and washed well

⅓ cup dry white wine

1 bay leaf

1½ teaspoons minced fresh thyme, or ½ teaspoon dried

1½ teaspoons minced fresh oregano, or ½ teaspoon dried

1 rib celery, diced

1½ tablespoons dry sherry

1 clove garlic, chopped

1½ teaspoons chopped flat-leaf parsley

1½ teaspoons grated lemon zest

1½ tablespoons minced fresh chives

¾ teaspoon salt

¼ teaspoon fresh-ground black pepper

1. If using canned chicken broth, skim off and discard any fat that floats to the surface. In a large stainless-steel pot, heat the oil over moderately high heat. Add the onions, shallots, and half the leeks. Cook, stirring, until soft and brown, about 10 minutes. Remove half of the onion mixture from the pot and puree in a blender or food processor until smooth. Return the puree to the pot. Stir in the wine, bay leaf, dried thyme and oregano, if using, and the stock. Bring to a boil, reduce the heat, and simmer for 10 minutes.

2. Stir in the celery, sherry, fresh thyme and oregano, if using, and the remaining leeks. Simmer the soup for 2 minutes. Remove the bay leaf.

3. In a small bowl, combine the garlic, parsley, and lemon zest. Remove the soup from the heat and stir in the chives. Add the salt and pepper. Ladle the soup into four bowls and sprinkle with the parsley mixture.

—JOHN ASH AND SID GOLDSTEIN

PER SERVING: CALORIES 137 kcal **TOTAL FAT** 2.7 gm **SATURATED FAT** .5 gm **CARBOHYDRATE** 20 gm **PROTEIN** 4 gm **CHOLESTEROL** 0 mg

CURRIED CAULIFLOWER AND LEEK SOUP

Pureed vegetables make a satisfyingly thick soup. Here, an earthy puree of potato, cauliflower, and leeks, and gets an extra hit of flavor from a garnish of tangy yogurt topped with a pinch of toasted curry powder.

4 SERVINGS

1½ cups Chicken Stock, page 61, or canned chicken broth

1 teaspoon olive oil

2 leeks, white and light-green parts only, halved lengthwise, cut crosswise into thin slices, and washed well

1 small baking potato (about ¼ pound), peeled and chopped coarse

2½ teaspoons curry powder

3 packed cups cauliflower florets (from about 1 pound cauliflower)

1½ cups water

1 bay leaf

1 teaspoon salt

Fresh-ground black pepper

¼ cup plain nonfat yogurt

1. If using canned chicken broth, skim off and discard any fat that floats to the surface. In a large pot, heat the oil over moderately low heat. Add the leeks; cook, stirring occasionally, until starting to soften, about 7 minutes. Add the potato and 1½ teaspoons of the curry powder. Cook for 1 minute. Add the cauliflower, stock, water, and bay leaf. Bring to a boil. Reduce the heat, cover, and simmer until the vegetables are very soft, about 30 minutes.

2. Meanwhile, in a small frying pan, toast the remaining 1 teaspoon curry powder over moderate heat, shaking the pan, until fragrant, about 1 minute.

3. Remove the bay leaf from the soup. In a blender or food processor, puree the vegetables and the cooking liquid until smooth. Add more water if the soup is thicker than you like. Season with the salt and with pepper to taste. Ladle the soup into four bowls and top with the yogurt and toasted curry powder.

—DIANA STURGIS

PER SERVING: CALORIES 100 kcal TOTAL FAT 2 gm SATURATED FAT .3 gm
CARBOHYDRATE 18 gm PROTEIN 4 gm CHOLESTEROL .3 mg

DOUBLE-MUSHROOM SOUP WITH SAUTÉED SHIITAKES

First white mushrooms and shiitake stems give their flavor to the stock and are strained out. They're replaced by sliced shiitake caps, which are sautéed in a little oil and added to the bowls of clear, elegant soup.

4 SERVINGS

2	teaspoons olive oil
3	shallots, minced
¼	cup dry marsala
2½	cups Chicken Stock, page 61, or canned chicken broth
1	pound white mushrooms, chopped
½	pound shiitake mushrooms, stems removed and reserved, caps sliced thin
1	teaspoon minced fresh thyme, or ½ teaspoon dried
	Salt and fresh-ground black pepper
2	teaspoons chopped flat-leaf parsley

1. In a medium stainless-steel pot, heat 1 teaspoon of the oil over moderate heat. Add the shallots and cook, stirring, until starting to soften, about 4 minutes. Add the marsala and cook until it evaporates, about 2 minutes.

2. If using canned chicken broth, skim off and discard any fat that floats to the surface. Add the white mushrooms, the shiitake stems, the thyme, ½ teaspoon salt, and ¼ teaspoon pepper and cook over moderately high heat, stirring occasionally, for 10 minutes. Add the stock and bring to a boil. Reduce the heat, cover, and simmer for 30 minutes. Strain the soup and then return it to the pot and keep warm.

3. In a large nonstick frying pan, heat the remaining teaspoon of oil over moderate heat. Add the sliced shiitake caps and cook, stirring occasionally, until soft and light brown, about 5 minutes. Season with salt and pepper.

4. Ladle the soup into four bowls and add the sliced shiitake caps. Sprinkle with the chopped parsley.

—DIANA STURGIS

MAKE IT AHEAD

The soup can be prepared through step three a day in advance. Cover and refrigerate. Reheat the soup and proceed with the recipe.

PER SERVING: CALORIES 120 kcal   TOTAL FAT 3.9 gm   SATURATED FAT .7 gm   CARBOHYDRATE 14 gm   PROTEIN 5.5 gm   CHOLESTEROL 0 mg

CORN CHOWDER

East meets West as pureed corn kernels give an interesting twist to what is essentially egg-drop soup. The familiar Asian flavor comes from a small quantity of grated fresh ginger, while the New World supplies the corn.

4 SERVINGS

4 cups Chicken Stock, page 61, or canned chicken broth

3 cups fresh corn kernels (from about 5 ears), or 1 pound frozen corn kernels, thawed

½ teaspoon grated fresh ginger

Salt and fresh-ground black pepper

3 egg whites, beaten

2 scallions including green tops, sliced thin on the diagonal

1. If using canned chicken broth, skim off and discard any fat that floats to the surface. In a blender or food processor, puree two thirds of the corn kernels with ¾ cup of the stock until almost smooth; there should still be some pieces of corn.

2. In a medium pot, combine the remaining 3¼ cups stock with the ginger, ¼ teaspoon salt, and ⅛ teaspoon pepper. Bring to a boil over high heat. Add the remaining corn kernels; bring back to a boil. Reduce the heat. Simmer, covered, for 5 minutes. Add the pureed corn; boil over high heat, stirring, until starting to thicken, about 2 minutes.

3. Add the egg whites to the soup in a thin stream, stirring, and remove the pot from the heat. Stir until the whites form thin opaque strands. Season with salt and pepper. Ladle the soup into four bowls and sprinkle with the scallions.

—EILEEN YIN-FEI LO

PER SERVING: CALORIES 145 kcal   TOTAL FAT 2.9 gm   SATURATED FAT .6 gm   CARBOHYDRATE 24 gm   PROTEIN .9 gm   CHOLESTEROL 0 mg

VEGETARIAN HOT-AND-SOUR SOUP

There's so much going on in a bowl of this hot-and-sour soup—so many intense flavors and interesting textures—that there's not much need for fat.

4 SERVINGS

40 dried lily buds (½ ounce),* (optional)

¼ cup dried tree ear mushrooms* or dried shiitake mushrooms

5 cups Chicken Stock, page 61, or canned chicken broth

½ cup drained and rinsed canned bamboo shoots, cut into thin strips

2 teaspoons minced fresh ginger

¼ teaspoon salt

3 tablespoons red-wine vinegar
    Dried red-pepper flakes

3 tablespoons cornstarch

3 tablespoons water

1 egg

1 egg white

2½ tablespoons black soy sauce,* or 3 tablespoons light soy sauce plus a pinch of sugar

4 ounces firm tofu, cut into ⅓-inch pieces

1 teaspoon Asian sesame oil

1 scallion including green top, sliced thin

    *Available at Asian markets

1. In a bowl, soak the lily buds and the mushrooms in hot water until softened, about 20 minutes. Drain, rinse, and squeeze them to remove as much water as possible. Cut the lily buds into thin slices. Discard the stems from the mushrooms; chop the caps.

2. If using canned chicken broth, skim off and discard any fat that floats to the surface. In a large stainless-steel pot, combine the stock, lily buds, mushrooms, bamboo shoots, ginger, and salt. Cover and bring to a boil. Reduce the heat and simmer for 10 minutes. Stir in the vinegar and 1½ teaspoons red-pepper flakes. Boil for 2 minutes.

3. In a small bowl, stir together the cornstarch and water and add to the soup. In another small bowl, combine the egg with the egg white. Pour the eggs into the soup in a thin stream, stirring. Stir in the soy sauce, tofu, and sesame oil. Reduce the heat to moderate and cook until warmed through. Season with additional red-pepper flakes to taste, ladle into four bowls, and scatter the scallion over the top.

—EILEEN YIN-FEI LO

PER SERVING: CALORIES 208 kcal TOTAL FAT 5.1 gm SATURATED FAT 1.3 gm CARBOHYDRATE 13 gm PROTEIN 23 gm CHOLESTEROL 53 mg

Spinach Soup with Bean-Thread Noodles

Spinach leaves and thin noodles swim in a flavorful ginger broth that is both quick and simple to prepare. A bit of Asian sesame oil stirred in at the end adds a burst of deep, rich flavor.

4 SERVINGS

1 ounce bean-thread noodles*

6 cups Chicken Stock, page 61, or canned chicken broth

1 tablespoon dry white wine

2 teaspoons minced fresh ginger

2 teaspoons minced garlic

1 pound spinach, stems removed, leaves washed and torn in half

1 teaspoon Asian sesame oil

Salt

*Available at Asian markets

1. In a small bowl, soak the noodles in warm water to cover until pliable, about 30 minutes. Drain and rinse. Cut the noodles into 4-inch lengths.

2. If using canned chicken broth, skim off and discard any fat that floats to the surface. In a large stainless-steel pot, combine the stock, wine, ginger, and garlic. Cover and bring to a boil over high heat. Stir in the spinach and boil until just tender, about 1 minute.

3. Stir the noodles into the soup and bring back to a boil. Remove the pan from the heat and stir in the sesame oil. Season with salt.

—Eileen Yin-Fei Lo

Variation

Instead of spinach, use bok choy: Cut the dark-green leaves and the crunchy white stalks into one-inch pieces, boil the stalks for two minutes, and then add the leaves and boil for an additional minute.

PER SERVING: CALORIES 111 kcal   TOTAL FAT 3.8 gm   SATURATED FAT .8 gm
CARBOHYDRATE 13 gm   PROTEIN 7 gm   CHOLESTEROL 0 mg

CABBAGE-ROLL SOUP

Little cabbage packages filled with a zesty pork mixture and tied with scallion greens are the centerpiece of this Vietnamese soup. Because the flavorful stock is such an important element, we don't advise using canned broth here.

4 SERVINGS

4 tender green cabbage leaves

2 scallions, white parts cut into thin slices, green tops left whole

2 teaspoons dried Chinese black mushrooms or dried shiitake mushrooms*

3 ounces ground pork

5 teaspoons Asian fish sauce (nuoc mam or nam pla)*

Fresh-ground black pepper

4 cups Chicken Stock, page 61

Salt

*Available at Asian markets

1. Bring a large pot of water to a boil. Add the cabbage leaves and boil gently until the leaves are wilted but still light green, about 2 minutes. Carefully remove the cabbage leaves with tongs and rinse with cold water. Drain thoroughly. Add the scallion tops to the boiling water and cook for 10 seconds. Drain. Rinse with cold water and drain thoroughly. Cut out the tough stems from the cabbage and cut each leaf in half. Cut each of the scallion tops lengthwise into four strips.

2. In a medium bowl, soak the mushrooms in hot water to cover until softened, about 20 minutes. Drain and rinse well to remove any remaining grit. Squeeze to remove as much water as possible. Discard the stems and mince the caps. Return the mushroom caps to the bowl and stir in the sliced scallions, pork, 1 teaspoon of the fish sauce, and 1/8 teaspoon pepper.

3. Put one eighth of the pork filling near the bottom of a cabbage-leaf half. Fold the two sides in and then roll up. Tie with a scallion strip. Repeat with the remaining filling and cabbage leaves.

4. In a large pot, bring the stock to a boil over moderately high heat. Reduce the heat to low and add the remaining 4 teaspoons fish sauce. Add the cabbage rolls and simmer, partially covered, until the cabbage is tender, 12 to 14 minutes. Season with salt and pepper. Ladle the soup into four bowls and put two cabbage rolls in each one.

—MARCIA KIESEL

PER SERVING: CALORIES 150 kcal TOTAL FAT 7.2 gm SATURATED FAT 2.4 gm CARBOHYDRATE 8.7 gm PROTEIN 12 gm CHOLESTEROL 20.4 mg

Spring Pea Soup with Scallops and Sorrel

Spring is the season for all things green—including this exceptional soup, which makes fine use of the springtime specialties fresh sorrel and early peas.

4 SERVINGS

1 teaspoon vegetable oil

4 shallots, chopped fine

1 sprig fresh thyme, or ¼ teaspoon dried

¼ cup dry white wine

4 cups fresh peas, or two 10-ounce packages frozen petite peas, thawed

2½ cups water

Salt and fresh-ground black pepper

4 sea scallops (about 3 ounces), sliced horizontally into thirds

¼ cup fresh sorrel leaves, cut into thin strips

2 tablespoons chopped fresh mint

1. In a medium stainless-steel pot, heat the oil over low heat. Add the shallots and thyme and cook, covered, until the shallots are translucent, about 5 minutes. Add the wine and simmer for 2 minutes. Add the peas and water and bring to a boil over high heat. Cover, reduce the heat, and simmer until the peas are just tender, about 4 minutes for fresh, 2 minutes for frozen.

2. In a blender or food processor, puree the soup and then strain it back into the pot. Press the vegetables firmly with a spoon to get all the puree.

3. Season the soup with salt and pepper and bring to a simmer. Add the scallops and simmer, stirring, until just cooked through, about 2 minutes. Ladle the soup into four bowls and top with the sorrel and mint.

—Marcia Kiesel

PER SERVING: CALORIES 173 kcal   **TOTAL FAT** 1.9 gm   **SATURATED FAT** .3 gm   **CARBOHYDRATE** 25 gm   **PROTEIN** 12 gm   **CHOLESTEROL** 7 mg

SHRIMP SOUP WITH CRISP TORTILLA STRIPS

Tortilla soups, while relatively unknown in America, are popular all over Mexico. This seafood version from the Veracruz region is based on a rich broth made with shrimp shells. It's packed with corn, tomatoes, poblanos, and shrimp and garnished with oil-free baked tortilla strips.

4 SERVINGS

- 2 medium poblano chiles
- 4 6-inch corn tortillas, halved and cut crosswise into ¼-inch strips
- ¾ pound medium shrimp, shelled and cut in half, shells reserved
- 2 cups water
- ½ cup dry white wine
- 3 scallions including green tops, cut into 1-inch pieces
- 1 sprig cilantro, plus 3 tablespoons chopped cilantro for serving
- 1 teaspoon dried oregano, preferably Mexican
- 1 bay leaf
- 1 teaspoon salt
- 1¼ cups Chicken Stock, page 61, or canned chicken broth
- 2 teaspoons olive oil
- 1 onion, cut into thin slices
- 4 cloves garlic, chopped
- 2 large tomatoes, peeled, seeded, and chopped
- 1 tablespoon hot paprika
- 1 cup fresh (cut from about 2 ears) or frozen corn kernels

Lime wedges, for serving

1. Roast the chiles over a gas flame or grill or broil them, turning with tongs until charred all over, about 10 minutes. When the chiles are cool enough to handle, pull off the skin. Remove the stems, seeds, and ribs and cut the chiles into thin strips.

2. Heat the oven to 325°. Spread the tortilla strips on a baking sheet in a single layer. Toast until crisp, about 10 minutes.

3. In a medium stainless-steel pot, combine the shrimp shells with the water, wine, scallions, the cilantro sprig, oregano, bay leaf, and salt. Bring to a boil over high heat. Reduce the heat, cover, and simmer for 15 minutes. Strain the shrimp stock into a bowl. Press to get all the liquid.

4. If using canned chicken broth, skim off and discard any fat that floats to the surface. In a large stainless-steel pot, heat the

PER SERVING: CALORIES 275 kcal TOTAL FAT 5.2 gm SATURATED FAT .7 gm CARBOHYDRATE 34 gm PROTEIN 20 gm CHOLESTEROL 106 mg

oil over moderate heat. Add the onion and garlic and cook, stirring, until starting to soften, about 3 minutes. Add the tomatoes and increase the heat to high. Cook, stirring frequently, until the liquid is almost evaporated, 4 to 5 minutes. Stir in the paprika and cook for 30 seconds. Stir in the shrimp stock and the chicken stock.

5. Bring the soup to a boil over moderately high heat. Add the shrimp, poblanos, and corn. Reduce the heat and simmer until the shrimp turn pink, 2 to 3 minutes. Ladle the soup into four bowls. Sprinkle with the chopped cilantro and scatter the tortilla strips over all. Serve with lime wedges.

—MARGE POORE

MAKE IT AHEAD

The soup can be prepared through step four a day ahead. Cover and refrigerate the soup and the poblanos separately. Store the tortilla strips in an airtight container.

THE TORTILLA TASTE TEST

FOOD & WINE tested several tortillas to find the best of an increasing number of available brands.

OUR PICKS: Maria & Ricardo white-corn tortillas (available by mail order from Harbar Corporation, 617-524-6107) had the best flavor and texture; Garden of Eating's yellow-corn version, found at health-food stores, was a close runner-up. Of the supermarket varieties, Mariachi yellow-corn had good flavor and Mission white-corn had good texture.

OUR PAN: Gringo Pete's, which was similar to soggy cardboard.

BORSCHT WITH GREENS AND CHICKPEAS

Both parts of the beet—the sweet red bulb and the nutrient-packed greens—go into this colorful, untraditional borscht. Be sure to leave a bit of stem on each beet so that the color won't leach out in cooking.

4 SERVINGS

1 pound beets with greens attached (about 3)

1½ cups Vegetable Stock, page 61, Chicken Stock, page 61, or canned broth

2 teaspoons olive oil

1 small onion, diced

1 carrot, diced

1 tomato, peeled, seeded, and chopped

¾ teaspoon salt

⅔ cup drained and rinsed canned chickpeas

1½ tablespoons dry sherry

1½ tablespoons lemon juice

Chopped fresh dill, for serving

1. Cut the greens off the beets, leaving about 1 inch of the stems attached. Rinse and chop the leaves and stems. In a large pot, cover the whole beets with water and bring to a boil. Reduce the heat and simmer, covered, until the beets are tender, 50 to 60 minutes. Drain, reserving the liquid. Let the beets cool, then peel them and cut into ¼-inch pieces.

2. If using canned chicken broth, skim off and discard any fat that floats to the surface. In a large stainless-steel pot, heat the oil over moderately high heat. Add the onion and cook until translucent, about 3 minutes. Add the carrot and cook for 1 minute. Stir in the tomato, stock, and ½ teaspoon of the salt. Bring to a boil. Cover, reduce the heat, and simmer for 15 minutes. Add the beet greens and cook, stirring, until tender, about 15 minutes.

3. Add 3 cups of the reserved beet-cooking liquid to the pot along with the chickpeas, diced beets, sherry, lemon juice, and the remaining ¼ teaspoon salt. Simmer for 5 minutes. Ladle the soup into four bowls and sprinkle with the dill.

—ANNEMARIE COLBIN

PER SERVING: CALORIES 166.8 kcal   TOTAL FAT 4.8 gm   SATURATED FAT .45 gm
CARBOHYDRATE 25.2 gm   PROTEIN 5.4 gm   CHOLESTEROL 0 mg

CARROT AND CHESTNUT SOUP

Nuts lend an irresistible flavor to almost anything, but they also bring a big dose of fat. All nuts, that is, except chestnuts. These soft, sweet morsels are wondrously low in fat and are perfect for adding a nutty taste to soups like this gingery carrot puree.

4 SERVINGS

½ pound fresh chestnuts, or ¾ cup canned unsweetened chestnut puree

½ cup chopped onion

¼ cup water

1½ pounds carrots, cut into ½-inch slices

1 rib celery, sliced

1 tablespoon chopped fresh ginger

6 cups Vegetable Stock, page 61, or canned vegetable broth

Salt and fresh-ground black pepper

Chopped fresh chives, for serving

1. If using fresh chestnuts, heat the oven to 450°. Cut an X through the shell on the flat side of each chestnut. Put the chestnuts on a baking sheet. Bake until the shell at each X lifts away from the chestnut, about 15 minutes. As soon as they are cool enough to handle, peel the chestnuts.

2. Put the onion and water in a large pot, bring to a simmer, and cook until translucent, about 8 minutes.

3. Set aside 1½ cups of the carrots. Add the remaining carrots, the celery, ginger, stock, and chestnuts to the pot. Simmer over moderate heat until the carrots are tender, about 25 minutes. Meanwhile, cook the reserved carrots in a steamer basket set over boiling water until tender, about 10 minutes.

4. In a blender or food processor, puree the soup until smooth. Season with salt and pepper. Ladle the soup into four bowls. Stir in the steamed carrots and sprinkle with the chopped chives.

—SALLY SAMPSON

PER SERVING: CALORIES 274 kcal TOTAL FAT 2 gm SATURATED FAT .4 gm CARBOHYDRATE 60 gm PROTEIN 6 gm CHOLESTEROL 0 mg

CALYPSO-BEAN SOUP

The spices and sweet potatoes in this soup evoke the tropics. Though the name *calypso bean* carries out the Caribbean theme, these beans can be replaced by black-eyed peas, cranberry beans, or navy beans. We like the soup with the flatbread shown here, recipe next page.

4 SERVINGS

⅓ pound dried calypso beans (about ⅔ cup)

5½ cups Vegetable Stock, page 61, Chicken Stock, page 61, or canned broth

1 sweet potato (about 6 ounces), peeled and diced

3 ounces green beans, cut into ½-inch pieces

4 teaspoons olive oil

1½ onions, chopped fine

3 cloves garlic, minced

2 teaspoons minced fresh ginger

1 bay leaf

¼ teaspoon ground coriander

¼ teaspoon ground cumin

⅛ teaspoon cayenne

¼ teaspoon tomato paste

¼ teaspoon grated orange zest

Salt and fresh-ground black pepper

2 tablespoons cilantro leaves

1. Soak the dried calypso beans overnight in cold water to cover by at least 2 inches. Drain.

2. If using canned chicken broth, skim off and discard any fat that floats to the surface. In a medium pot, bring the stock to a boil over high heat. Add the sweet potato and cook until tender, about 5 minutes. Remove the sweet potato with a slotted spoon. Add the green beans to the pot and cook until tender, about 4 minutes. Remove the green beans with a slotted spoon. Remove the stock from the heat.

3. In a large pot, heat the oil over moderately high heat. Add the onions, garlic, and ginger and cook, stirring occasionally, until the onions are translucent, about 5 minutes. Add the calypso beans, bay leaf, and the reserved stock. Bring to a boil, reduce the heat, and simmer, skimming occasionally, until the calypso beans are very tender, about 1 hour, adding water if necessary.

4. Stir in the sweet potato and green beans. Reduce the heat to low.

5. In a small heavy frying pan, toast the coriander, cumin, and cayenne over moderately high heat, shaking the pan, until fragrant, about 1 minute. Stir in the tomato

PER SERVING: CALORIES 387.8 kcal TOTAL FAT 8.1 gm SATURATED FAT 1 gm CARBOHYDRATE 65.7 gm PROTEIN 16.4 gm CHOLESTEROL 0 mg

paste and cook 1 minute longer. Whisk the spice mixture into the soup. Stir in the orange zest and whisk well. Season with salt and pepper. Ladle the soup into four bowls and sprinkle with the cilantro leaves.

—Marcia Kiesel

Onion Parmesan Flatbread

Prepared bread dough is available in the refrigerator or freezer section of most supermarkets. If you like, substitute pizza dough; you can usually buy it at your local pizzeria. Our nutritional analysis is based on dough with four grams of fat per four-ounce serving.

4 SERVINGS

- 1 tablespoon olive oil
- 1 pound cold prepared bread dough
- ¼ cup chopped onion
- 2 tablespoons grated Parmesan cheese
- 2 teaspoons chopped fresh rosemary
- ½ teaspoon coarse salt

1. Heat the oven to 450°. Brush a baking sheet with ½ teaspoon of oil. Stretch the dough into a 9-by-12-inch rectangle and transfer to the prepared baking sheet. Brush the dough with the remaining 2½ teaspoons oil and scatter the onion, Parmesan, rosemary, and salt over the top.

2. Bake until the flatbread is crisp and light brown, about 20 minutes. Transfer to a rack to cool slightly. Cut into pieces and serve warm or at room temperature.

—Diana Sturgis

PER SERVING: CALORIES 350 kcal　TOTAL FAT 9.8 gm　SATURATED FAT 2.3 gm
CARBOHYDRATE 55 gm　PROTEIN 10 gm　CHOLESTEROL 8 mg

BEAN AND BASIL SOUP

The basil-and-garlic puree that flavors this delectable combination of tomatoes, cannellini beans, and pasta is reminiscent of pesto—but, with only two teaspoons of oil, it's considerably lower in fat.

4 SERVINGS

4 cups Chicken Stock, page 61, or canned chicken broth

2 cups chopped canned tomatoes with their juice (from a 28-ounce can)

1 onion, chopped fine

½ teaspoon dried oregano

4 cups drained and rinsed canned cannellini beans (two 19-ounce cans)

1 clove garlic

½ cup fresh basil leaves, plus 4 leaves shredded, for serving

2 teaspoons olive oil

1 cup tubetti or ditalini

Salt and fresh-ground black pepper

1. If using canned chicken broth, skim off and discard any fat that floats to the surface. In a large pot, bring the stock to a boil over moderately high heat. Add the tomatoes, onion, and oregano. Reduce the heat and simmer for 10 minutes. Add the beans and simmer for 10 minutes longer.

2. In a blender or food processor, combine the garlic and the ½ cup basil. Pulse to chop. Add the oil and puree. Using a slotted spoon, transfer half of the beans and vegetables to the blender. Puree until smooth and then return the mixture to the pot.

3. Meanwhile, in a medium pot of boiling, salted water, cook the pasta until just done, about 6 minutes. Reserve 1 cup of the cooking water and drain the pasta.

4. Stir the pasta into the soup and season with salt and pepper. If the soup seems too thick, add some of the reserved pasta-cooking water.

5. Ladle the soup into four bowls and sprinkle with the shredded basil.

—MICHELE SCICOLONE

PER SERVING: CALORIES 413 kcal   TOTAL FAT 5.5 gm   SATURATED FAT .6 gm
CARBOHYDRATE 71 gm   PROTEIN 23 gm   CHOLESTEROL 0 mg

Smoky Black-Bean and Vegetable Soup

The smokiness and spicy Southwestern flavor in this soup come from chipotle chiles. A spoonful of yogurt on top provides welcome relief from the heat.

4 SERVINGS

1 large onion, chopped

2 ribs celery, halved lengthwise, sliced thin

2 carrots, cut into 1/3-inch pieces

4 cloves garlic, chopped

1/2 cup water

2 canned chipotle chiles *en adobo*,* rinsed, seeded, and chopped

2 bay leaves

2 teaspoons ground cumin

2 teaspoons dried basil

1 teaspoon chili powder

1 teaspoon dried oregano

8 cups Vegetable Stock, page 61, Chicken Stock, page 61, or canned broth

5 cups drained and rinsed canned black beans (from three 16-ounce cans)

3 1/2 cups canned chopped tomatoes with their juice (one 28-ounce can)

Salt and fresh-ground black pepper

1/2 cup plain nonfat yogurt

Chopped fresh cilantro, for serving

4 lime or orange wedges (optional)

*Available at Latin American markets and specialty-food stores

1. In a large pot, simmer the onion, celery, carrots, and garlic in the water until the vegetables are soft, about 12 minutes. Stir in the chiles, bay leaves, cumin, basil, chili powder, and oregano. Cook for 3 minutes.

2. If using canned chicken broth, skim and discard any fat that floats to the surface. Stir the beans, the tomatoes, and the stock into the pot and bring to a boil. Simmer, partially covered, for 1 hour, stirring occasionally.

3. Remove the bay leaves. In a blender or food processor, puree 3 cups of the soup until smooth. Stir the puree back into the soup. Season with salt and pepper. Ladle the soup into four bowls and top each serving with 2 tablespoons yogurt, some chopped cilantro, and a lime or orange wedge, if you like.

—SALLY SAMPSON

PER SERVING: CALORIES 363 kcal TOTAL FAT 3 gm SATURATED FAT .3 gm
CARBOHYDRATE 69 gm PROTEIN 20 gm CHOLESTEROL .6 mg

CHICKEN STOCK

Canned low-fat chicken broth is a great convenience, but it can't quite match the flavor of homemade stock. Make this recipe when you have the time and keep the stock on hand for use in soups, sautés, and other dishes.

MAKES ABOUT 2 QUARTS

5¼ pounds chicken carcasses, backs, wings, and/or necks, plus gizzards (optional)

3 onions, quartered

3 carrots, quartered

3 ribs celery, quartered

10 parsley stems

6 peppercorns

2½ quarts water

Put all the ingredients in a large pot. Bring to a boil and skim the foam that rises to the surface. Reduce the heat and simmer, partially covered, for 2 hours. Strain. Press the bones and vegetables firmly to get all the liquid. Skim the fat from the surface if using immediately. If not, the stock can be refrigerated for up to a week or frozen. Scrape off the fat before using.

PER 1-CUP SERVING: CALORIES 22 kcal **TOTAL FAT** 0 gm **SATURATED FAT** 0 gm
CARBOHYDRATE 1.5 gm **PROTEIN** 3 gm **CHOLESTEROL** 0 mg

VEGETABLE STOCK

The high ratio of vegetables to water gives this stock delicious flavor. It will keep in the refrigerator for up to one week, or can be frozen for months.

MAKES ABOUT 2 QUARTS

2 pounds leeks (about 6), cut into ½-inch slices and washed well

1 pound carrots, chopped

3 ribs celery, chopped

3 quarts water

6 sprigs fresh parsley

6 cloves garlic

1 large bay leaf

1½ teaspoons salt

1 teaspoon peppercorns

In a large pot, combine all the ingredients and bring to a boil. Reduce the heat and simmer, partially covered, for 1 hour. Strain. Press on the vegetables to get all the liquid.

PER 1-CUP SERVING: CALORIES 22 kcal **TOTAL FAT** .1 gm **SATURATED FAT** 0 gm
CARBOHYDRATE 5 gm **PROTEIN** .6 gm **CHOLESTEROL** 0 mg

chapter 3

SALADS

Pear, Arugula, and Pecorino Salad, page 65

Pear, Arugula, and Pecorino Salad

A trio of complementary ingredients—sweet pears, salty Pecorino Romano, and sharp arugula—harmonizes beautifully in a salad that's simple yet sublime.

4 SERVINGS

2 medium pears, such as Bartlett, quartered, cored, and sliced into ⅛-inch wedges

4 teaspoons lemon juice

2 teaspoons olive oil

Salt and fresh-ground black pepper

1¾ cups arugula with stems removed (from a 3-ounce bunch)

1 cup Pecorino Romano cheese shavings (about 1 ounce), or ½ cup grated

1. In a medium bowl, toss the pear slices with the lemon juice and oil. Season with salt and pepper.

2. Mound the arugula on four plates. Arrange the pear slices on top and scatter the cheese shavings over all.

—Michele Scicolone

Variations

Experiment with different combinations of greens, grating cheeses, and crisp fall or winter fruits. Our favorite substitutions:
• Slices of Granny Smith apple for the pears
• Watercress for the arugula
• Another Italian cheese, such as Asiago or Parmesan, for the Pecorino

Cheese Tip

Hard cheeses such as Parmesan and Pecorino Romano are important ingredients in low-fat dishes, but that's not because they're particularly low-fat themselves. Ounce for ounce, they're about as high in fat as any other cheese. However, an ounce is all you'll need for a salad that serves four. Because of their strong flavors, grating cheeses can make a big impression in small amounts, and that's a real advantage when every ounce counts.

PER SERVING: CALORIES 105 kcal   TOTAL FAT 4.8 gm   SATURATED FAT 1.7 gm   CARBOHYDRATE 14 gm   PROTEIN 3 gm   CHOLESTEROL 7 mg

Garlic Caesar Salad

The great Caesar gets a makeover in this garlicky version that's long on flavor but short on fat. Blanched garlic—a key ingredient in the egg-free dressing—can replace roasted in almost any dressing or condiment. But, unlike roasting, blanching requires no oil whatsoever.

4 SERVINGS

2   ½-inch slices country bread or sourdough bread, crusts trimmed, bread cut into ½-inch cubes

5   teaspoons olive oil

3   tablespoons Chicken Stock, page 61, Vegetable Stock, page 61, or canned broth

1½ tablespoons Blanched-Garlic Puree, opposite page

1   small shallot, minced

1   anchovy fillet, minced, or ½ teaspoon anchovy paste

1   teaspoon Dijon mustard

2   teaspoons lemon juice

2   teaspoons red-wine vinegar

    Salt and fresh-ground black pepper

6   cups romaine lettuce, torn into bite-size pieces (about 1 head)

3   tablespoons grated Parmesan cheese

1. Heat the oven to 350°. In a small bowl, toss the bread cubes with 1 teaspoon of the oil. Spread the bread cubes on a baking sheet in a single layer. Bake until crisp and golden brown, about 8 minutes.

2. In a small bowl, whisk together the stock, garlic puree, shallot, anchovy, mustard, lemon juice, vinegar, and the remaining 4 teaspoons oil. Season the dressing with salt and pepper.

3. In a large bowl, toss the lettuce with the croutons and the dressing. Sprinkle with the Parmesan and toss again.

—Jim Ackard

PER SERVING: CALORIES 127 kcal   TOTAL FAT 7.4 gm   SATURATED FAT 1.6 gm   CARBOHYDRATE 10.4 gm   PROTEIN 4.7 gm   CHOLESTEROL 3.5 mg

Blanched-Garlic Puree

MAKES ABOUT ¹/₂ CUP

2 large heads garlic, cloves separated
   and peeled

1. Put the garlic cloves in a small saucepan with enough water to cover. Bring to a boil over high heat. Drain the garlic and return it to the pan.

2. Repeat the process three times, or until the garlic is softened. Transfer the garlic to a bowl and mash with a fork until smooth.

Make It Ahead

• **CROUTONS:** Make a few days in advance and store in an airtight container.
• **DRESSING:** Prepare several days ahead and keep refrigerated. Let return to room temperature before using.
• **LETTUCE:** Wash and tear into pieces a day in advance; store wrapped in paper towels in a large resealable plastic bag to retain crispness.

Variation

For a main-course Caesar salad, add strips of boneless, skinless chicken breast. If the chicken is poached or broiled rather than cooked with oil, one small breast (about 4 ounces) per person will add around 125 calories to each serving.

BIBB LETTUCE WITH WARM ROSEMARY DRESSING

Halving the small heads of lettuce rather than tearing them into bite-size pieces ensures that they won't wilt too much with the warmth of the rosemary-scented dressing. A sprinkling of Parmesan would make a fine finishing touch.

4 SERVINGS

- 5 teaspoons olive oil
- 1 large clove garlic, quartered lengthwise
- 1 teaspoon fresh rosemary, or
  ½ teaspoon dried
- 1½ tablespoons balsamic vinegar
  Salt and fresh-ground black pepper
- 4 small heads Bibb lettuce (about
  1 pound in all), halved lengthwise
  and cored

MAKE IT AHEAD

Prepare the dressing several hours ahead of time and keep it at room temperature. Reheat before serving.

1. In a small frying pan, combine the oil, garlic, and rosemary. Cook over moderate heat until the garlic softens, 1 to 2 minutes. Remove from the heat and let cool slightly. Whisk in the vinegar. Season with salt and pepper.

2. Put two lettuce halves, cut-side up, on each of four plates. Drizzle the warm dressing over the lettuce.

—SALLY SCHNEIDER

PER SERVING: CALORIES 72.9 kcal   TOTAL FAT 6 gm   SATURATED FAT .8 gm
CARBOHYDRATE 4.6 gm   PROTEIN 1.5 gm   CHOLESTEROL 0 mg

WATERCRESS AND RADICCHIO SALAD

The contrasting flavors and colors of radicchio and watercress offer a change of pace from the usual lettuce salad. A mellow sesame dressing plays off the mildly bitter radicchio.

4 SERVINGS

- 4 teaspoons sesame seeds
- 1 head radicchio (about 5 ounces)
- 3½ cups watercress with tough stems removed (from a 7-ounce bunch)
- ¼ cup Chicken Stock, page 61, Vegetable Stock, page 61, or canned broth
- 3 tablespoons flat-leaf parsley leaves
- 2 teaspoons lemon juice
- 2 teaspoons cider vinegar
- Salt

1. In a small frying pan, toast the sesame seeds over moderate heat, stirring frequently, until light brown and fragrant, about 2 minutes. Remove from the pan to cool.

2. Remove four outer leaves from the radicchio and reserve. Cut the remainder of the head in half lengthwise, remove the core, and cut the leaves into thin strips. In a large bowl, toss the radicchio strips with the watercress.

3. In a food processor or blender, puree the toasted sesame seeds with the stock, parsley, lemon juice, and vinegar. Season with salt. Add half of this dressing to the salad and toss.

4. Put one of the reserved radicchio leaves on each of four plates and then mound the salad in the center and drizzle with the remaining dressing.

—ANNEMARIE COLBIN

PER SERVING: CALORIES 30 kcal TOTAL FAT 1.7 gm SATURATED FAT .2 gm CARBOHYDRATE 3 gm PROTEIN 2 gm CHOLESTEROL 0 mg

GRILLED-MUSHROOM SALAD

Bold flavors predominate in this unusual salad, which features roasted red bell pepper, arugula, a minty tomato-and-orange dressing, and skewers of warm shiitake mushrooms.

4 SERVINGS

1	large red bell pepper
½	pound plum tomatoes (about 4), peeled, seeded, and chopped
1	clove garlic, minced
1½	tablespoons orange juice
1	teaspoon lemon juice
1½	teaspoons sherry vinegar
1	teaspoon soy sauce
1	tablespoon chopped fresh mint or basil
¾	pound shiitake mushrooms, stems removed
1½	teaspoons olive oil
	Salt and fresh-ground black pepper
1¼	cups arugula, stems removed and leaves torn into bite-size pieces (from a 2-ounce bunch)
1½	cups Boston lettuce, torn into bite-size pieces (about ¼ head)

1. Roast the pepper over a gas flame or grill or broil, turning with tongs until charred all over, about 10 minutes. When the pepper is cool enough to handle, pull off the skin. Remove the stem, seeds, and ribs. Cut the pepper into thin strips.

2. In a food processor or blender, puree the tomatoes with the garlic. Pour the tomato puree into a small bowl and stir in the orange juice, lemon juice, vinegar, soy sauce, and mint.

3. Heat the grill or broiler. Thread the mushrooms onto four bamboo skewers, piercing the center of each mushroom cap at an angle. Brush the mushrooms with the oil. Sprinkle with salt and pepper. Grill or broil the mushrooms until tender and brown, turning once, about 3 minutes.

4. In a large bowl, toss the arugula and Boston lettuce with the tomato dressing. Mound the salad on four plates. Scatter the roasted pepper strips over the salads and top each with a mushroom skewer.

—MARCIA KIESEL

PER SERVING: CALORIES 68 kcal TOTAL FAT 2 gm SATURATED FAT .3 gm
CARBOHYDRATE 11 gm PROTEIN 4 gm CHOLESTEROL 0 mg

Swiss-Cheese Crisp with Mixed Greens

It takes just half a cup of grated Gruyère and one tablespoon of Parmesan to make the cheese crisp that gives this salad its extra crunch. The dressing, a puree of roasted tomatoes, balsamic vinegar, and mustard, adds no fat to the tally; it's made without a drop of oil.

4 SERVINGS

½   pound plum tomatoes (about 4), cored and halved lengthwise

1   shallot, minced (about 1 tablespoon)

2   tablespoons balsamic vinegar

1   teaspoon Dijon mustard

   Salt and fresh-ground black pepper

½   cup grated Gruyère cheese

1   tablespoon grated Parmesan cheese

1½ quarts mixed salad greens (about ¼ pound)

2   tablespoons chopped fresh chives

1. Heat the broiler. Put the tomatoes, cut-side down, on a baking sheet; broil for 5 minutes. Remove the skin and broil just browned, about 2 minutes. Turn the tomatoes and broil until blackened, about 4 minutes longer. Transfer the tomatoes and any accumulated juices to a food processor or blender and pulse to chop. Add the shallot, vinegar, and mustard and puree until smooth. Transfer the dressing to a small bowl and season with salt and pepper.

2. In another small bowl, toss the Gruyère and Parmesan with ⅛ teaspoon each of salt and pepper. Put a large nonstick skillet over moderate heat. Sprinkle the cheese mixture into the pan in an even layer to form an 8-inch disk. Cook, spooning off any fat, until the cheese is lightly browned, about 4 minutes. Drain the cheese crisp on a paper towel.

3. Toss the greens with the chives and dressing. Mound the greens on four plates and crumble the cheese crisp over the salads.

—Bob Chambers

PER SERVING: CALORIES 85 kcal   TOTAL FAT 4.5 gm   SATURATED FAT 2.8 gm
CARBOHYDRATE 5 gm   PROTEIN 7 gm   CHOLESTEROL 14 mg

CRISP SALAD WITH ORANGE MISO DRESSING

Miso, the fermented soybean paste that's a mainstay of Japanese cooking, adds body and a slight saltiness to this citrusy dressing. Miso should be kept in an airtight container and stored in the refrigerator.

4 SERVINGS

- 2 teaspoons grated orange zest (from 1 orange)
- ½ cup orange juice (from about 2 oranges)
- 2 tablespoons medium- or light-colored miso (soybean paste)*
- 2 teaspoons Asian sesame oil
- 1½ teaspoons light tamari*
- 4 cups romaine lettuce, torn into bite-size pieces (1 small head)
- 1½ cups watercress with tough stems removed (1 small head)
- 1 carrot, grated
- 6 radishes, cut in half and sliced thin

*Available at Asian markets

1. In a small bowl, whisk together the orange zest, orange juice, miso, sesame oil, and tamari.

2. Put the romaine and watercress on four plates. Top the greens with the carrot and radishes and drizzle with the dressing.

—DIANA STURGIS

VARIATION

We don't often recommend iceberg lettuce, but here is one of the rare places where it works well. Use iceberg instead of the romaine; its crunchiness makes it a fine backdrop for the flavorful orange miso dressing.

PER SERVING: CALORIES 81 kcal TOTAL FAT 3 gm SATURATED FAT .4 gm CARBOHYDRATE 11 gm PROTEIN 3 gm CHOLESTEROL 0 mg

SPINACH AND CHERRY-TOMATO SALAD

As the tomatoes macerate in a mixture of balsamic vinegar, mustard, salt and pepper, sugar, and just a little oil, their juices come out and, with the other ingredients, form a tasty dressing for the salad. We use cherry tomatoes here, since they're good all year round, but feel free to use other varieties when you can get them at their peak.

4 SERVINGS

- 1 tablespoon balsamic vinegar
- 2 teaspoons Dijon mustard
- 1 teaspoon olive oil
- ½ pound cherry tomatoes, quartered
- ¼ teaspoon sugar
  Salt and fresh-ground black pepper
- 6 cups spinach, stems removed, leaves washed and torn into 1-inch pieces (from about ¾ pound)
- 2½ cups watercress with tough stems removed (about 5 ounces)

1. In a large bowl, whisk together the vinegar, mustard, and oil. Add the tomatoes, sugar, and ¼ teaspoon each of salt and pepper. Toss gently. Set aside for 30 minutes, stirring once or twice.

2. Add the spinach and watercress to the tomatoes and toss. Season the salad with salt and pepper.

—DIANA STURGIS

VARIATIONS

- Take advantage of whatever greens are available: Substitute arugula, red-leaf lettuce, or torn romaine leaves for the watercress or spinach.
- Make the salad more colorful by using a combination of red and yellow cherry tomatoes.

LOW-FAT DRESSINGS

The loss of rich ingredients can leave low-fat salad dressings a little thin in the flavor department. To give them greater taste and texture, try adding one of the following:
- A puree of blanched garlic or shallots, fresh herbs, or reconstituted sun-dried tomatoes (not oil-packed, obviously)
- Prepared mustard
- Nonfat yogurt
- Tomato paste
- Salsa

PER SERVING: CALORIES 43 kcal   TOTAL FAT 1.7 gm   SATURATED FAT .2 gm
CARBOHYDRATE 6 gm   PROTEIN 3 gm   CHOLESTEROL 0 mg

ENDIVE SALAD WITH ROASTED PEPPERS

The sweetness of red and yellow bell peppers balances the bitterness of the Belgian and curly endive used here. Sautéed leeks join the peppers to add enough juiciness to the salad so that you can do without a dressing.

4 SERVINGS

1½ teaspoons olive oil

2 leeks, white and light-green parts only, split lengthwise, cut crosswise into ½-inch slices, and washed well

3 cloves garlic, cut into thin slices

3 tablespoons lemon juice

2 yellow bell peppers

1 red bell pepper

Salt and fresh-ground black pepper

¼ cup thin-sliced basil leaves

2 heads Belgian endive, cored and cut crosswise into ½-inch pieces

2 cups curly endive or frisée, torn into bite-size pieces (about ¼ pound)

1. Heat the oil in a medium nonstick frying pan. Add the leeks and cook over low heat, stirring, for 5 minutes. Add the garlic and cook until the leeks are soft, about 5 minutes longer. Remove from the heat and stir in the lemon juice.

2. Roast the peppers over a gas flame or grill or broil them, turning with tongs until charred all over, about 10 minutes. When the peppers are cool enough to handle, pull off the skin, working over a bowl to catch the juices. Remove the stems, seeds, and ribs. Cut the peppers lengthwise into ½-inch strips and set aside. Strain the pepper juices into the leeks and season with salt and pepper. Stir in the basil.

3. In a large bowl, toss the Belgian endive with one third of the leeks. Arrange the salad in a ring on each of four plates. Put the curly endive in the bowl and toss with half of the remaining leeks. Mound a quarter of this mixture in the center of each plate. Toss the roasted pepper strips with the remaining leeks and scatter over all.

—BOB CHAMBERS

PER SERVING: CALORIES 98 kcal TOTAL FAT 2.2 gm SATURATED FAT .3 gm CARBOHYDRATE 19.1 gm PROTEIN 2.7 gm CHOLESTEROL 0 mg

Thai Mushroom Salad

Lots of mint leaves lend a refreshing note to this earthy mushroom mixture. Serve it as a first course, or offer it with Thai sticky rice or jasmine rice as a low-fat main dish. If oyster or portobello mushrooms are unavailable, white mushrooms will work just fine.

4 SERVINGS

½ pound portobello mushrooms, stems removed and caps chopped coarse

½ pound oyster mushrooms, stems removed and caps chopped coarse

1 clove garlic

½ teaspoon sugar

1 to 2 teaspoons crumbled dried red chile pepper or dried red-pepper flakes

3 tablespoons lime juice

2 tablespoons Asian fish sauce (nam pla or nuoc mam)*

2 tablespoons sliced shallots

1½ cups fresh mint leaves

*Available at Asian markets and many supermarkets

1. In a large saucepan, bring 2 inches of water to a boil. Add the mushrooms; cook, partially covered, until tender, about 4 minutes. Drain and transfer to a large bowl.

2. In a mortar with a pestle, pound the garlic clove with the sugar to a paste. Add the chile and pound to blend. Stir in the lime juice and fish sauce.

3. Add the shallots to the mushrooms along with the dressing and toss gently. Add the mint and toss again.

—Jeffrey Alford and Naomi Duguid

Some Like It Hot

A teaspoon or two of crumbled dried red chile may not sound like a lot, but it actually makes the salad quite spicy. If you're not sure you can take the heat, start with one-quarter to one-half teaspoon, and work your way up.

PER SERVING: CALORIES 53.7 kcal   TOTAL FAT 1.3 gm   SATURATED FAT .2 gm   CARBOHYDRATE 8.6 gm   PROTEIN 3.5 gm   CHOLESTEROL 0 mg

Zucchini Salad with Mint and Lemon

In this taste-of-summer salad, bright-green steamed zucchini is cooled quickly with cold water and then tossed with a light, mint-spiked dressing. Grated zest and juice add to the lemony flavor.

4 SERVINGS

- 5 small zucchini (about 6 ounces each), cut into approximately 1-by-$\frac{1}{3}$-inch sticks
- 3 scallions including green tops, sliced thin
- 3 tablespoons sliced mint leaves
- 2 teaspoons olive oil
- 1 teaspoon grated lemon zest (from 1 lemon)
- 1 teaspoon lemon juice
- $\frac{1}{8}$ teaspoon salt
- $\frac{1}{4}$ teaspoon fresh-ground black pepper

1. In a steamer basket set over a saucepan of boiling water, steam the zucchini until just tender, about 3 minutes. Rinse the zucchini with cold water and drain thoroughly.

2. In a medium bowl, toss the zucchini with the scallions, mint, oil, lemon zest, lemon juice, salt, and pepper.

—Jean Galton

Variations

Go to the garden for ideas to change this simple salad:
- Replace the zucchini with summer squash, carrots, green or wax beans, or snow peas.
- Batons of cucumber can also stand in for the zucchini; you don't even have to cook them.
- Substitute fresh basil or chopped dill for the mint, if you prefer.

Steaming

Not only is it one of the fastest and easiest methods of cooking, but steaming is also one of the few that doesn't require fat. Most of the food's vitamins and minerals are retained, instead of being lost to the water in boiling, making steaming a perfect technique for health-conscious cooks.

PER SERVING: CALORIES 55 kcal TOTAL FAT 2.7 gm SATURATED FAT .4 gm CARBOHYDRATE 7gm PROTEIN 2.7 gm CHOLESTEROL 0 mg

ASPARAGUS AND PEPPER SALAD WITH GINGER DRESSING

Fresh ginger, rice-wine vinegar, and sesame oil make for a dressing with an unmistakably Asian accent. Add some asparagus and strips of red and yellow bell pepper, and you have a dish that's pleasing to the eye as well as the palate.

4 SERVINGS

6 scallions, green part only, minced (about ½ cup)

2 tablespoons minced fresh ginger

2 tablespoons rice-wine vinegar

1 tablespoon Asian sesame oil

1 clove garlic, minced

1½ pounds thick asparagus, peeled

1 red bell pepper, cut into approximately 2-by-¼-inch strips

1 yellow bell pepper, cut into approximately 2-by-¼-inch strips

Salt and fresh-ground black pepper

1. In a small bowl, combine the scallions, ginger, rice-wine vinegar, Asian sesame oil, and garlic. Cut the asparagus stalks into ¼-inch diagonal slices, leaving the asparagus tips whole.

2. In a large pot of boiling, salted water, cook the asparagus until just done, about 1 minute. Drain. Rinse with cold water and drain thoroughly.

3. In a large bowl, mix the sliced asparagus with the bell-pepper strips. Toss with the ginger dressing and season the salad with salt and pepper.

—JANET HAZEN DE JESUS

VARIATIONS

Replace the asparagus with steamed Chinese cabbage, bok choy, snow peas, carrots, or a combination of these.

PER SERVING: CALORIES 93 kcal   TOTAL FAT 4 gm   SATURATED FAT .6 gm
CARBOHYDRATE 13 gm   PROTEIN 5 gm   CHOLESTEROL 0 mg

JICAMA ORANGE SALAD WITH JALAPEÑO DRESSING

Jicama strips, red-onion wedges, and navel-orange segments dressed with a zesty mixture of roasted jalapeños, cilantro, and cumin offer a bright variety of colors, textures, and tastes.

4 SERVINGS

1	small red onion, cut into thin wedges
2	large jalapeño peppers
3	navel oranges
3	tablespoons chopped cilantro
1	tablespoon olive oil
¼	teaspoon ground cumin
	Salt and fresh-ground black pepper
2½	cups watercress with tough stems removed (from a 5-ounce bunch)
½	small jicama (about ¾ pound), peeled and cut into ¼-inch sticks

1. Soak the onion in ice water for 15 minutes. Drain; transfer to a medium bowl.

2. Roast the jalapeños over a gas flame or grill or broil them, turning with tongs until charred all over. When the peppers are cool enough to handle, pull off the skin. Remove the stems, seeds, and ribs. Mince the peppers.

3. Using a small stainless-steel knife, peel the oranges down to the flesh, removing all of the white pith. Working over a small bowl to catch the juice, cut the orange sections away from the membranes. Add the orange sections to the onion wedges. Squeeze the membranes over the bowl. You should get about 3 tablespoons of juice.

4. Add the roasted jalapeños to the bowl with the orange juice. Whisk in the cilantro, oil, cumin, ½ teaspoon of salt, and ⅛ teaspoon of pepper.

5. Put the watercress on four plates. Add the jicama sticks to the onion wedges and oranges; toss with the dressing. Season with salt and pepper. Mound the salad on top of the watercress.

—JANET HAZEN DE JESUS

PER SERVING: CALORIES 124 kcal TOTAL FAT 4 gm SATURATED FAT .5 gm CARBOHYDRATE 22 gm PROTEIN 3 gm CHOLESTEROL 0 mg

Tomato, Cucumber, and Red-Onion Salad

Use the Middle Eastern flatbread served here to scoop up bites of the tasty salad—an easy-to-assemble combination of cucumber, tomato, and red onion.

4 SERVINGS

½ medium red onion, cut into thin slices

2 tablespoons red-wine vinegar

   Salt

1 large tomato, diced

1 medium cucumber, cut into thin slices

2 teaspoons olive oil

1 tablespoon chopped fresh basil, plus whole sprigs for serving

   Fresh-ground black pepper

2 6-inch pitas, halved, or 4 ounces of another Middle Eastern flatbread cut into pieces

1. In a medium bowl, toss the onion with the vinegar and ¼ teaspoon salt. Let sit for 10 minutes.

2. Drain the onion and return it to the bowl. Add the tomato, cucumber, oil, and the chopped basil. Toss gently to combine. Season with salt and pepper. Put on four plates, top with basil sprigs, and serve each portion with half a pita.

—Janet Hazen De Jesus

VARIATIONS

• For a salad suggestive of Italian *panzanella*, toast the pita in the oven until dry, break it up into pieces, and toss it with the salad.

• Substitute other plentiful herbs, such as dill, chives, or tarragon, for the chopped basil.

• A handful of torn sorrel leaves or arugula would add a delicious flavor component.

• If you feel like splurging and using a little more fat, add a sprinkling of crumbled feta cheese to the salad. Just a tiny amount will give substantial flavor.

PER SERVING: CALORIES 125 kcal TOTAL FAT 2.9 gm SATURATED FAT .4 gm CARBOHYDRATE 22 gm PROTEIN 4 gm CHOLESTEROL 0 mg

Black-Bean Salad

Lime juice and rice-wine vinegar, balanced by a touch of oil, add a refreshing zing to this Southwestern favorite. A cilantro-mint combo enhances the effect.

4 SERVINGS

1½ cups cooked black beans, rinsed if canned

½ pound jicama, peeled and cut into small dice

1 medium tomato, seeded and chopped

1 cucumber, peeled, halved, seeded, and cut into small dice

1 serrano chile, minced

1 tablespoon minced onion

½ teaspoon grated lime zest

2 tablespoons lime juice

2 teaspoons olive oil

1 teaspoon rice-wine vinegar

½ teaspoon ground cumin

Salt and fresh-ground black pepper

1 tablespoon chopped cilantro

1 tablespoon chopped fresh mint

SERVING SUGGESTION

You can treat this versatile salad as a first course, a side dish, or even a salsa, using it to top grilled chicken breasts, broiled or grilled fish, or pork tenderloin.

1. In a large bowl, combine the beans, jicama, tomato, cucumber, serrano, and onion. In a small bowl, whisk together the lime zest and juice, oil, vinegar, and cumin.

2. Toss the dressing with the bean salad and season with salt and pepper. Add the chopped cilantro and mint; toss again.

—MARGE POORE

PER SERVING: CALORIES 113 kcal   TOTAL FAT 3.1 gm   SATURATED FAT .4 gm   CARBOHYDRATE 17 gm   PROTEIN 6 gm   CHOLESTEROL 0 mg

NEW-POTATO AND WAX-BEAN SALAD

Our lighter version of potato salad replaces high-fat mayo with a mustardy vinaigrette and throws in wax beans and arugula for good measure.

4 SERVINGS

½ pound yellow wax beans or green beans, cut diagonally into 1-inch pieces

½ pound small new potatoes, quartered

4 teaspoons white-wine or Champagne vinegar

1½ teaspoons Dijon mustard

1 tablespoon olive oil

1 clove garlic, minced

1 teaspoon chopped fresh thyme

1 teaspoon chopped fresh rosemary

Salt and fresh-ground black pepper

2½ cups arugula with stems removed (from a 4-ounce bunch)

1. In a medium pot of boiling, salted water, cook the beans until just tender, about 3 minutes. Using a slotted spoon, transfer the beans to a strainer and rinse with cold water. Drain thoroughly and transfer to a medium bowl.

2. Cook the potatoes in the same boiling water until just done, about 10 minutes. Drain, let cool, and add to the beans.

3. In a small bowl, whisk together the vinegar, mustard, oil, garlic, thyme, rosemary, a pinch of salt, and ¼ teaspoon pepper.

4. Put the arugula on four plates. Whisk the dressing and toss it gently with the beans and potatoes. Season with salt and pepper. Mound the salad on top of the arugula.

—JANET HAZEN DE JESUS

VARIATION

Use one of the many delicious grainy or flavored mustards available now (such as peppercorn) in place of the Dijon. Be sure to taste the mustard first so that you can gauge how much punch it will deliver.

PER SERVING: CALORIES 98 kcal   TOTAL FAT 4 gm   SATURATED FAT .5 gm   CARBOHYDRATE 15 gm   PROTEIN 3 gm   CHOLESTEROL 0 mg

Vietnamese Cabbage Slaw with Chicken and Grapefruit

Vietnamese salads are some of the most interesting and delicious in the world. Their complementary textures and flavors constitute a wake-up call for the mouth. The main components of most Vietnamese salad dressings—fish sauce, lime juice, sugar, and chile—strike a perfect balance of salty, tart, sweet, and hot. And Vietnamese dressings never include oil. The flavor combinations are so exciting that you'll never miss it.

4 SERVINGS

1   large bone-in chicken breast (about ¾ pound)

4   teaspoons sesame seeds

1   large pink grapefruit

1 to 2 serrano chiles, preferably red, seeded and minced

1   clove garlic, minced

2   teaspoons sugar

2   tablespoons plus 1 teaspoon Asian fish sauce (nuoc mam or nam pla)*

2   tablespoons lime juice

1   carrot, cut into thin 2-inch-long strips

1½   cups shredded red cabbage (about ⅓ pound)

1½   cups shredded green cabbage (about ⅓ pound)

¼   cup chopped fresh mint, plus whole sprigs for serving

3   tablespoons chopped cilantro, plus whole sprigs for serving

4   teaspoons chopped peanuts

*Available at Asian markets and many supermarkets

1. Put the chicken in a large saucepan of salted water. Bring just to a boil over moderate heat, skimming the surface. Cover, reduce the heat, and simmer until the chicken is just done, about 15 minutes. Let the chicken cool in the broth.

2. Meanwhile, in a small heavy frying pan, toast the sesame seeds over moderate heat, stirring frequently, until light brown and fragrant, about 2 minutes. Remove from the pan to cool.

3. Using a stainless-steel knife, peel the grapefruit down to the flesh, removing all of the white pith. Cut the sections away from the membranes. Using a fork, flake apart half of the grapefruit sections.

4. Drain the chicken. Discard the skin and bones and tear the chicken into ¼-inch shreds.

5. In a mortar with a pestle, pound the serrano, garlic, and sugar to a paste. Transfer the paste to a small bowl and add the fish

PER SERVING: CALORIES 171 kcal   TOTAL FAT 5.2gm   SATURATED FAT .9 gm
CARBOHYDRATE 19.1 gm   PROTEIN 13.6 gm   CHOLESTEROL 24.4 mg

sauce and lime juice. Stir until the sugar is dissolved.

6. In a large bowl, toss together the chicken, flaked grapefruit, carrot, red and green cabbage, chopped mint and cilantro, and toasted sesame seeds. Add the lime dressing and toss. Let sit until the vegetables start to soften, about 10 minutes.

7. Using tongs, transfer the salad to a large platter or four individual dishes, leaving behind any excess liquid. Top the salad with the whole grapefruit sections, mint and cilantro sprigs, and chopped peanuts.

—JOYCE JUE

TOASTING SESAME SEEDS

Toasting enhances the nutty flavor of sesame seeds, but watch out—if you don't remove them from the pan to cool, they'll keep cooking and go right past toasted to burnt. Take care, too, when handling the toasted seeds; they're little, but they retain a surprising amount of heat and just might burn you.

SUBSTITUTION

Can't find **fish sauce**? This Asian staple is now available in many supermarkets, but if you can't locate it, use soy sauce in its place.

SALMON AND POTATO SALAD WITH HORSERADISH DRESSING

Salmon is a fairly fatty fish, but it doesn't take much of it to make this skinny main-dish salad into something special. The fish is sliced, seared, and served on a bed of horseradish-spiced potatoes.

4 SERVINGS

1½ pounds small waxy potatoes, such as Yukon Gold

1 cup low-fat buttermilk

2 scallions including green tops, chopped

¼ cup bottled horseradish, drained

Salt and fresh-ground black pepper

2½ cups watercress with tough stems removed (from a 5-ounce bunch)

¾ pound salmon fillet, cut into thin slices on the diagonal

1. Put the potatoes in a medium saucepan of salted water. Bring to a boil; simmer until tender, about 20 minutes. Drain the potatoes and cut them into ¼-inch slices.

2. In a small bowl, combine the buttermilk, scallions, and horseradish. Season with salt and pepper.

3. In a large bowl, combine the potatoes and the watercress. Add half the dressing and toss. Mound the salad on four plates and drizzle with the remaining dressing.

4. Lightly coat a grill pan or a large non-stick frying pan with vegetable-oil cooking spray and heat over high heat. Season the salmon with salt and pepper and put it in the hot pan. Sear the salmon, without turning, until browned on the bottom, about 30 seconds. Put the salmon slices, browned-side up, on top of the salads.

—MICHELE SCICOLONE

LIGHT LIQUIDS

Oil and vinegar aren't the only liquids suitable for salad dressings. For leaner, lighter dressings, try adding:
• Orange, grapefruit, tomato, or carrot juice; reduced chicken stock; or rice-wine vinegar. These flavorful liquids can be used instead of or in addition to regular vinegar, and they need less oil to balance them.
• Buttermilk. Despite its name, today's buttermilk is actually low in fat, and it gives dressings a creamy consistency.

PER SERVING: CALORIES 296 kcal TOTAL FAT 6.7 gm SATURATED FAT 1.4 gm CARBOHYDRATE 26 gm PROTEIN 23 gm CHOLESTEROL 47 mg

Skinny Salad Dressings

Low-fat dressings line plenty of supermarket shelves these days, but finding one that tastes good is still a challenge. That is, unless you make your own with one of our fat-reducing, flavor-enhancing techniques. Here are three examples of delicious possibilities.

In the first, reducing fresh vegetable or fruit juices intensifies their sweetness, providing a good balance for whatever acid the dressing contains. A case in point is our Sweet-and-Sour Carrot Dressing. Try it with watercress, spinach, Boston or romaine lettuce, or cabbage slaw.

Roasting or smoking vegetables, as in Smoked-Tomato Dressing, concentrates their taste. When pureed, they add body. Toss this dressing with watercress, spinach, steamed potatoes, or grilled white-fleshed fish.

Roasted chiles add a big burst of flavor without a lot of fat. Our Roasted-Poblano Dressing takes advantage of this and will go well with spinach, romaine lettuce, steamed potatoes, or tomatoes.

Sweet-and-Sour Carrot Dressing

MAKES ABOUT 1/2 CUP

- 2 cups fresh carrot juice
- 2 teaspoons lemon juice
- 4 teaspoons rice-wine vinegar
- 1 teaspoon soy sauce
- 1 teaspoon vegetable oil
- 2 drops hot-chili oil
- Salt
- 1 scallion including green top, minced

1. In a small stainless-steel saucepan, bring the carrot and lemon juices to a boil over moderately high heat. Cook until the solids separate from the liquid, about 5 minutes. Strain the liquid and return it to the pan. Boil until reduced to ⅔ cup, about 20 minutes. Transfer to a bowl and let cool.

2. Whisk in the vinegar, soy sauce, and the oils. Season the dressing with salt. Whisk in the scallion just before serving.

—Grace Parisi

PER 1-TABLESPOON SERVING: CALORIES 31 kcal TOTAL FAT .7 gm SATURATED FAT .1 gm CARBOHYDRATE 6 gm PROTEIN .6 gm CHOLESTEROL 0 mg

SMOKED-TOMATO DRESSING

MAKES ABOUT ¹/₂ CUP

¼ pound plum tomatoes (about 2)

¼ teaspoon minced garlic

1½ teaspoons water

1½ teaspoons olive oil

1½ teaspoons balsamic vinegar

¼ teaspoon Worcestershire sauce

¼ teaspoon Dijon mustard

    Salt and fresh-ground black pepper

1 teaspoon chopped flat-leaf parsley

1. Heat a grill pan or heavy frying pan. Add the tomatoes and cover with a metal bowl or pan lid. Cook over high heat, turning once, until the skins are charred, about 10 minutes. Remove from the heat and let sit, covered, for 30 minutes.

2. Peel the tomatoes and put them in a food processor. Add the garlic, water, oil, vinegar, Worcestershire sauce, and mustard. Process until smooth. Season with salt and pepper. Let the dressing stand at room temperature for 3 to 5 hours. Stir in the parsley just before serving.

—GRACE PARISI

PER 1-TABLESPOON SERVING: CALORIES 11 kcal TOTAL FAT .9 gm SATURATED FAT .2 gm
CARBOHYDRATE .7 gm PROTEIN .1 gm CHOLESTEROL 0 mg

ROASTED-POBLANO DRESSING

MAKES ABOUT ¹/₂ CUP

1 medium poblano chile

1 scallion including green top, chopped

1 small clove garlic, chopped

2 tablespoons chopped cilantro

1½ teaspoons lime juice

¼ cup low-fat buttermilk

1½ tablespoons olive oil

    Pinch sugar

    Salt and fresh-ground black pepper

1. Roast the poblano over a gas flame or grill or broil it, turning with tongs until charred all over. When the poblano is cool enough to handle, pull off the skin. Remove the stem, seeds, and ribs.

2. Chop the poblano and put it in a blender or food processor. Add the scallion, garlic, cilantro, and lime juice; pulse to chop. Add the buttermilk, oil, and sugar and puree until smooth. Season with salt and pepper.

—GRACE PARISI

PER 1-TABLESPOON SERVING: CALORIES 27 kcal TOTAL FAT 2.4 gm SATURATED FAT .4 gm
CARBOHYDRATE 1.2 gm PROTEIN .4 gm CHOLESTEROL .4 mg

chapter *4*

PASTA & GRAINS

Saffron Pasta with Coriander and Clams Steamed in Sake, page 101

BROCCOLI RABE WITH ORECCHIETTE

A bitter green that's best with lots of garlic, broccoli rabe is often served dripping in oil. Here, just a tablespoon and a half is ample. We've paired the green with orecchiette, but you can use pasta shells, if you prefer.

WINE RECOMMENDATION
While the bitterness of broccoli rabe can be tricky to pair with wine, whites with assertive aromas often work well. Try a riesling, chenin blanc, or pinot blanc. Avoid cabernet sauvignon and other red wines with high tannin.

4 SERVINGS

1½ tablespoons olive oil

6 cloves garlic, cut into thin slices

1 large red bell pepper, diced

½ teaspoon dried red-pepper flakes

Salt

1¼ pounds broccoli rabe, tough stems removed, cut into 1-inch lengths

½ pound orecchiette

1. In a large frying pan, heat the oil over moderate heat. Add the garlic, bell pepper, and red-pepper flakes. Cook, stirring, until the bell pepper is soft, 10 to 12 minutes. Stir in ½ teaspoon salt.

2. Meanwhile, in a large pot of boiling, salted water, cook the broccoli rabe until almost tender, about 3 minutes. Drain. Add to the frying pan and cook, stirring, for 2 minutes. Season with salt.

3. In a large pot of boiling, salted water, cook the orecchiette until just done, about 15 minutes. Drain and toss with the broccoli-rabe mixture.

—DIANA STURGIS

PER SERVING: CALORIES 316 kcal   TOTAL FAT 7 gm   SATURATED FAT .9 gm
CARBOHYDRATE 55 gm   PROTEIN 12 gm   CHOLESTEROL 0 mg

WILD-MUSHROOM LINGUINE

A combination of dried porcini and fresh oyster and shiitake mushrooms lends a deep, earthy flavor to this autumnal dish. The sauce gets its creaminess from drained nonfat yogurt.

WINE RECOMMENDATION
Though low in fat, this is a full-flavored dish with a creamy texture. Pair it with a big chardonnay, or go for a hearty red such as a Chianti Classico Riserva.

4 SERVINGS

- 1   cup plain nonfat yogurt
- ½   ounce dried porcini or other dried mushrooms
- 1   cup hot water
- 1   tablespoon olive oil
- 1   pound oyster mushrooms, stems removed and tops quartered
- 1   pound shiitake mushrooms, stems removed and caps quartered
-     Salt and fresh-ground black pepper
- 1   carrot, cut into approximately 2-by-¼-inch strips
- 5   shallots, cut into thin slices
- 3   cloves garlic, minced
- ½   cup dry white wine
- 1½ teaspoons chopped fresh thyme, or ½ teaspoon dried
- ¾   pound linguine
- ¼   cup chopped fresh parsley
- ¼   cup grated Parmesan cheese

1. Put the yogurt in a strainer lined with cheesecloth, a coffee filter, or a paper towel set over a bowl. Let drain for at least 1 hour. Throw away the liquid and put the yogurt in the bowl.

2. Meanwhile, put the porcinis in a small bowl and pour the hot water over them. Soak until softened, about 20 minutes. Remove the porcinis and strain the soaking liquid into a bowl through a sieve lined with a paper towel. Rinse the porcinis well to remove any grit and chop them.

3. In a large stainless-steel frying pan, heat 1 teaspoon of the oil over moderately high heat. Add the oyster mushrooms, stir, cover, and cook until done, about 7 minutes. Transfer the oyster mushrooms to a bowl. Repeat with 1 teaspoon of the remaining oil and the shiitakes. Add the chopped porcinis to the other mushrooms. Season with salt and pepper.

4. In a steamer basket set over a saucepan of boiling water, steam the carrot strips until just tender, about 3 minutes. Rinse the carrot with cold water and drain thoroughly.

PER SERVING: CALORIES 505 kcal   TOTAL FAT 7.6 gm   SATURATED FAT 1.9 gm
CARBOHYDRATE 85 gm   PROTEIN 22 gm   CHOLESTEROL 5 mg

5. Heat the remaining teaspoon of oil in the frying pan over low heat. Add the shallots, cover, and cook, stirring occasionally, until translucent, about 5 minutes. Add the garlic and cook, stirring, for 1 minute. Increase the heat to high, stir in the wine, and boil until the wine has almost evaporated, about 2 minutes. Add the mushroom-soaking liquid, carrot, and thyme and cook until heated through, 1 to 2 minutes.

6. Meanwhile, in a large pot of boiling, salted water, cook the linguine until just done, about 12 minutes. Reserve about ½ cup of the pasta-cooking water. Drain the linguine and return it to the pot.

7. Add the carrot mixture and the mushrooms to the linguine. Toss to combine. Stir in the drained yogurt and the parsley. If the sauce seems too thick, add some of the reserved pasta-cooking water. Season with salt and pepper. Serve sprinkled with the Parmesan.

—MARCIA KIESEL

CLEANING WILD MUSHROOMS

Wild mushrooms often arrive in stores with bits of the forest still clinging to them; they almost always require careful cleaning.

• Start by trimming away unwanted parts: Discard any stems that are tough and fibrous, slice off the base of the tender stems, and cut out any damaged parts of the caps.

• Next, wash the mushrooms. Despite what you may have heard, this can be done without damaging their flavor or texture. Simply rinse the mushrooms in a colander under cold running water, tossing gently to dislodge dirt. If you soak the mushrooms, however, they will indeed absorb water and get mushy.

• Any stubborn bits of dirt can be brushed away with a damp cloth or your fingers. Take extra care when cleaning mushrooms with pitted surfaces (such as morels) or with deep gills, both of which tend to collect dirt.

ROASTED-VEGETABLE RAVIOLI WITH YELLOW-PEPPER MOLE SAUCE

Store-bought egg-roll wrappers are real time-savers in this Southwest-inspired vegetable ravioli. The mole sauce is thickened with a corn tortilla, a common technique in Mexican cooking.

WINE RECOMMENDATION
Sauvignon blanc, with its forthright aroma of citrus and herbs, is a good choice for balancing the many flavors in this dish. Wines from California or New Zealand should have the requisite qualities.

4 SERVINGS

1 large yellow bell pepper

3 tomatillos, husked, rinsed, and halved

1 small onion, chopped

3 cloves garlic, minced

½ 6-inch corn tortilla

1 ⅓-pound piece butternut squash, peeled, seeded, and diced

⅓ pound rutabaga, peeled and diced

1 small Japanese eggplant, peeled and diced

1 rib celery, diced

1 small zucchini, diced

1 teaspoon balsamic vinegar

1 teaspoon tomato paste

½ teaspoon Dijon mustard

Salt and fresh-ground black pepper

¼ teaspoon cumin seeds

¼ teaspoon coriander seeds

Pinch aniseed

⅔ cup Vegetable Stock, page 61, Chicken Stock, page 61, or canned broth

½ teaspoon pure chile powder

Pinch ground allspice

1 red bell pepper, cut into ¼-inch strips

4 teaspoons lime juice

4 teaspoons dry white wine

1½ teaspoons sugar

2 teaspoons cornstarch

8 egg-roll wrappers

1½ tablespoons crumbled soft goat cheese

3 tablespoons cilantro leaves

1. Heat the oven to 450°. Roast the yellow bell pepper over a gas flame or grill or broil it, turning with tongs until charred all over, about 10 minutes. When the bell pepper is cool enough to handle, pull off the skin. Remove the stem, seeds, and ribs. Chop the bell pepper.

PER SERVING: CALORIES 305 kcal   TOTAL FAT 2.4 gm   SATURATED FAT .6 gm
CARBOHYDRATE 61 gm   PROTEIN 10.3 gm   CHOLESTEROL 7.2 mg

2. Put the tomatillos and half the onion in a small baking dish and roast in the oven until tender, about 15 minutes. Stir in half the garlic and roast 5 minutes longer. Put the tortilla directly on an oven rack; bake until crisp, about 4 minutes. Cool slightly and then break the tortilla into pieces. Increase the oven temperature to 500°.

3. Heat a large roasting pan in the oven for 5 minutes. Add the squash, rutabaga, eggplant, celery, zucchini, and the remaining onion. Roast, stirring occasionally, until the vegetables are tender, about 30 minutes. Remove from the oven and stir in the remaining garlic, the vinegar, tomato paste, and mustard. Season with salt and pepper. Let the vegetables cool.

4. In a small frying pan, toast the cumin, coriander, and aniseed over moderately high heat, shaking the pan, until fragrant, about 30 seconds. Grind the spices in a mortar with a pestle or in a spice grinder.

5. In a blender or food processor, combine the roasted yellow bell pepper, the tomatillo mixture, the tortilla, the ground spice mixture, the stock, chile powder, and allspice. Puree until smooth. Transfer the sauce to a small stainless-steel saucepan and bring to a boil over moderate heat. Reduce the heat and simmer, stirring, until thickened, about 20 minutes. Season the mole sauce with salt and pepper.

6. In a small stainless-steel saucepan, combine the red-bell-pepper strips with the lime juice, wine, and sugar. Bring just to a boil over moderately high heat. Reduce the heat and simmer until the liquid has thickened, about 15 minutes. Season with salt.

7. Dust a baking sheet with the cornstarch. Put four of the egg-roll wrappers on a work surface. Spoon one quarter of the roasted vegetables into the center of each wrapper. Brush the edges of the wrappers with water, place one of the remaining wrappers on top of each, and press the edges to seal. Transfer the ravioli to the prepared baking sheet, cover with plastic, and refrigerate until chilled, for up to 3 hours.

8. In a large pot of boiling, salted water, cook the ravioli until tender, about 3 minutes. Drain them carefully. Put the ravioli in four shallow bowls and add the mole sauce. Top with the red-bell-pepper mixture, goat cheese, and cilantro leaves.

—CHARLES WILEY

BAKED VEGETABLE PASTA

Peppers, squash, mushrooms, eggplant, leek, onion, arugula, tomatoes—a virtual extravaganza of nutrients fills this luscious layered pasta. Could there be a more delicious way to get your daily servings of vegetables?

WINE RECOMMENDATION
A wine that's understated but not mouth-puckeringly dry will help link the creamy, cheesy flavor and the bite of the arugula and cherry tomatoes. A Loire Valley Pouilly-Fumé or Sancerre would be good, as would a somewhat more aromatic white wine from Germany's Mosel region.

4 SERVINGS

1	red bell pepper
1	yellow bell pepper
1	1-pound piece butternut squash, seeded
1½	teaspoons cooking oil
1	small eggplant, cut into ½-inch cubes
2	ounces mushrooms, stems removed and caps cut into ½-inch pieces
	Salt and fresh-ground black pepper
1	leek, white and light-green parts only, washed well and chopped
1	small onion, chopped
1	clove garlic, minced
2	cups 2-percent milk
1	tablespoon butter
3	tablespoons flour
1¼	cups arugula with stems removed (about 2 ounces)
6	ounces penne
½	cup cherry tomatoes, halved
3	tablespoons grated Parmesan cheese

1. Heat the oven to 450°. Roast the bell peppers over a gas flame or grill or broil them, turning with tongs until charred all over, about 10 minutes. When the peppers are cool enough to handle, pull off the skin. Remove the stems, seeds, and ribs. Cut the bell peppers into ½-inch squares and put them in a large bowl.

2. Put the squash, flesh-side down, in a baking dish. Add ½ inch of hot water to the dish. Bake until the squash is just tender and light brown, about 50 minutes. Remove the skin and cut the squash into ½-inch cubes. Add the squash to the bell peppers.

3. Meanwhile, brush a nonstick baking sheet with ½ teaspoon of the oil. Spread the eggplant and mushrooms out on the baking sheet. Roast until tender and brown, about 25 minutes. Toss the eggplant and mushrooms with the bell peppers and squash and season with salt and pepper. Decrease the oven temperature to 400°.

PER SERVING: CALORIES 406 kcal   TOTAL FAT 9.8 gm   SATURATED FAT 4.5 gm
CARBOHYDRATE 65 gm   PROTEIN 17 gm   CHOLESTEROL 21 mg

4. In a medium saucepan, heat the remaining teaspoon of oil over moderately high heat. Add the leek and onion and cook, stirring, until translucent, about 5 minutes. Add the garlic and cook 1 minute longer. Stir in the milk and bring to a simmer. Remove the pan from the heat, cover, and let stand for 5 minutes. Strain, reserving the liquid and the leek mixture separately.

5. Wipe out the saucepan and melt the butter in it over moderate heat. Whisk in the flour; cook, whisking, until light brown, about 3 minutes. Add the reserved leek-cooking liquid slowly, whisking. Increase the heat to moderately high, add the leek mixture, and cook, stirring, until the sauce is thickened, about 4 minutes. Season with salt and pepper.

6. In a large pot of boiling, salted water, cook the arugula for 30 seconds. Remove the arugula with a slotted spoon, rinse with cold water, and squeeze out the excess liquid. Return the water to a boil and cook the penne until almost done, about 11 minutes. Drain the penne.

7. Add the tomatoes and arugula to the bell peppers, squash, eggplant, and mushrooms. Spread one third of the leek sauce over the bottom of a large gratin or baking dish. Cover with one third of the penne, half of the vegetables, and 1 tablespoon of the Parmesan. Repeat with another layer of leek sauce, penne, vegetables, and Parmesan. Top with the remaining penne and leek sauce and sprinkle the remaining tablespoon of Parmesan over the top. Bake the pasta until heated through and golden brown on top, about 35 minutes.

—BOB CHAMBERS

MAKE IT AHEAD

You can complete the recipe through step five a day in advance. Refrigerate the vegetables and sauce separately. Reheat the sauce before proceeding.

SAFFRON PASTA WITH CORIANDER AND CLAMS STEAMED IN SAKE

Beautiful yellow-tinted saffron noodles provide a stunning showcase for clams steamed in Japanese rice wine. Though making fresh pasta is time-consuming, your efforts will be rewarded by the flavor and elegance of the final dish.

WINE RECOMMENDATION
The classic wine to serve with clams is a crisp, light-bodied Muscadet from the Loire Valley in France.

4 SERVINGS

3 cups sake

2 pounds small clams, such as littleneck or Manila, scrubbed, or mussels, scrubbed and debearded

   Saffron Pasta, next page

2 tablespoons butter

2 teaspoons minced shallot

   Salt

¼ cup chopped fresh cilantro, basil, or parsley

1. In a medium stainless-steel saucepan, simmer the sake until reduced to approximately 1½ cups, about 10 minutes. Discard any clams that have broken shells or that do not clamp shut when tapped. Add the clams to the pot. Cover, raise the heat to high, and bring to a boil. Cook, shaking the pot occasionally, just until the clams begin to open, about 5 minutes. Remove the open clams. Continue to cook, uncovering the pot as necessary to remove the clams as soon as their shells open. Discard any clams that do not open.

2. Meanwhile, in a large pot of boiling, salted water, cook the pasta until just done, about 3 minutes. Drain.

3. Transfer the pasta to four shallow bowls. Top the pasta with the clams. Add the butter, shallot, and a pinch of salt to the liquid remaining in the saucepan and bring to a boil over high heat. Boil for 30 seconds and then pour the sauce over the pasta and clams. Sprinkle with the cilantro.

—SALLY SCHNEIDER

PER SERVING: CALORIES 335 kcal   TOTAL FAT 9.5 gm   SATURATED FAT 4.5 gm   CARBOHYDRATE 50 gm   PROTEIN 11.6 gm   CHOLESTEROL 133 mg

SAFFRON PASTA

MAKES ABOUT 1/2 POUND

1 cup plus 2 tablespoons flour, more for dusting

2 eggs

1 teaspoon saffron threads, crushed

½ teaspoon olive oil

⅛ teaspoon salt

1. Put the flour in a large bowl and make an indentation in the center. Beat the eggs to combine them and pour them into the indentation. Add the saffron, oil, and salt.

2. With a fork, gradually pull the flour into the egg mixture. (You can also use your fingers to do this.) When the dough is a rough mass, transfer it to a floured work surface. Knead the dough, sprinkling with more flour if the dough is sticky, until it forms a smooth and elastic ball, about 10 minutes.

3. Divide the dough into two pieces and wrap the piece you're not working with in plastic. Set the rollers of a pasta machine on the widest notch. Flatten the piece of dough with your hands and pass it through the rollers of the pasta machine. Fold the dough in thirds, press it together, and dust lightly with flour. Feed one of the open ends of the dough through the pasta machine. Repeat the whole process about eight times.

4. Move the setting of the machine to the next notch. This time, don't fold the dough. Dust with flour on one side and roll it through. Continue to flatten the pasta, moving the rollers one notch closer each time. When the rollers are on the thinnest setting, dust the dough with flour on both sides and pass it through the machine. Put it on a floured surface. Repeat with the remaining dough.

5. Let the pasta dry for 10 minutes. Flip the dough and let it dry about 10 minutes longer. When the dough is ready to cut, it should look somewhat leathery but not be so dry that it cracks.

6. Loosely roll each sheet of pasta into a flattened cylinder about 2 inches wide. With a large knife, cut each rolled sheet crosswise into ¼-inch-wide strips. Unravel the strips and put on a baking sheet dusted with flour. Alternatively, pass the pasta through the ¼-inch-wide cutter on the pasta machine. Let the pasta dry for at least 10 minutes.

PASTA WITH FRESH TUNA AND TOMATOES

Top bow-tie pasta with an uncooked tomato sauce redolent of roasted peppers and capers. Chunks of sautéed tuna make this a substantial meal, and a sprinkling of toasted rosemary-seasoned bread crumbs adds yet another taste and texture.

WINE RECOMMENDATION

There are two ways to highlight the bold flavors of this dish: Contrast them with a refreshing wine, such as a Muscadet, or match them with a correspondingly bold wine that can stand up to the acidity of tomatoes and capers, such as a sauvignon blanc, a sparkling wine, or even a mild red such as Valpolicella.

4 SERVINGS

- 2   red bell peppers
- 1   small red onion, chopped
- 6   plum tomatoes, seeded and chopped
- 1   clove garlic, minced
- 2   tablespoons drained capers, chopped
- 2   tablespoons olive oil
- 2   tablespoons red-wine vinegar
- ⅛   teaspoon dried red-pepper flakes
- ¾   cup fresh bread crumbs
- 1½   teaspoons chopped fresh rosemary, or ½ teaspoon dried, crumbled
- ½   pound tuna steak, about ½ inch thick

Salt and fresh-ground black pepper

¾   pound bow-tie pasta

1. Roast the bell peppers over a gas flame or grill or broil them, turning with tongs until charred all over, about 10 minutes. When the peppers are cool enough to handle, pull off the skin. Remove the stems, seeds, and ribs. Chop the peppers. In a large bowl, combine the roasted peppers with the onion, tomatoes, garlic, capers, oil, vinegar, and red-pepper flakes. Let the sauce stand for at least 10 minutes.

2. Coat a small nonstick frying pan with vegetable-oil cooking spray. Add the bread crumbs; cook over moderately high heat, stirring, until browned, about 2 minutes. Add the rosemary; cook, stirring, for 1 minute. Transfer the crumbs to a small bowl.

3. Wipe out the frying pan, coat it with vegetable-oil cooking spray, and heat it over high heat. Season the tuna with ½ teaspoon each salt and pepper. Cook the tuna over high heat, turning once, until browned

PER SERVING: CALORIES 523 kcal   TOTAL FAT 12 gm   SATURATED FAT 2 gm
CARBOHYDRATE 77 gm   PROTEIN 26 gm   CHOLESTEROL 22 mg

but still pink inside, about 2 minutes per side. Transfer the tuna to a plate.

4. Break up the tuna into 1-inch chunks and stir it into the sauce. Season with salt and pepper.

5. In a large pot of boiling, salted water, cook the bow-ties until just done, about 15 minutes. Drain the bow ties and toss with the tomato sauce. Sprinkle the herbed bread crumbs over the top.

—JEAN GALTON

LOW-FAT TUNA

Fresh tuna, unlike canned tuna packed in oil, is low in fat. You can reduce the fat even further by selecting the right variety. Yellowfin has very little total fat, only .3 grams for each ounce of raw fish. On the other end of the scale, bluefin has almost five times as much fat—1.4 grams per ounce.

MAKE IT AHEAD

You can make the uncooked tomato sauce a day in advance, but wait to add the onion until closer to serving time. Adding it a few hours ahead is okay, but if the onion is in the sauce overnight, its flavor will dominate.

VEAL AND LINGUINE ALLA PIZZAIOLA

Veal scallops are often breaded and fried—hardly a low-fat preparation. Here, they're browned and simmered with crushed tomatoes, garlic, and oregano, the aromatic ingredients of *pizzaiola* sauce.

WINE RECOMMENDATION
Avoid high-tannin wines with this dish; the tomatoes can cause them to taste astringent. Barbera, a simple Beaujolais, or a Chilean merlot will work better.

4 SERVINGS

1½ tablespoons olive oil

¾ pound veal scaloppine, pounded to ⅛ inch thick

Salt and fresh-ground black pepper

2 cloves garlic, minced

½ cup dry white wine

2 cups canned crushed tomatoes with their juice (from a 28-ounce can)

½ cup water

2 tablespoons chopped fresh parsley

½ teaspoon dried oregano, crumbled

¾ pound linguine

1. In a large nonstick frying pan, heat the oil over moderately high heat. Season the veal with salt and pepper and add it to the pan. Cook until browned, about 2 minutes. Turn the veal, add the garlic to the pan, and cook until the veal is browned on the second side, about 2 minutes longer. Transfer the veal to a plate.

2. Add the wine to the pan and boil until reduced to approximately 2 tablespoons, 2 to 3 minutes. Stir in the tomatoes with their juice, the water, parsley, and oregano. Season with salt and pepper. Bring just to a simmer over moderately low heat. Return the veal and any accumulated juices to the pan and cook, stirring occasionally, until the sauce is thickened and the veal is tender, about 15 minutes. Remove the veal from the pan.

3. Meanwhile, in a large pot of boiling, salted water, cook the linguine until just done, about 12 minutes. Drain the linguine and toss with the tomato sauce. Serve the veal alongside the linguine.

—MICHELE SCICOLONE

PER SERVING: CALORIES 481 kcal TOTAL FAT 9.4 gm SATURATED FAT 1.4 gm CARBOHYDRATE 70 gm PROTEIN 30 gm CHOLESTEROL 66 mg

POTATO GNOCCHI WITH TOMATO PROSCIUTTO SAUCE

Baking potatoes, usually called Idahos or russets, are the best to use for making gnocchi. Because they're drier than other varieties, they produce lighter dumplings. Baking the potatoes rather than boiling helps to make the dough drier still.

WINE RECOMMENDATION The soft, comforting taste and texture of gnocchi finds its perfect companion in a smooth red, such as a pinot noir or a mellow merlot. Or you can opt for a Chianti Classico Riserva as a counterpoint to the tartness of the tomato sauce.

4 SERVINGS

- 2 pounds baking potatoes (about 4)
  Salt
- 1 cup flour
- 1 tablespoon olive oil
- 1 onion, minced
- 3½ cups canned crushed tomatoes (one 28-ounce can)
  Fresh-ground black pepper
- 2 ounces thin-sliced prosciutto, cut into thin strips
- 2 tablespoons minced fresh basil

1. Heat the oven to 400°. Prick the potatoes with a fork and bake until they are tender, about 45 minutes. Let the potatoes cool slightly.

2. Peel the potatoes and work them through a ricer or a coarse sieve into a large bowl. Let them cool completely. Stir in 1 teaspoon salt. Gradually mix in about half the flour, until the dough becomes stiff. Put the dough on a lightly floured work surface and knead in as much of the remaining flour as necessary so that the dough is no longer sticky.

3. Line two baking sheets with wax paper and dust with flour. Dust your hands and the work surface with flour and divide the dough into four parts. Using both hands, roll each piece of dough into a ½-inch-thick rope and cut the rope into ¾-inch pieces. Shape as directed in "Shaping Gnocchi," opposite page. Put the gnocchi on the prepared baking sheets in a single layer.

4. In a large stainless-steel frying pan, heat the oil over moderately high heat. Add the onion. Cook, stirring, until translucent, about 3 minutes. Add the tomatoes; season with salt and pepper. Bring the sauce to a simmer, reduce the heat, and continue simmering, stirring occasionally, for 20 minutes.

PER SERVING: CALORIES 326 kcal TOTAL FAT 6.3 gm SATURATED FAT 1.1 gm
CARBOHYDRATE 58 gm PROTEIN 12 gm CHOLESTEROL 12 mg

5. In a large pot of boiling, salted water, cook half the gnocchi until they rise to the surface, about 40 seconds. Remove with a slotted spoon and repeat with the remaining gnocchi.

6. Stir the prosciutto and basil into the tomato sauce. Serve the gnocchi topped with the sauce.

—MICHELE SCICOLONE

SHAPING GNOCCHI

For traditional gnocchi, roll one side of each piece of dough along the inside curve of a fork, pressing the opposite side of the gnocchi gently with your thumb. The dough will flatten out slightly and then, as it falls off the fork into your hand, curl in on itself. The finished gnocchi should be oval, with ridges on one side and an indentation on the other. It takes a bit of practice to get this right. Don't worry about it. The ridges and indentation are nice to collect the sauce, but even if you just roll the gnocchi into ovals or flatten them by pressing lightly with a fork, they'll taste just as good.

PEPPERY POLENTA WITH WILD MUSHROOMS

Polenta made with cornmeal, stock, and low-fat milk is an ideal bed for roasted fennel and sautéed mushrooms. We call for coarse-ground cornmeal, but regular is fine, too. Avoid the fine grind, however; instead of fluffy polenta, you'll get a gluey mess.

WINE RECOMMENDATION
Mushrooms can easily stand up to a reasonably big red wine. Try a dolcetto or zinfandel. If you prefer white, go for a full-flavored, buttery chardonnay.

4 SERVINGS

3 large red bell peppers

4 teaspoons olive oil

1 small onion, minced

3 large tomatoes, peeled, seeded, and chopped

2 cloves garlic, minced

1 teaspoon honey

1 tablespoon minced fresh basil

¼ teaspoon minced fresh thyme
Salt and fresh-ground black pepper

1 fennel bulb, halved, cored, and cut lengthwise into ⅓-inch-thick slices

1½ pounds wild mushrooms, such as cremini, chanterelle, or shiitake, or a combination

6½ cups Vegetable Stock, page 61, Chicken Stock, page 61, or canned broth

1½ cups coarse cornmeal

½ cup 2-percent milk

¼ cup grated Romano cheese

2 tablespoons sliced scallion including green tops

1. Roast the peppers over a gas flame or grill or broil them, turning with tongs until charred all over, about 10 minutes. When the peppers are cool enough to handle, pull off the skin. Remove the stems, seeds, and ribs. Chop the peppers.

2. Heat the oven to 400°. In a medium stainless-steel saucepan, heat 2 teaspoons of the oil over moderately high heat. Add the onion and cook, stirring, until translucent, about 5 minutes. Add the roasted peppers, the tomatoes, garlic, honey, basil, and thyme. Season with salt and pepper. Cook, stirring, until thickened, about 15 minutes. Puree the sauce in a blender or food processor.

3. Put the fennel slices in a small baking dish and season with salt and pepper. Roast

PER SERVING: **CALORIES** 457 kcal **TOTAL FAT** 9.6 gm **SATURATED FAT** 1.3 gm **CARBOHYDRATE** 81 gm **PROTEIN** 15 gm **CHOLESTEROL** 8 mg

the fennel in the oven until it is tender and light brown, about 20 minutes.

4. If using shiitake mushrooms, remove the stems. In a large nonstick frying pan, heat the remaining 2 teaspoons oil over moderately high heat. Add the mushrooms and season with salt and pepper. Cook the mushrooms, stirring occasionally, until soft, about 10 minutes.

5. In a heavy medium saucepan, bring the stock to a boil. Add the cornmeal in a slow stream, whisking constantly. Simmer, stirring frequently with a wooden spoon, until the polenta is very thick and pulls away from the sides of the pan, about 20 minutes. Stir in the milk and cook, stirring, until the polenta is creamy, about 10 minutes longer. Remove from the heat and stir in the cheese. Season well with pepper.

6. Meanwhile, reheat the sauce, fennel, and mushrooms. Divide the polenta among four plates. Top the polenta with the fennel and mushrooms and spoon some sauce onto the plates. Sprinkle with the scallion. Pass any remaining sauce.

—HUBERT KELLER

MAKE IT AHEAD

Make the red-pepper and tomato sauce several days in advance. Keep it refrigerated until ready to use. Thin with a little vegetable stock before rewarming.

HOW TO PEEL AND SEED A TOMATO

For easy peeling, cut out the core of a tomato and slash an X in the tomato's base. Then drop the tomato into boiling water and leave just until the skin begins to curl away from the X, ten to fifteen seconds. Transfer the tomato to a bowl of cold water and, when cool enough to handle, strip away the skin. Cut the tomato in half crosswise and squeeze out the seeds, or scoop them out with your fingertips.

ASPARAGUS RISOTTO

Tender spears of asparagus take center stage in a light, tasty risotto that sings of springtime. Toss any asparagus trimmings into the simmering stock to give it an extra dose of flavor.

WINE RECOMMENDATION
The asparagus's sharp flavor is rounded off by the sherry and the nutty brown rice. Serve the risotto with a wine that has good acidity and aroma such as a sauvignon blanc, a pinot blanc, or a chardonnay from Oregon.

4 SERVINGS

- 8 cups Vegetable Stock, page 61, Chicken Stock, page 61, or canned broth
- ¼ teaspoon saffron threads
- 2 tablespoons olive oil
- 3 shallots, minced
- 2 cloves garlic, minced
- 2 cups short-grain brown rice
  Salt
- 1 pound asparagus, tough ends snapped off, stalks cut into ¾-inch pieces, and tips left whole
- 1 tablespoon cider vinegar
- 1 tablespoon dry sherry (optional)
  Fresh-ground black pepper

1. In a medium saucepan, bring the stock to a simmer. Transfer ¼ cup of the stock to a small bowl and add the saffron threads.

2. In a large stainless-steel pot, heat the oil over moderate heat. Add the shallots and garlic and cook, stirring, until starting to soften, about 3 minutes. Add the rice and stir until it begins to turn opaque, about 2 minutes. Add about ½ cup of the simmering stock and 1 teaspoon salt; cook, stirring frequently, until the stock has been absorbed. The rice and stock should bubble gently; adjust the heat as needed. Continue cooking the rice, adding the stock ½ cup at a time and allowing the rice to absorb the stock before adding the next ½ cup. Cook the rice in this way for 30 minutes.

3. Add the saffron liquid; cook, stirring frequently, until the rice is almost tender, about 15 minutes. Add ½ cup more stock as needed. Stir in the asparagus and cook until tender, adding more stock if needed, about 10 minutes longer. The stock that hasn't been absorbed should be thickened by the starch from the rice. You may not need to use all of the liquid, or you may need more stock or some water.

4. Stir in the vinegar, sherry, and salt and pepper. Cook for 2 minutes.

—ANNEMARIE COLBIN

PER SERVING: CALORIES 491 kcal   TOTAL FAT 10.2 gm   SATURATED FAT 1.7 gm
CARBOHYDRATE 88.5 gm   PROTEIN 13.5 gm   CHOLESTEROL 0 mg

ZUCCHINI AND LEMON RISOTTO

The zingy combination of grated lemon zest, lemon juice, and chopped parsley brightens the flavor of this risotto, thick with slices of fresh zucchini.

WINE RECOMMENDATION Almost any dry white wine will accent the tang of lemon zest here, but a red wine wouldn't be out of place either. A light Chinon from the Loire Valley in France or a soft merlot would be good.

4 SERVINGS

- 3 cups Chicken Stock, page 61, or canned chicken broth
- 5 cups water
- 4 teaspoons olive oil
- 4 zucchini (about 2 pounds), sliced
- 1 onion, chopped
- 3 cloves garlic, minced
  Salt
- 2 cups arborio rice
- ½ cup dry white wine
- 3 tablespoons chopped fresh parsley
- 1 tablespoon grated lemon zest
- 1 tablespoon lemon juice
  Fresh-ground black pepper

1. In a medium saucepan, bring the stock and water to a simmer. In a large non-stick frying pan, heat 2 teaspoons of the oil over high heat. Add the zucchini, onion, garlic, and ½ teaspoon salt and cook, stirring frequently, until the vegetables start to soften, about 5 minutes.

2. In a large stainless-steel pot, heat the remaining 2 teaspoons oil over moderate heat. Add the rice and stir until the rice begins to turn opaque, about 2 minutes. Add the wine and cook, stirring frequently, until all the wine has been absorbed. Add the zucchini, ½ cup of the stock, and 1 teaspoon salt and cook, stirring frequently, until the liquid has been absorbed.

3. Continue cooking the rice, adding the stock ½ cup at a time and allowing the rice to absorb the stock before adding the next ½ cup. The rice and stock should bubble gently; adjust the heat as needed. Cook the rice this way until tender, 25 to 30 minutes in all. The stock that hasn't been absorbed should be thickened by the starch from the rice. You may not need to use all of the liquid, or you may need to add more stock or water.

4. Stir the parsley, lemon zest, and lemon juice into the risotto. Season with salt and pepper.

—JEAN GALTON

PER SERVING: CALORIES 332 kcal   TOTAL FAT 4.3 gm   SATURATED FAT .7 gm
CARBOHYDRATE 62 gm   PROTEIN 8 gm   CHOLESTEROL 0 mg

TOMATO RISOTTO

Cherry tomatoes make a break from the salad bowl and turn up quartered and just heated through in this bright-red risotto. Their fresh flavor is heightened by the tomato juice in the cooking liquid.

WINE RECOMMENDATION
Serve a flavorful white wine such as riesling, gewürztraminer, or chenin blanc.

4 SERVINGS

- 1 large onion, chopped
- 4 teaspoons olive oil
- 4 cups tomato juice
- 3¼ cups Chicken Stock, page 61, or canned chicken broth
- 3 shallots, minced
- 2 cups arborio rice
- 1⅓ cups dry white wine
  Salt
- 1¼ pounds cherry tomatoes, quartered
  Fresh-ground black pepper
- ½ cup shredded fresh basil leaves
- 3 tablespoons grated Pecorino Romano cheese

1. Heat the oven to 375°. Toss the onion with 2 teaspoons of the oil and spread on a baking sheet. Roast until brown, about 20 minutes.

2. In a medium stainless-steel saucepan, bring the tomato juice and stock to a simmer.

3. In a large stainless-steel pot, heat the remaining 2 teaspoons oil over moderate heat. Add the shallots and cook, stirring, until translucent, about 4 minutes. Add the rice and stir until the rice begins to turn opaque, about 2 minutes.

4. Add the wine and cook, stirring frequently, until all has been absorbed. Add about ½ cup of the simmering liquid and 1 teaspoon salt. Cook, stirring frequently, until the liquid has been completely absorbed. The rice and liquid should bubble gently; adjust the heat as needed. Continue cooking the rice, adding the liquid ½ cup at a time and allowing the rice to absorb the liquid before adding the next ½ cup. Cook the rice this way until tender, 25 to 30 minutes in all. The liquid that hasn't been absorbed should be thickened by the starch from the rice. You may not need to use all of the liquid, or you may need to add more liquid or some water.

5. Stir the tomatoes and the roasted onions into the risotto and cook until heated through. Season with salt and pepper. Serve with the basil and the Pecorino Romano sprinkled over the top.

—MATTHEW KENNEY

PER SERVING: CALORIES 534 kcal TOTAL FAT 6.9 gm SATURATED FAT 1.6 gm CARBOHYDRATE 104 gm PROTEIN 14 gm CHOLESTEROL 3.8 mg

SHRIMP AND FENNEL RISOTTO

A quick, thrifty stock made with shrimp shells and fennel trimmings is the basis for this unique risotto. Just a pinch of saffron adds to the depth of flavor.

WINE RECOMMENDATION

A refreshing and uncomplicated white wine, such as a Chilean chardonnay, would best show off the heady aromas and flavors of the shrimp, saffron, and fennel.

4 SERVINGS

- 2 medium fennel bulbs, stalks and fronds chopped separately, bulbs cut into ½-inch dice
- ½ pound medium shrimp, shelled and halved lengthwise, shells reserved
- 2 onions, chopped
- 1 carrot, sliced
- 1 tablespoon fennel seeds
- 1 bay leaf
- 9 cups water
  Salt
- ¼ teaspoon saffron threads
- ½ cup dry white wine
- 1 tablespoon olive oil
- 3 plum tomatoes, seeded and diced
- 2 cloves garlic, minced
- 2 cups arborio rice
- 2 tablespoons chopped fresh parsley
  Fresh-ground black pepper

1. In a medium saucepan, combine the chopped fennel stalks and all but 1 tablespoon of the fronds with the shrimp shells, half the onions, the carrot, fennel seeds, bay leaf, water, and 1½ teaspoons salt. Bring to a boil. Reduce the heat and simmer for 30 minutes. Strain the stock and return it to the pan. Keep warm over low heat.

2. In a small bowl, crumble the saffron into the wine. In a large stainless-steel pot, heat the oil over moderately high heat. Add the diced fennel bulbs, the remaining onion, and ½ teaspoon salt. Cook, stirring occasionally, until the fennel and onion start to brown, about 8 minutes. Reduce the heat to moderate.

3. Stir in the tomatoes and garlic and cook for 1 minute. Add the rice and stir until it begins to turn opaque, about 2 minutes. Add the wine mixture; cook, stirring frequently, until all the wine has been absorbed.

4. Bring the stock to a simmer. Add about ½ cup of the simmering stock and cook, stirring frequently, until the stock has been completely absorbed. The rice and stock should bubble gently; adjust the heat as needed. Continue cooking the rice,

PER SERVING: CALORIES 519 kcal   TOTAL FAT 5.3 gm   SATURATED FAT .8 gm
CARBOHYDRATE 93 gm   PROTEIN 19 gm   CHOLESTEROL 71 mg

adding the stock ½ cup at a time and allowing the rice to absorb the stock before adding the next ½ cup. Cook the rice this way until tender, 25 to 30 minutes in all. The stock that hasn't been absorbed should be thickened by the starch from the rice. You may not need to use all of the liquid, or you may need to add more stock or some water.

5. Stir the shrimp and parsley into the risotto. Cook until the shrimp are just done, about 2 minutes. Season with salt and pepper. Sprinkle the reserved fennel fronds over the risotto.

—JEAN GALTON

MAKE IT AHEAD

To enjoy risotto's famous creamy texture without the last-minute fuss, cook the rice until it is almost done and set it and the remaining stock aside. Five to ten minutes before you want to serve, reheat the stock and proceed with the recipe.

Savoy-Cabbage and Lentil Risotto

Unexpected ingredients for risotto—tender lentils, strips of cabbage, pancetta, and sliced carrots—come together to create an interesting low-fat main dish.

WINE RECOMMENDATION
Either a full-flavored white or a rustic red will suit this wine-friendly dish. Try a California chardonnay, or a zinfandel or inexpensive Australian shiraz.

4 SERVINGS

½ cup lentils (about 3 ounces)

2½ cups Chicken Stock, page 61, or canned chicken broth

6½ cups water

1½ teaspoons olive oil

2 carrots, chopped

1 onion, chopped

3 ounces pancetta, chopped

Salt and fresh-ground black pepper

3 cloves garlic, minced

1¼ pounds Savoy cabbage, shredded (about 5 cups)

2 cups arborio rice

¼ cup grated Parmesan cheese

1. In a medium saucepan, combine the lentils with 1 cup of the stock. Bring the stock to a boil. Reduce the heat and simmer, covered, until the lentils are tender, about 20 minutes.

2. In another medium saucepan, bring the remaining stock and the water to a simmer. In a large pot, heat the oil over moderately high heat. Add the carrots, onion, pancetta, and ¾ teaspoon salt. Cook, stirring occasionally, until starting to soften, about 3 minutes. Stir in the garlic. Reduce the heat; add about 3½ cups of the cabbage. Cook, stirring occasionally, until the cabbage wilts, about 5 minutes. Add the rice; stir until it begins to turn opaque, about 2 minutes. Stir in the lentils and any cooking liquid.

3. Add about ½ cup of the simmering stock and 1 teaspoon salt and cook, stirring frequently, until the stock has been completely absorbed. The rice and stock should bubble gently; adjust the heat as needed. Continue cooking the rice, adding the stock ½ cup at a time and allowing the rice to absorb the stock before adding more. Cook the rice this way until tender, 25 to 30 minutes in all. The stock that hasn't been absorbed should be thickened by the starch from the rice. You may not need to use all of the liquid, or you may need to add more stock or some water. Stir in the remaining cabbage; cook until starting to wilt. Add the Parmesan and season with salt and pepper.

—Jean Galton

PER SERVING: CALORIES 588 kcal TOTAL FAT 5.7 gm SATURATED FAT 1.8 gm CARBOHYDRATE 109.5 gm PROTEIN 25 gm CHOLESTEROL 14.6 mg

chapter 5

FISH & SHELLFISH

Lemon Red Snapper, page 127

FISH WRAPPED IN RICE PAPER

These lean fish fillets are spread with a bold ginger paste, wrapped in edible rice paper, and cooked until crisp. Serve the fish bundles on steamed spinach for an unusual main dish. Any leftover ginger paste can be brushed on grilled chicken or pork.

WINE RECOMMENDATION

The candied ginger and orange juice make this a difficult dish to pair with wine because they can muffle a wine's sweetness and fruitiness. However, a full-flavored dry riesling will hold its own here.

4 SERVINGS

- ½ cup candied ginger in heavy syrup,* drained
- 1 chipotle chile *en adobo*,* seeded and minced
- 1 clove garlic, minced
- 1 tablespoon soy sauce
- ½ teaspoon cornstarch
- 1 tablespoon water
- 1 cup orange juice
- 1 cup carrot juice
- 4 9-inch rice-paper rounds*
- 4 lean fish fillets (about 4 ounces each), such as red snapper, striped bass, or orange roughy, ¾ inch thick
  Salt
- 2 tablespoons cilantro leaves

*Available at specialty-food stores and some supermarkets

1. In a blender or miniprocessor, puree the ginger with the chipotle, garlic, and soy sauce. In a small bowl, dissolve the cornstarch in the water.

2. In a small stainless-steel saucepan, boil the orange juice and carrot juice until reduced to approximately ¾ cup, about 15 minutes. Whisk in the cornstarch mixture and simmer until thickened. Reduce the heat to very low and stir in 1 teaspoon of the ginger puree.

3. Heat the oven to 375°. Dip the rice-paper rounds in a bowl of water to moisten them. Let sit on a work surface until pliable, about 2 minutes.

4. Season the fish with salt; spread 1 teaspoon of the ginger paste over each fillet. Top each with a quarter of the cilantro. Set one fillet, skin-side up, in the center of each of the rice-paper rounds. Fold the sides of the rice paper over the fish to enclose it.

5. Coat a large nonstick ovenproof frying pan with vegetable-oil cooking spray. Heat the pan over moderate heat. Add the

PER SERVING: CALORIES 327 kcal   TOTAL FAT 2.5 gm   SATURATED FAT .4 gm   CARBOHYDRATE 50 gm   PROTEIN 27.5 gm   CHOLESTEROL 42 mg

fish packets, seam-side down, and cook until crisp and brown, about 3 minutes. Spray the fish packets with vegetable-oil cooking spray and turn them. Cook until golden brown, about 3 minutes. Turn the packets over once more and bake until the fish is just done, 3 to 5 minutes. Serve the fish with the carrot sauce.

—GRACE PARISI

NONSTICK PANS

They're an indispensable part of any low-fat cook's equipment, but nonstick pans do need a little care to keep them in top condition. Some tips:
• Remove empty pans from hot burners immediately after cooking.
• Let hot pans cool before putting them in water.
• Don't put nonstick pans in the dishwasher—dishwashing detergent can damage their coatings.
• Dry pans after washing.
• If you stack pans for storage, protect the nonstick surfaces paper towels.

SEA BASS WITH CITRUS COUSCOUS

A tangy sauce made from sliced red onions and fresh-squeezed orange juice tops grilled sea bass. The couscous, cooked in citrus-spiked vegetable broth, makes an ideal accompaniment.

WINE RECOMMENDATION
Highlight the lively flavors of orange and lemon zest with a clean, crisp sauvignon blanc or an Italian Soave or Orvieto.

4 SERVINGS

- 5 teaspoons olive oil
- 2 red onions, cut into 1/4-inch slices
- 1 1/3 cups orange juice (from about 3 oranges)
- 1 1/2 tablespoons chopped fresh parsley
  Pinch ground coriander
  Dash Tabasco sauce
  Salt and fresh-ground black pepper
- 2 cups Vegetable Stock, page 61, or canned vegetable broth
- 3/4 teaspoon grated orange zest
- 1/2 teaspoon grated lemon zest
- 1/2 teaspoon grated lime zest
- 1/4 teaspoon Asian chili paste
- 1 1/4 cups couscous (about 7 ounces)
- 4 sea-bass fillets (about 5 ounces each) or other lean fish fillets, such as red snapper, striped bass, or orange roughy, 1 inch thick
- 4 teaspoons lemon juice

1. In a medium stainless-steel saucepan, heat 2 teaspoons of the oil over moderately low heat. Add the onions and cook, stirring, until translucent, about 5 minutes. Add the orange juice and simmer until reduced to approximately 3/4 cup, about 8 minutes. Add the parsley, coriander, Tabasco, and salt and pepper to taste.

2. In another medium stainless-steel saucepan, combine the stock, citrus zests, chili paste, and 2 teaspoons of the remaining oil. Bring to a boil. Stir in the couscous. Cover, remove from the heat, and let sit for 5 minutes. Fluff the couscous with a fork and season with salt and pepper.

3. Light the grill or heat the broiler. Rub the fish with the remaining teaspoon of oil and season with salt and pepper. Grill or broil the fish until starting to brown, about 3 minutes. Turn the fish and drizzle the lemon juice over the top. Cook until just done, 3 to 5 minutes longer. Put a mound of couscous on each of four plates. Top with the fish and the orange sauce.

—HANS RÖCKENWAGNER

PER SERVING: CALORIES 459 kcal   TOTAL FAT 9 gm   SATURATED FAT 1.5 gm
CARBOHYDRATE 58.3 gm   PROTEIN 34.8 gm   CHOLESTEROL 58 mg

STEAMED FISH
WITH GINGER AND SCALLIONS

Coated with soy sauce, wine, and white-wine vinegar and then steamed on a bed of ginger and scallions, this is a beautifully flavored whole fish. Plain steamed rice is all you need to go along with it.

WINE RECOMMENDATION
Riesling and gewürztraminer are ideal with an Asian dish such as this. A festive alternative would be Champagne or another sparkling wine.

4 SERVINGS

  2 tablespoons soy sauce

  2 tablespoons dry white wine

  2 teaspoons white-wine vinegar

  2 teaspoons peanut oil
     Salt and fresh-ground black pepper

2½ tablespoons matchstick strips of fresh ginger

  3 scallions including green tops, 2 cut into 2-inch pieces, 1 sliced thin

  1 2-pound red snapper, striped bass, or sea bass, cleaned

  1 teaspoon Asian sesame oil

1½ tablespoons minced cilantro

1. In a small bowl, combine the soy sauce, wine, vinegar, and peanut oil. Season with a pinch each of salt and pepper.

2. Sprinkle 1 tablespoon of the ginger and half the scallion pieces over the bottom of a 10-inch glass pie plate. Put the fish in the pie plate and rub the soy-sauce mixture all over the fish, inside and out. Sprinkle 1½ teaspoons of the remaining ginger and the remaining scallion pieces in the cavity of the fish. Sprinkle the remaining tablespoon of ginger over the top.

3. Put a wire rack in the bottom of a wok or large roasting pan. Pour about ¾ inch of water into the wok. Bring to a simmer over moderately high heat. Put the pie plate with the fish on the rack. Cover the wok and steam the fish until just done, about 20 minutes.

4. Turn off the heat and remove the lid. Using two large metal spatulas, transfer the fish from the pie plate to a platter. Pour the juices from the pie plate over the fish and drizzle with the sesame oil. Scatter the sliced scallion and the cilantro over the top.

—EILEEN YIN-FEI LO

PER SERVING: CALORIES 140 kcal   TOTAL FAT 5.7 gm   SATURATED FAT 1 gm
CARBOHYDRATE 2 gm   PROTEIN 18 gm   CHOLESTEROL 78 mg

FISH IN A FOIL PACKET

For a nearly effortless meal, seal fish fillets, bell-pepper strips, and herbs in foil packets and pop them onto the grill or into the oven. In a quarter of an hour, you'll have juicy fish that's made its own sauce. Serve it with rice.

WINE RECOMMENDATION
The simple, straightforward flavors of this dish call for an equally uncomplicated white wine. An Italian pinot grigio, a vinho verde from Portugal, or a crisp Muscadet from France would add the right note.

4 SERVINGS

- 1 red bell pepper, cut into approximately 2-by-3/8-inch strips
- 1 yellow bell pepper, cut into approximately 2-by-3/8-inch strips
- 2 cloves garlic, cut into thin slices
- 2 teaspoons chopped fresh thyme
- 2 teaspoons chopped fresh rosemary
- 1/4 teaspoon dried red-pepper flakes
  Salt
- 4 lean fish fillets (about 6 ounces each), such as red snapper, striped bass, or orange roughy, 1/2 inch thick
- 1 teaspoon olive oil
  Fresh-ground black pepper
- 2 tablespoons dry white wine
- 2 teaspoons chopped fresh parsley

1. Light the grill or heat the oven to 400°. In a medium bowl, toss the bell pepper with the garlic, thyme, rosemary, red-pepper flakes, and 1/2 teaspoon salt. Rub the fish with the oil and season it with salt and black pepper.

2. Put four 18-by-12-inch rectangles of heavy-duty aluminum foil on a work surface, each with a short side toward you. Spoon a quarter of the bell-pepper mixture onto the lower half of each rectangle. Put a fish fillet on top of the peppers, and drizzle each fillet with 1 1/2 teaspoons of the wine. Fold the top half of each sheet of foil over the fish and crimp the edges to secure.

3. Put the foil packets on the grill and cover the grill. Cook for 6 minutes. Rotate the packets and cook until the fish is just done, about 6 minutes longer. Alternatively, bake the fish for 15 minutes.

4. Cut open the packets. Transfer the fish to four plates and spoon the bell peppers and cooking juices over the top. Sprinkle with the parsley.

—JANET HAZEN DE JESUS

PER SERVING: CALORIES 199 kcal TOTAL FAT 3.5 gm SATURATED FAT .6 gm CARBOHYDRATE 3.2 gm PROTEIN 35 gm CHOLESTEROL 62.3 mg

LEMON RED SNAPPER

Tropical coconut rice with spinach and cilantro accompanies this lovely lemon-scented fish. If you prefer, make the citrusy marinade with lime or orange juice instead of lemon juice.

WINE RECOMMENDATION
A dish with such complex yet delicate flavors would harmonize well with a white wine such as a chardonnay, sauvignon blanc, or pinot blanc.

4 SERVINGS

- 4 teaspoons olive oil
- 1 large onion, chopped
- 1 cup long-grain rice
- 1 jalapeño pepper, minced
- 1 clove garlic, minced
- 2/3 cup chopped spinach
- 3 tablespoons canned unsweetened coconut milk
- 1/2 teaspoon ground cumin
  Salt and fresh-ground black pepper
- 2 cups water
- 1 1/2 tablespoons shredded unsweetened coconut*
- 1 1/2 tablespoons minced cilantro
- 1/2 teaspoon fine slivers of lime zest
- 1 tablespoon lime juice
- 3 tablespoons pine nuts
- 4 teaspoons fine slivers of lemon zest
- 1/3 cup lemon juice

- 4 teaspoons dry sherry
- 4 red-snapper fillets with skin (about 5 ounces each) or other lean fish fillets, such as striped bass or orange roughy, 3/4 inch thick
- 1 1/2 teaspoons minced fresh chives

*Available at health-food stores

1. Heat the oven to 350°. In a medium saucepan, heat 2 teaspoons of the oil over moderate heat. Add half the onion and cook, stirring, until translucent, about 5 minutes. Stir in the rice, jalapeño, and garlic. Add the spinach, coconut milk, cumin, 1 teaspoon salt, 1/4 teaspoon pepper, and the water. Bring to a boil. Cover, reduce the heat, and simmer until all the liquid is absorbed and the rice is tender, about 20 minutes. Fluff the rice with a fork and stir in the coconut, cilantro, lime zest, and lime juice.

2. Meanwhile, in a small ovenproof saucepan, toss the pine nuts with the lemon zest. Cook until the nuts are brown and fragrant, about 8 minutes.

3. In a glass or stainless-steel baking dish, combine the remaining 2 teaspoons oil with

PER SERVING: CALORIES 457 kcal **TOTAL FAT** 13.5 gm **SATURATED FAT** 4.5 gm **CARBOHYDRATE** 47 gm **PROTEIN** 35 gm **CHOLESTEROL** 52 mg

the remaining onion, the lemon juice, and sherry. Season with salt and pepper. With a sharp knife, make three ½-inch-deep cuts in each snapper fillet. Add the fish to the marinade and turn the fish to coat. Let stand for 5 minutes. With a spoon, transfer half the marinade from the baking dish to a small bowl.

4. Bake the fish, basting once with the reserved marinade, until just done, about 15 minutes. Transfer the fish to four plates and spoon the pan juices over the top. Sprinkle the toasted pine nuts and chives over the fish and serve with the coconut rice.

—ALLEN SUSSER

KITCHEN TIP

Allen Susser, of Chef Allen's in Miami, has a simple philosophy when it comes to low-fat cooking: Don't try to cut out oil and rich foods altogether, just use small amounts and make sure they're top quality. Coconut milk, for instance, is a high-fat ingredient, but by using a mere three tablespoons in the coconut rice, we get the benefit of its flavor without going overboard on the fat.

COD STEAKS WITH RED-PEPPER SAUCE

Both the red bell peppers and the fish are steamed, so cooking this dish is extremely simple. The peppers are then pureed with olive oil, wine vinegar, and garlic to make a sauce for the fish. As long as you're using the steamer, put in some thin green beans to serve as a side dish.

WINE RECOMMENDATION
Either a crisp sauvignon blanc from New Zealand or a white wine from Bordeaux would provide a nice counterpoint to the sharp, earthy flavors of the red-bell-pepper puree.

4 SERVINGS

- 1 red bell pepper, halved, cored, and seeded
- 1 tablespoon olive oil
- ½ teaspoon wine vinegar
- 1 clove garlic, minced
   Salt
- 4 cod steaks (about 6 ounces each) or other lean fish steaks, such as halibut, 1 inch thick
- 2 teaspoons chopped fresh parsley

1. In a large saucepan, bring 2 inches of water to a boil. Put the bell-pepper halves in a steamer basket, skin-side up, and put it over the boiling water. Cover and cook the peppers over moderate heat for 15 minutes. Remove the peppers. When the peppers are cool enough to handle, peel the peppers. Leave the water in the pan.

2. In a blender or food processor, puree the steamed peppers with the oil, vinegar, garlic, and ¼ teaspoon salt. Transfer the sauce to a small stainless-steel saucepan. Keep warm over low heat.

3. Return the water in the saucepan to a boil. Arrange the cod steaks in the steamer basket in a single layer. Season with salt. Put the steamer basket over the boiling water. Cover and steam over moderate heat until the fish is just done, about 10 minutes. Transfer the fish to paper towels to drain. Remove the skin, if desired. Serve the cod topped with the red-pepper sauce and the chopped parsley sprinkled over all.

—STEPHANIE LYNESS

PER SERVING: CALORIES 176 kcal   TOTAL FAT 4.5 gm   SATURATED FAT .7 gm
CARBOHYDRATE 1.5 gm   PROTEIN 31 gm   CHOLESTEROL 73 mg

POACHED COD
WITH TOMATOES AND FENNEL

A tomato-based broth accented with the Provençal flavors of garlic, fennel, and orange zest serves as a poaching liquid for fillets of cod. Serve with pasta or rice.

WINE RECOMMENDATION
In Provence, the wine of choice is often rosé. Almost any full-bodied white would also be compatible, as would low-tannin reds like Côtes-du-Rhône Villages or barbera, a fruity Italian red.

4 SERVINGS

½ teaspoon fennel seeds

2 teaspoons olive oil

1 large fennel bulb, chopped

1 leek, white and light-green parts only, halved lengthwise, chopped, and washed well

2 cloves garlic, minced

3½ cups canned chopped tomatoes with their juice (one 28-ounce can)

½ teaspoon grated orange zest

1 bay leaf

Salt and fresh-ground black pepper

4 cod fillets (about 6 ounces each) or other lean fish fillets, such as halibut or whitefish, ¾ inch thick

2 tablespoons chopped fresh basil

1. Grind the fennel seeds in a mortar with a pestle or in a spice grinder.

2. In a large stainless-steel frying pan, heat the oil over moderately low heat. Add the fennel, leek, and garlic; cook, covered, stirring occasionally, until translucent, about 10 minutes. Add the tomatoes with their juice, the ground fennel, orange zest, bay leaf, and a pinch each of salt and pepper. Bring to a boil over moderately high heat. Reduce the heat and simmer, covered, for 20 minutes.

3. Sprinkle the fillets with salt and pepper; put them in the tomato sauce. Spoon some sauce over the fish, cover, and simmer gently until just done, 8 to 10 minutes.

4. With a slotted spoon, transfer the fish to a platter and cover with aluminum foil. Discard the bay leaf. Bring the sauce to a boil over moderately high heat; cook until thickened, about 3 minutes. Stir in any juices from the fish. Season with salt and pepper and stir in the basil. Spoon the sauce over the fish.

—GEORGIA CHAN DOWNARD

PER SERVING: CALORIES 221 kcal TOTAL FAT 4 gm SATURATED FAT .6 gm
CARBOHYDRATE 13 gm PROTEIN 33 gm CHOLESTEROL 73 mg

LEMON-SCENTED POMPANO ON SPINACH AND LEEKS

Pompano, a beautiful firm-fleshed fish, needs only to be steamed to bring out its mild sea flavor. Perfume the steaming liquid with bay leaves and slices of lemon and lime. This recipe also works well for sea scallops.

WINE RECOMMENDATION
The delicacy of this steamed fish would be lost if it were served with an overbearing wine. Choose a flinty Sancerre from the Loire Valley in France, a restrained chardonnay from Oregon or Washington State, or a French Chablis.

4 SERVINGS

12   bay leaves

 2   lemons, cut into thin slices

 2   limes, cut into thin slices

 2   cups water

 2   leeks, white and light-green parts only, halved lengthwise, cut crosswise into thin slices, and washed well

 2   pounds spinach or Swiss chard, tough stems removed and leaves washed

 4   pompano fillets (about 4 ounces each) or other thin, lean fish fillets, such as flounder or trout

     Salt

 2   teaspoons soy sauce

     Fresh-ground black pepper

1. In a large saucepan, combine the bay leaves, lemon and lime slices, and water. Bring to a simmer over low heat. Cook, covered, for 2 minutes.

2. Uncover the pan and bring the water to a boil over high heat. Put the leeks in a steamer basket and set it over the boiling water. Cover and cook until tender, about 3 minutes. Pack the spinach into the steamer basket, cover, and steam until wilted, about 4 minutes. Transfer the steamer basket to the sink and press the spinach gently to extract some of the excess liquid. Transfer the spinach and leeks to a large frying pan.

3. Return the steaming liquid to a boil. Sprinkle the fish with salt, put the fish in the steamer basket, and set it over the boiling water. Cover and cook until the fish is just done, 3 to 4 minutes.

4. Reheat the spinach and leeks over high heat. Add the soy sauce and toss to combine; season with pepper. Serve the fish on the warm spinach.

—MARCIA KIESEL

PER SERVING: CALORIES 258 kcal   TOTAL FAT 11.5 gm   SATURATED FAT 4.1 gm
CARBOHYDRATE 14 gm   PROTEIN 27 gm   CHOLESTEROL 57 mg

HALIBUT WITH SPICY VEGETABLE SAUCE

The zesty Caribbean-style sauce here, made from tomatoes, sweet potatoes, green bell peppers, and Scotch bonnet chile, tastes great with halibut. Use more or less of the chile pepper according to your taste.

WINE RECOMMENDATION
Hot peppers can numb the palate, dulling the fruity flavors of most wines, but a bold gewürztraminer or riesling, or even a good Vouvray (made in France's Loire Valley from the chenin blanc grape), can take the heat.

4 SERVINGS

- 2 sweet potatoes (about ¾ pound in all), peeled and cut into ½-inch dice
- 2 teaspoons cooking oil
- 1 large onion, chopped
- 2 green bell peppers, chopped
- 2 ribs celery, chopped
- 3 scallions, white parts minced and green tops sliced
- 3 cloves garlic, minced
- 2 tablespoons minced fresh ginger
- ½ teaspoon minced Scotch bonnet chile, or 1 teaspoon minced serrano chile
- 3½ cups canned crushed tomatoes with their juice (one 28-ounce can)
- 2½ teaspoons chopped fresh thyme
- ¼ teaspoon ground allspice
- Salt and fresh-ground black pepper

- 4 halibut fillets (about 6 ounces each) or other lean fish fillets, such as cod or whitefish, ¾ inch thick

1. Heat the oven to 450°. Put the sweet potatoes in a steamer basket and set it over a saucepan of boiling water. Cover; cook over moderate heat until tender, about 5 minutes.

2. In a large stainless-steel frying pan, heat the oil over moderately high heat. Add the onion, bell peppers, celery, minced scallions, garlic, ginger, and chile. Cook, stirring occasionally, until the vegetables start to brown, about 8 minutes. Stir in the tomatoes, 2 teaspoons of the thyme, and the allspice. Bring to a boil. Reduce the heat to low; simmer until starting to thicken, 4 to 5 minutes. Stir in the sweet potatoes; season with salt and pepper. Spoon the sauce into a 9-by-13-inch glass or ceramic baking dish.

3. Add the fish and cover with aluminum foil. Bake until the fish is just done and the sauce bubbles, about 10 minutes. Sprinkle with the remaining scallions and thyme.

—MARCIA KIESEL

PER SERVING: CALORIES 357 kcal TOTAL FAT 7.1 gm SATURATED FAT 1 gm CARBOHYDRATE 34 gm PROTEIN 40 gm CHOLESTEROL 54 mg

HALIBUT WITH CHILE MUSTARD SAUCE AND CILANTRO CHUTNEY

A pungent marinade of mustard seeds, jalapeño, and turmeric makes the fish come out spicy and full-flavored. A simple no-cook chutney completes the dish.

WINE RECOMMENDATION
High-acid foods, such as the chutney spiked with lemon juice that accompanies this dish, shine when matched with a crisp, sparkling wine. Sauvignon blanc or chardonnay from a cool-climate region such as Washington State would also fill the bill.

4 SERVINGS

 1 teaspoon cumin seeds

1½ cups packed cilantro leaves

 ¼ cup chopped red onion

 ¼ cup lemon juice

1½ teaspoons sugar

 2 teaspoons minced jalapeño pepper

4½ tablespoons water

 2 teaspoons black* or yellow mustard seeds, ground

 2 teaspoons cooking oil

 ¼ teaspoon turmeric

 Salt

 4 halibut fillets (about 6 ounces each) or other lean fish fillets, such as cod or whitefish, ¾ inch thick

*Available at Indian markets

1. In a small heavy frying pan, toast the cumin seeds over moderately high heat, shaking the pan, until fragrant, about 1 minute. Grind in a mortar with a pestle or in a spice grinder.

2. In a blender or food processor, combine the cilantro, onion, lemon juice, sugar, 1 teaspoon of the minced jalapeño, and the ground cumin. Add 2 tablespoons of the water and puree the chutney until smooth.

3. In a small bowl, combine the ground mustard seeds with the remaining 2½ tablespoons water. Stir in the remaining teaspoon jalapeño, the oil, turmeric, and ¼ teaspoon salt. Put the halibut in a medium glass or stainless-steel baking dish and spread the mustard-seed marinade over the fillets, turning to coat. Cover and refrigerate for 1 hour.

4. Heat a large nonstick frying pan over low heat. Add the fish and marinade; cook, covered, for 5 minutes. Turn; cook, covered, until just done, about 5 minutes more. Season with salt. Put the fish on plates; spoon the pan sauce over. Serve with the chutney.

—BHARTI KIRCHNER

PER SERVING: CALORIES 235 kcal TOTAL FAT 6.9 gm SATURATED FAT .9 gm CARBOHYDRATE 4.9 gm PROTEIN 36.5 gm CHOLESTEROL 54 mg

HOT-AND-SOUR FISH STEW

Serve this quick, satisfying Vietnamese fish stew with the steamed jasmine rice on the side, or mound the rice in bowls and top with the fish and broth.

WINE RECOMMENDATION
Hot and sour are two very difficult taste sensations to match with wine, but there is one simple solution: Serve the fish stew and rice with an inexpensive sparkling wine.

4 SERVINGS

¼ cup plus 2 teaspoons Asian fish sauce (nuoc mam or nam pla)*

1 teaspoon minced fresh ginger

½ teaspoon turmeric

2 halibut or cod steaks (about 10 ounces each), ¾ inch thick

5 cups water

2 stalks lemongrass,* bottom third only, cut into 2-inch pieces, or two 3-inch strips lemon zest

1 tomato, quartered

½ teaspoon grated lime zest

¼ cup lime juice

1 small dried red chile pepper, or ½ teaspoon dried red-pepper flakes

2 scallions including green tops, sliced

2 tablespoons chopped cilantro

Fresh-ground black pepper

4 cups steamed white rice, preferably jasmine, for serving

*Available at Asian markets and many supermarkets

1. In a small bowl, combine the 2 teaspoons fish sauce with the ginger and turmeric. Rub the fish on both sides with the mixture and let stand for 5 minutes.

2. In a large stainless-steel saucepan, bring the water and lemongrass to a simmer over moderate heat. Add the fish steaks and simmer until just done, about 8 minutes. Transfer the fish to a plate and let cool. Set the pan aside. Discard the skin and bones from the fish and separate each steak into two pieces.

3. Bring the cooking liquid back to a simmer. Stir in the tomato, lime zest, lime juice, and chile. Simmer for 2 minutes. Add the ¼ cup fish sauce and the fish. Remove the pan from the heat; stir in the scallions and cilantro. Season with black pepper. Put a piece of fish in each of four bowls and ladle the broth over the top. Serve with the rice.

—MARCIA KIESEL

PER SERVING: CALORIES 450 kcal TOTAL FAT 5.4 gm SATURATED FAT 1 gm
CARBOHYDRATE 64 gm PROTEIN 32.8 gm CHOLESTEROL 36.7 mg

CARIBBEAN FISH STEW WITH GREEN BANANAS

Bananas, allspice, and a fiery Scotch bonnet chile provide an island accent here. Don't peel the bananas before slicing them. They're eaten skins and all.

WINE RECOMMENDATION
The forceful flavors of tomato, saffron, bell pepper, and okra will be complemented by a full-bodied chardonnay or a light fruity red, such as a gamay or a light pinot noir.

4 SERVINGS

- 4 lean fish steaks (about 6 ounces each), such as halibut or cod, 1 inch thick
- 5½ cups water
- 2 teaspoons olive oil
- 1 large rib celery, sliced
- 1 small onion, chopped
- 1 small green bell pepper, chopped
- 1 tomato, chopped
- 1 scallion including green top, chopped
- 1 clove garlic, minced
- Pinch saffron threads
- Salt and fresh-ground black pepper
- 1 Scotch bonnet chile, pierced with a knife
- 3 sprigs fresh thyme, or ½ teaspoon dried
- 2 3-inch strips lime zest
- ¾ teaspoon ground allspice
- 3 large green bananas, unpeeled, rinsed, and cut into thin slices
- ⅔ cup okra cut into ⅓-inch slices (about 2½ ounces)
- 1 small zucchini, halved lengthwise and cut crosswise into ¼-inch slices
- 4 teaspoons lime juice
- 4 cups steamed white rice, for serving
- Lime wedges, for serving

1. Put the fish and water in a large sauce-pan. Bring just to a boil over moderately high heat. Reduce the heat and simmer, skimming, until the fish is just done, about 8 minutes. Transfer the fish to a plate, let cool, and discard the skin and bones. Strain the fish broth.

2. In a large heavy saucepan, heat the oil over moderately low heat. Add the celery, onion, and bell pepper and cook, stirring, until soft, about 10 minutes. Increase the heat to moderately high. Add the tomato, scallion, and garlic and cook, stirring, for 2 minutes. Add the fish broth and saffron and season with salt and pepper. Bring to a simmer. Add the Scotch bonnet, thyme, lime zest, and allspice. Simmer for 10 minutes.

PER SERVING: CALORIES 565 kcal TOTAL FAT 6.7 gm SATURATED FAT 1.1 gm CARBOHYDRATE 88.8 gm PROTEIN 36.8 gm CHOLESTEROL 44.1 mg

3. Meanwhile, in a small saucepan of simmering water, cook the bananas until tender, about 10 minutes. Remove the bananas with a slotted spoon. Add the okra to the simmering water; cook until tender, about 4 minutes. Drain the okra.

4. Stir the zucchini into the stew and simmer until just tender, about 4 minutes. Discard the Scotch bonnet and lime zest. Add the bananas, okra, lime juice, and the fish. Simmer until just heated through. Season with salt and pepper. Serve the stew over the rice with lime wedges.

—Marcia Kiesel

Scotch Bonnet Chiles

If there is such a thing as a distinctly Caribbean flavor, it is probably that of the stingingly hot, slightly fruity Scotch bonnet chile. Considered one of the hottest chiles in the world, this cousin of the spicy habañero can be red, yellow, or orange. The Scotch bonnet gets its unlikely name from its slightly flat-tened rounded shape, which looks like a Scotsman's tam-o'-shanter. Though its taste is unique, there are other fresh chiles that can be substituted for the Scotch bonnet, including (from hottest to mildest) Thai or bird, serrano, hot cherry pepper, or jalapeño.

LOBSTER AMÉRICAINE WITH RICE AND HARICOTS VERTS

Every bit of the lobster is used to make this elegant dish. The chunks of meat served in a tarragon-infused sauce are from the tail and claws; the shells and head are sautéed to flavor the stock that's the base of the sauce.

WINE RECOMMENDATION
The concentrated flavors of the sauce demand a full-flavored wine. A rich white from Burgundy or a big chardonnay from California would be good. Alternatively, try a white from the Rhône in France, such as viognier or marsanne.

4 SERVINGS

- 2 live lobsters (about 1½ pounds each)
- 1 tablespoon olive oil
- 1 onion, chopped
- 1 carrot, chopped
- 1 clove garlic, sliced
- ¼ cup cognac
- ¾ cup dry white wine
- 2 plum tomatoes, chopped
- 3 sprigs flat-leaf parsley
- 1 sprig fresh thyme, or ¼ teaspoon dried
- 1 bay leaf
  Salt
- 5 cups water
  Fresh-ground black pepper
- ¾ pound *haricots verts* or thin green beans

- 1 teaspoon butter
- 1½ teaspoons flour
- 1 tablespoon minced fresh tarragon
- 1 tablespoon minced fresh chives
- 4 cups steamed white rice, preferably jasmine, for serving

1. In a large pot of boiling, salted water, cook the lobsters until just done, about 10 minutes. Remove from the pot. When cool enough to handle, twist the lobsters to separate the tail section and the "arms" and claws from the bodies. Turn the tails upside down. Using scissors or a large sharp knife, cut through the underside of the shells. Remove the tail meat from the shells. Crack the claws and remove the meat from the claws and "arms." Cut all the lobster meat into ½-inch pieces and put in a bowl. Reserve the shells and heads.

2. In a large heavy stainless-steel saucepan, heat the oil over moderately high heat. Add the onion and carrot and cook, stirring occasionally, until starting to brown, about 5 minutes. Add the lobster shells and heads

PER SERVING: CALORIES 458 kcal TOTAL FAT 5.7 gm SATURATED FAT 1.3 gm
CARBOHYDRATE 72 gm PROTEIN 24 gm CHOLESTEROL 57 mg

and the garlic and cook until fragrant, about 3 minutes. Add the cognac and warm for 20 seconds. Carefully ignite the cognac with a match and cook until the flame burns out, about 1 minute.

3. Add the wine, tomatoes, parsley, thyme, bay leaf, $\frac{1}{4}$ teaspoon salt, and the water to the pan. Bring to a boil. Reduce the heat; simmer, covered, stirring occasionally, for 50 minutes. Strain the stock into a large saucepan. Discard the vegetables, shells, and herbs. Add any accumulated liquid from the lobster meat, and boil over high heat until reduced to 1 cup, about 15 minutes. Season with salt and pepper.

4. Meanwhile, in a medium saucepan of boiling, salted water, cook the *haricots verts* until tender, about 5 minutes. Drain.

5. In a small bowl, work the butter and flour into a paste. Whisk the paste into the boiling lobster stock. Reduce the heat to low and stir in the lobster meat, the tarragon, and half the chives. Cook until warmed through, about 3 minutes.

6. To serve, spoon the lobster and the sauce over the rice and arrange the *haricots verts* on top. Sprinkle with the remaining chopped chives.

—Diana Sturgis

Quick Seafood Stock

Shrimp and lobster shells are loaded with seafood flavor. Even if the recipe doesn't call for it, save your shells and whip up a batch of quick shellfish stock. Simply simmer the shells in water with a splash of wine, some chopped onion and celery, parsley, and a bay leaf for about forty-five minutes. Strain the stock and use it as a poaching liquid or to make a sauce, or freeze it for later.

CILANTRO SHRIMP
WITH GINGER DIPPING SAUCE

Simmering shrimp shells with cilantro, scallions, and ginger makes a flavorful poaching liquid. The cooked shrimp are served with a tasty dipping sauce. A side of steamed white rice would be in order.

WINE RECOMMENDATION
The saltiness of the soy in the dipping sauce calls for a wine with a reasonably high level of acidity. A riesling from Alsace or from New York State's Finger Lakes region would be a good choice, as would an Oregon pinot gris.

4 SERVINGS

1½ pounds medium shrimp, shelled, shells reserved

1 cup packed cilantro leaves

5 scallions including green tops, 4 cut into 3 pieces each, 1 sliced thin

1 3-inch piece fresh ginger, smashed, plus ½ teaspoon grated fresh ginger

¼ cup plus 2 tablespoons dry white wine

2 teaspoons white vinegar

2 teaspoons sugar

1 teaspoon salt

¼ teaspoon peppercorns

5 cups water

2 teaspoons soy sauce

3 tablespoons Chicken Stock, page 61, or canned chicken broth

1. In a medium stainless-steel saucepan, combine the shrimp shells with the cilantro, scallion pieces, smashed ginger, the ¼ cup wine, 1 teaspoon of the vinegar, the sugar, salt, and peppercorns. Add the water, cover, and bring to a boil over high heat. Reduce the heat and simmer for 30 minutes.

2. In a small bowl, combine the sliced scallion, the grated ginger, the remaining 2 tablespoons wine, the remaining teaspoon of vinegar, the soy sauce, and chicken stock.

3. Strain the shrimp stock into a large bowl and return it to the pan, along with the smashed ginger. Bring to a boil over high heat. Add the shrimp and cook, stirring once or twice, until just done, 2 to 3 minutes. Remove the shrimp with a slotted spoon and serve with the ginger dipping sauce.

—EILEEN YIN-FEI LO

PER SERVING: CALORIES 172 kcal TOTAL FAT 2.5 gm SATURATED FAT .5 gm CARBOHYDRATE 5.9 gm PROTEIN 29 gm CHOLESTEROL 210.5 mg

PAELLA WITH SEAFOOD AND CHICKEN

Chock-full of goodies, this paella offers lobster, shrimp, clams, mussels, chicken, and smoked ham. We call for the traditional medium-grain rice, but more readily available long-grain will do just fine.

WINE RECOMMENDATION
Nothing could be better with a Spanish paella than a classic red wine from the Rioja region of Spain—unless it's a zesty, fresh white from Spain's Penedès region.

6 SERVINGS

1 live lobster (about 1½ pounds)

½ pound medium shrimp, shelled, shells reserved

1 tablespoon tomato paste

3 tablespoons brandy

1 smoked ham hock (about 1 pound)

8 cups water

2 bone-in chicken breasts (about 1 pound in all), skin removed, breasts cut into 2 pieces each

   Salt and fresh-ground black pepper

1 onion, chopped

1 clove garlic, minced

1 cup canned crushed tomatoes, drained

1½ cups medium-grain rice

¾ teaspoon paprika

¼ teaspoon saffron threads, crumbled

6 littleneck clams, scrubbed

6 mussels, scrubbed and debearded

¼ cup fresh or frozen peas

¼ pound sugar snap peas

1. In a large pot of boiling, salted water, cook the lobster for 2 minutes. (It will be only partially cooked, but the meat will be cooked again later.) Drain.

2. When cool enough to handle, twist the lobster to separate the tail section and the "arms" and claws from the body. Turn the tail upside down. Using scissors or a large sharp knife, cut through the underside of the shell. Remove the tail meat from the shell and cut it into four pieces. Crack the claws. Remove the claw meat, keeping it whole if possible. Remove the "arm" meat. Reserve the lobster shells and head.

3. Heat a large saucepan over high heat. Add the lobster shells and head and the shrimp shells and cook, stirring occasionally, for 5 minutes. Stir in the tomato paste, brandy, ham hock, and water and bring to a boil. Reduce the heat and simmer until the liquid is reduced to approximately 4 cups, about 45 minutes. Remove the ham hock and cut enough lean meat from the

PER SERVING: CALORIES 346 kcal TOTAL FAT 2.9 gm SATURATED FAT .6 gm CARBOHYDRATE 46 gm PROTEIN 32 gm CHOLESTEROL 105 mg

bone to measure approximately ½ cup. Strain the broth and skim off any fat from the surface.

4. Heat the oven to 350°. Coat a large nonstick ovenproof frying pan with vegetable-oil cooking spray. Heat the pan over high heat. Season the chicken with salt and pepper. Add the chicken to the pan; cook, turning once, until brown, about 2 minutes per side. Remove the chicken. Coat the pan with additional cooking spray. Add the onion and garlic and cook until translucent, about 3 minutes. Stir in the tomatoes, rice, paprika, and saffron. Cook until the liquid is absorbed, about 4 minutes.

5. Stir in the broth, ham, chicken, 1 teaspoon salt, and ½ teaspoon pepper. Cover and bring to a boil over high heat. Reduce the heat and simmer, shaking the pan occasionally, for 10 minutes. Discard any clams or mussels that have broken shells. Add the clams, mussels, and lobster meat to the pan. Cover and bake until the clams and mussels start to open, about 10 minutes. Stir in the shrimp, peas, and sugar snaps. Continue to bake, covered, until the shrimp are just done, about 5 minutes. Discard any clams or mussels that do not open. Let the paella stand for 10 minutes before serving.

—GRACE PARISI

SEAFOOD STEW WITH ROASTED-PEPPER SAUCE

Capped with garlicky croûtes spread with a pesto-like red-pepper sauce, this light shellfish stew will waft you to the Mediterranean.

WINE RECOMMENDATION
Like most tomato-based seafood stews, this one is well suited to rosé or even a light red such as Bardolino or Beaujolais. White-wine alternatives include sauvignon blanc or a simple chardonnay from France's Languedoc-Roussillon.

4 SERVINGS

1   small red bell pepper
½   cup fresh basil leaves
5   cloves garlic, 3 chopped, 2 left whole
2   teaspoons grated Parmesan cheese
1½ tablespoons olive oil
½   teaspoon balsamic vinegar
1½ cups canned tomatoes with their juice
¼   teaspoon fennel seeds
2   leeks, white and light-green parts only, halved lengthwise, chopped, and washed well
1   onion, chopped
3   cups fish stock, or 1½ cups bottled clam juice and 1½ cups water
1   cup dry white wine
1½ teaspoons minced fresh thyme, or ½ teaspoon dried

1   bay leaf
    Salt and fresh-ground black pepper
8   ¾-inch slices French bread
12 mussels, scrubbed and debearded
½   pound sea scallops
½   pound large shrimp, shelled

1. Roast the bell pepper over a gas flame or grill or broil it, turning with tongs until charred all over, about 10 minutes. When the pepper is cool enough to handle, pull off the skin. Remove the stem, seeds, and ribs.

2. In a blender or food processor, combine the roasted bell pepper with the basil, 1 whole garlic clove, the Parmesan, ½ tablespoon of the oil, and the vinegar. Puree until almost smooth. Transfer to a bowl.

3. In a blender or food processor, puree the tomatoes with their juice. Grind the fennel seeds in a mortar with a pestle or in a spice grinder.

4. In a large pot, heat the remaining 1 tablespoon olive oil over moderately low

PER SERVING: CALORIES 383 kcal   TOTAL FAT 8.9 gm   SATURATED FAT 1.5 gm   CARBOHYDRATE 46 gm   PROTEIN 30 gm   CHOLESTEROL 99 mg

heat. Add the leeks, onion, and chopped garlic. Cover and cook, stirring occasionally, until soft, about 10 minutes. Add the pureed tomatoes, ground fennel seeds, stock, wine, thyme, bay leaf, and ¼ teaspoon each of salt and pepper. Bring to a boil, reduce the heat, and simmer, stirring occasionally, for 20 minutes.

5. Meanwhile, heat the broiler. Broil the bread until it starts to brown, about 1 minute. Turn and broil until golden brown, about 2 minutes longer. Rub the toasted bread with the remaining whole garlic clove.

6. Discard any mussels that have broken shells or do not clamp shut when tapped. Add the mussels to the pot. Cover, raise the heat to high, and bring to a boil. Cook, shaking the pot occasionally, just until the mussels begin to open, about 3 minutes. Remove the open mussels. Continue to cook, uncovering the pot as necessary to remove the mussels as soon as their shells open. Discard any mussels that do not open. When the mussels are cool enough to handle, remove them from their shells, holding them over the pot to catch all the juices. Set aside.

7. Add the scallops and the shrimp to the pot, bring to a simmer, and simmer, stirring occasionally, until just done, 3 to 5 minutes.

8. Discard the bay leaf. Return the mussels to the stew. Season the stew with salt and pepper.

9. Ladle the stew into four shallow bowls. Serve with the toast, each piece topped with a dollop of the roasted-pepper sauce. Serve the remaining sauce alongside.

—GEORGIA CHAN DOWNARD

PAN BAGNAT

As the *pan bagnat* rests, the dressing saturates the bread and the gutsy flavors have time to meld. This Provençal classic is perfect for lunch or a light dinner.

WINE RECOMMENDATION
A summery sandwich calls for a summery wine—try a rosé from Southern France's Provence or Languedoc-Roussillon regions, or a simple white from Portugal.

4 SERVINGS

2 red bell peppers, or one 7-ounce jar roasted red peppers, drained

1 tablespoon olive oil

1 tablespoon red-wine vinegar

¼ teaspoon fresh-ground black pepper

1 loaf crusty French or Italian bread

1 clove garlic, cut in half

1 tomato, cut into thin slices

1 red onion, cut into thin slices

1 6½-ounce can water-packed tuna, drained

1 2-ounce tin anchovy fillets, drained and patted dry

6 basil leaves

1. If using fresh bell peppers, roast them over a gas flame or grill or broil them, turning with tongs until charred all over, about 10 minutes. When the peppers are cool enough to handle, pull off the skin. Remove the stems, seeds, and ribs. Cut into thick slices.

2. In a small bowl, combine the oil, vinegar, and black pepper. Cut off the upper third of the loaf of bread. Remove the soft center from the top, leaving a ½-inch shell. Rub the garlic over the inside of the bread, top and bottom, and drizzle the oil-and-vinegar dressing over it.

3. Top the bottom of the bread with the tomato and onion slices, tuna, roasted peppers, anchovies, and basil. Cover with the top of the bread.

4. Wrap the sandwich tightly in aluminum foil. Weigh the sandwich down with a cutting board and let stand at room temperature for an hour. Cut the sandwich into quarters before serving.

—MICHELE SCICOLONE

PER SERVING: CALORIES 383 kcal TOTAL FAT 7.4 gm SATURATED FAT 1.3 gm CARBOHYDRATE 54 gm PROTEIN 24 gm CHOLESTEROL 26 mg

chapter 6

POULTRY & MEAT

Pork-Tenderloin Tostadas with Red-Onion Marmalade, page 169

CHICKEN WITH CHIPOTLE CHUTNEY AND GRILLED POTATOES

A head of sweet roasted garlic and a skewer of grilled potato halves accompany each serving of these simple grilled chicken breasts. The smoky, fruity chutney adds a Southwestern kick.

WINE RECOMMENDATION
The big, spicy flavors of the garlic and chutney call for a big, spicy wine, such as a gewürztraminer from Alsace or a chenin blanc from California.

4 SERVINGS

- 4 heads garlic, unpeeled
- 8 small red new potatoes (about 1½ pounds), halved
- 2½ teaspoons olive oil
  Salt and fresh-ground black pepper
- ½ teaspoon chopped fresh thyme
- 4 boneless, skinless chicken breasts (about 1⅓ pounds in all)
- 4 sprigs fresh rosemary (optional)
  Chipotle Chutney, next page

1. Light a grill or heat the oven to 325°. Grill the garlic heads over moderately low heat, turning frequently, until the cloves are soft and the skin is brown, about 45 minutes. Alternatively, wrap the garlic loosely in aluminum foil and roast in the oven until tender, about 1 hour.

2. If using the oven, increase the temperature to 450°. Put the potatoes in a medium saucepan of salted water. Bring to a boil and cook over high heat until just tender, about 4 minutes. Drain and pat dry with paper towels. Toss the potatoes with 1½ teaspoons of the oil. Thread four halves on each of four skewers. Season with salt and pepper.

3. Grill the potatoes or roast in a roasting pan in the oven, turning once, until tender and browned, about 20 minutes. Sprinkle with the thyme. Keep warm.

4. Rub the chicken with the remaining teaspoon of oil and season with salt and pepper. Grill, turning occasionally, until browned and cooked through, about 12 minutes. Alternatively, cook the chicken in a grill pan or heavy frying pan over moderately high heat, turning once, for about 8 minutes.

5. Transfer the chicken to four plates. Put the roasted garlic and potato skewers alongside. Top each breast with a rosemary sprig, if using. Serve with the chutney.

—VINCENT GUERITHAULT

PER SERVING: CALORIES 574 kcal TOTAL FAT 5.5 gm SATURATED FAT .9 gm
CARBOHYDRATE 90 gm PROTEIN 43 gm CHOLESTEROL 90 mg

CHIPOTLE CHUTNEY

MAKES ABOUT ³/₄ CUP

3   Anaheim or poblano chiles

1   medium tart apple, such as Granny Smith, chopped fine

½   cup sherry vinegar

½   cup light-brown sugar

¼   cup granulated sugar

1   chipotle chile *en adobo**, seeded and minced

1   teaspoon minced garlic

*Available at Latin American markets and specialty-food stores

1. Roast the Anaheim chiles over a gas flame or grill or broil them, turning with tongs until charred all over, about 10 minutes. When the chiles are cool enough to handle, pull off the skin. Remove the stems, seeds, and ribs. Chop the chiles fine.

2. In a medium stainless-steel saucepan, combine the roasted chiles with the apple, vinegar, brown sugar, granulated sugar, chipotle, and garlic. Cook over moderately low heat, stirring occasionally, until the apple is tender and almost all of the liquid is evaporated, about 25 minutes. Let the chutney cool.

PER 3-TABLESPOON SERVING: CALORIES 189 kcal   TOTAL FAT .3 gm   SATURATED FAT 0 gm   CARBOHYDRATE 48 gm   PROTEIN .6 gm   CHOLESTEROL 0 mg

CITRUS-GRILLED CHICKEN WITH MESQUITE HONEY

Mesquite honey adds an extra touch of smoky flavor to this grilled chicken. If your supermarket doesn't carry it, though, you can use any type of honey.

WINE RECOMMENDATION
Rieslings from the Alsace region in northeastern France are dry yet have subtle honeylike flavors that will tie in nicely with the hint of honey in this dish.

4 SERVINGS

¼ teaspoon coriander seeds

⅛ teaspoon aniseed

⅓ cup honey, preferably mesquite

2 tablespoons plus 2 teaspoons lemon juice

2 tablespoons orange juice

2 tablespoons lime juice

1 scallion including green top, minced

¾ teaspoon chopped fresh thyme

¾ teaspoon chopped fresh rosemary

¾ teaspoon chopped fresh sage

4 boneless, skinless chicken breasts (about 1⅓ pounds in all)

Salt and fresh-ground black pepper

1. In a small frying pan, toast the coriander seeds and the aniseed over moderate heat, stirring, until fragrant, about 4 minutes. Grind the seeds in a mortar with a pestle or in a spice grinder.

2. In a large shallow glass dish or stainless-steel pan, whisk the honey, lemon juice, orange juice, lime juice, scallion, thyme, rosemary, sage, and ground spice mixture. Pound the chicken to a uniform thickness, about ¾ inch. Add the chicken to the honey mixture and turn to coat. Let marinate at room temperature for 30 minutes.

3. Light a grill or heat a grill pan or heavy frying pan over moderately high heat. Remove the chicken from the marinade and season with salt and pepper. Cook the chicken for 4 minutes, brushing with the marinade. Turn and cook, brushing with the marinade, until just done, about 3 minutes longer.

—CHARLES WILEY

PER SERVING: CALORIES 260 kcal   TOTAL FAT 2 gm   SATURATED FAT .5 gm   CARBOHYDRATE 25.5 gm   PROTEIN 35 gm   CHOLESTEROL 87.6 mg

GRILLED CHICKEN BREASTS WITH CARAMELIZED-ONION MARMALADE

Here's a simple dish that makes a perfect weeknight dinner. Both the glaze on the chicken and the accompanying caramelized onions have zero fat.

WINE RECOMMENDATION
Dijon mustard and the wines of Burgundy have a traditional affinity for each other. Try a light red Burgundy with this mustard-marinated chicken, or a California pinot noir. If you prefer white wine, two good regional Burgundians to look for are Saint-Véran and Macon.

4 SERVINGS

1 large red onion, cut into thin slices
1½ tablespoons brown sugar
6 tablespoons red wine
1½ tablespoons balsamic vinegar
   Salt and fresh-ground black pepper
3 tablespoons Dijon mustard
1½ teaspoons lemon juice
1 teaspoon Worcestershire sauce
1 teaspoon minced garlic
4 boneless, skinless chicken breasts (about 1⅓ pounds in all)
8 scallions including green tops, trimmed

1. In a large heavy stainless-steel saucepan, combine the onion and brown sugar. Cook over moderate heat, stirring frequently, until the onion begins to turn golden and caramelize, about 20 minutes.

2. Stir in the wine and vinegar. Increase the heat to moderately high and bring to a boil. Reduce the heat and cook, stirring, until most of the liquid evaporates, about 10 minutes. Season with salt and pepper and let the marmalade cool.

3. Light a grill or heat the broiler. In a medium stainless-steel bowl, whisk together the mustard, lemon juice, Worcestershire sauce, garlic, and ½ teaspoon pepper. Pound the chicken to a uniform thickness, about ¾ inch. Put the chicken in the mustard mixture and turn to coat.

4. Grill or broil the chicken, brushing with the mustard mixture, for 3 minutes. Turn and cook, brushing with the mustard mixture, until just done, about 4 minutes longer. Grill or broil the scallions alongside, turning, for about 4 minutes. Serve the chicken with the scallions and the onion marmalade.

—LAURIE BURROWS GRAD

PER SERVING: CALORIES 249 kcal   TOTAL FAT 2 gm   SATURATED FAT .5 gm
CARBOHYDRATE 14 gm   PROTEIN 36.5 gm   CHOLESTEROL 87.6 mg

CHICKEN KABOBS

Yogurt makes a great low-fat marinade for these exotic kabobs. Spiked with saffron, garlic, and mint, the yogurt gives the dish its Middle Eastern flair.

WINE RECOMMENDATION
Sauvignon blanc, a white that often has a faint aroma of herbs, will emphasize the flavors of mint and saffron in this dish. A simple, light Beaujolais-Villages is a red-wine alternative.

4 SERVINGS

Large pinch saffron threads

4 teaspoons water

⅔ cup plain low-fat yogurt

2 teaspoons minced garlic

2 teaspoons dried mint, crumbled

¼ teaspoon salt

¼ teaspoon fresh-ground black pepper

1⅓ pounds boneless, skinless chicken legs or breasts, cut into 1-inch pieces

1. In a small bowl, combine the saffron and water. Let sit for about 2 minutes.

2. In a large shallow glass dish or stainless-steel pan, combine the saffron mixture with the yogurt, garlic, mint, salt, and pepper. Add the chicken and stir to coat. Refrigerate the chicken for at least 3 hours and up to 24.

3. Light a grill or heat the broiler. Loosely thread the chicken on skewers. Grill the chicken over moderate heat, turning occasionally, until just done, about 10 minutes. Alternatively, broil the chicken about 6 inches from the heat. Serve hot or at room temperature.

—JEFFREY ALFORD AND NAOMI DUGUID

TEST-KITCHEN TIP

If you're using bamboo skewers, soak them in a shallow dish of water for about fifteen minutes before threading the chicken on them. That way, they won't char.

PER SERVING: CALORIES 208 kcal **TOTAL FAT** 6.3 gm **SATURATED FAT** 1.8 gm **CARBOHYDRATE** 3.3 gm **PROTEIN** 32.5 gm **CHOLESTEROL** 123 mg

STEAMED CHICKEN WITH CHINESE MUSHROOMS

It tastes like a stir-fry, but this sweet-and-sour mixture of chicken, mushrooms, and scallions is not fried; it's simply steamed in a gingery sauce. Fried Rice with Peas and Sun-Dried Tomatoes, page 211, is an ideal accompaniment.

WINE RECOMMENDATION
A fruity riesling or a gewürztraminer will hold its own with the slight sweetness here.

4 SERVINGS

1 ½-inch piece fresh ginger, grated

7 dried shiitake or Chinese black mushrooms

3 tablespoons Chicken Stock, page 61, or canned chicken broth

1 tablespoon oyster sauce

1 tablespoon dry white wine

2 teaspoons cooking oil

1½ teaspoons light soy sauce

1½ teaspoons sugar

1 teaspoon white vinegar

1 teaspoon Asian sesame oil

2 teaspoons cornstarch

½ teaspoon salt

Pinch fresh-ground black pepper

1 pound boneless, skinless chicken breasts (about 3), cut into 1-inch pieces

4 scallions, bulbs cut into 1-inch lengths, 2 green tops chopped

½ red bell pepper, cut into ⅛-inch strips

1. Put the ginger in a fine-mesh sieve set over a bowl and press firmly with the back of a spoon to get all the juice. Discard the pulp. In a small bowl, soak the mushrooms in hot water to cover until softened, about 20 minutes. Remove the mushrooms. Remove the stems from the mushrooms; cut the caps into ¼-inch slices.

2. In a 9-inch glass pie plate, combine the ginger juice, stock, oyster sauce, wine, cooking oil, soy sauce, sugar, vinegar, and sesame oil. Stir in the cornstarch, salt, and pepper. Add the chicken, the mushrooms, and the scallion pieces and stir to coat. Refrigerate for 1 hour.

3. Put a rack in a wok or steamer and add enough water to come within 1 inch of the rack. Cover and bring to a boil. Put the pie plate on the rack, cover, and steam the chicken over moderate heat, turning once, until just done, about 20 minutes. Top with the red pepper and the scallion tops.

—EILEEN YIN-FEI LO

PER SERVING: CALORIES 194 kcal TOTAL FAT 5 gm SATURATED FAT .9 gm
CARBOHYDRATE 8 gm PROTEIN 28 gm CHOLESTEROL 66 mg

CHICKEN WITH PEPPERS

In this Spanish-style sauté, chicken is topped with a zesty sauce of onion, red and green bell peppers, jalapeños, and garlic. Serve it with Baked Rice with Chickpeas, page 213, or with plain steamed rice.

Baked Rice with Chickpeas, page 213

WINE RECOMMENDATION
A boldly flavored wine from the sun-filled Mediterranean will accent the pungent flavors of the peppers. A good choice is a Spanish Rioja or a merlot or cabernet from the Languedoc-Roussillon. For a white, try a big chardonnay from sunny California.

4 SERVINGS

1 tablespoon olive oil

4 boneless, skinless chicken breasts (about 1⅓ pounds in all)

Salt and fresh-ground black pepper

1 cup Chicken Stock, page 61, or canned chicken broth

2 red bell peppers, cut into ⅓-inch strips

1 green bell pepper, cut into ⅓-inch strips

1 onion, chopped fine

2 jalapeños, minced

1 clove garlic, minced

1. In a large nonstick frying pan, heat the olive oil over moderate heat. Season the chicken with salt and pepper and add to the pan. Cook the chicken, turning once, until browned, about 6 minutes. Remove the chicken.

2. If using canned chicken broth, skim off and discard any fat that floats to the surface. Add the bell peppers, onion, jalapeños, garlic, and stock to the pan. Cover and cook, stirring occasionally, until the vegetables are tender, about 15 minutes. Season with salt and pepper.

3. Add the chicken to the pan and cook, turning occasionally, until just done, about 3 minutes. Serve the chicken topped with the bell-pepper sauce.

—MICHELE SCICOLONE

PER SERVING: CALORIES 228 kcal **TOTAL FAT** 5.6 gm **SATURATED FAT** .9 gm **CARBOHYDRATE** 8 gm **PROTEIN** 35 gm **CHOLESTEROL** 82 mg

Herb-Crusted Chicken with Toasted Almonds

The bread-crumb coating on these baked chicken breasts makes them as crunchy as if they were fried. They're topped with sliced almonds and served on a bed of lettuce for a main dish that's light but satisfying.

WINE RECOMMENDATION
Italian wines tend to go well with crisp, breaded meats; try a light-bodied barbera or an earthy Chianti. Alternatively, choose a fairly robust white such as an Arneis or Soave Classico.

4 SERVINGS

- 4 teaspoons sliced almonds
  Salt and fresh-ground black pepper
- ½ cup fresh bread crumbs
- ¾ teaspoon dried thyme, crumbled
- ¾ teaspoon dried basil, crumbled
- ¼ teaspoon dried marjoram, crumbled
  Pinch dried red-pepper flakes
- 4 boneless, skinless chicken breasts (about 1⅓ pounds in all)
- 1 egg white, beaten
- 4 teaspoons olive oil
- 2 teaspoons balsamic vinegar
- 1½ quarts mixed salad greens (about ¼ pound)

1. Heat the oven to 400°. Put the almonds in a pie plate; sprinkle with a pinch each of salt and pepper. Toast the almonds in the oven until golden brown, about 3 minutes. Remove and let cool.

2. On a plate, combine the bread crumbs with the thyme, basil, marjoram, and red-pepper flakes; season with salt and pepper. Brush the chicken on all sides with the egg white and then press only the tops into the seasoned bread crumbs.

3. Coat a baking sheet with vegetable-oil cooking spray. Heat 1½ teaspoons of the oil in a large nonstick frying pan over moderately high heat. Add the chicken to the pan, breaded-side down, and cook, without turning, until browned, about 1 minute. Transfer the chicken to the prepared baking sheet, breaded-side up. Bake until just done, about 10 minutes.

4. In a large bowl, whisk the remaining 2½ teaspoons oil with the vinegar. Add the greens and salt and pepper to taste and toss. Mound the salad on four plates, top with the chicken, and sprinkle with the almonds.

—MATTHEW KENNEY

PER SERVING: CALORIES 248.5 kcal   TOTAL FAT 7.9 gm   SATURATED FAT 1.2 gm
CARBOHYDRATE 5 gm   PROTEIN 37 gm   CHOLESTEROL 87.8 mg

CHICKEN SHEPHERD'S PIE

A British classic, shepherd's pie is typically chopped meat beneath a crust of mashed potatoes. To trim the fat, we've used chicken breasts rather than the traditional lamb, added vegetables, and mashed the potatoes with buttermilk rather than butter and milk.

WINE RECOMMENDATION
Bordeaux is a favorite of the British. There's no need to invest in a very expensive label for this simple dish—a modestly priced Bordeaux Supérior, Cru Bourgeois, or plain Bordeaux will be a congenial match. White Bordeaux (a blend of sauvignon blanc and sémillon grapes) would be equally appropriate.

4 SERVINGS

2½ pounds baking potatoes (about 5), peeled and cut into 1-inch cubes

½ cup nonfat buttermilk

Salt and fresh-ground black pepper

1 cup fresh or thawed frozen peas

2½ teaspoons olive oil

1 pound skinless, boneless chicken breasts (about 3), cut into ½-inch slices

2½ cups Chicken Stock, page 61, or canned chicken broth

6 scallions including green tops, sliced thin

4 large shallots, cut into thin slices

2 ribs celery, cut into thin slices

3 cloves garlic, minced

¼ pound shiitake mushrooms, stems removed and caps cut into ¼-inch slices

⅓ cup dry white wine

3 carrots, cut into matchstick strips

2 teaspoons arrowroot

3 tablespoons water

¼ cup chopped flat-leaf parsley

½ teaspoon chopped fresh thyme

2 teaspoons grated Parmesan cheese

1. Put the potatoes in a large saucepan of salted water. Bring to a boil, reduce the heat, and simmer until tender, about 15 minutes. Drain the potatoes and put them back into the saucepan along with the buttermilk and salt and pepper to taste. Mash until smooth.

2. If using fresh peas, cook them in a small saucepan of boiling, salted water for 1 minute. Drain.

3. In a large deep nonstick frying pan, heat ½ teaspoon of the oil over high heat. Season the chicken with salt and pepper. Cook, turning once, until browned, about 4 minutes. Remove the chicken. ➤

PER SERVING: CALORIES 484 kcal   TOTAL FAT 6.6 gm   SATURATED FAT 1.4 gm
CARBOHYDRATE 68 gm   PROTEIN 38 gm   CHOLESTEROL 68 mg

4. If using canned chicken broth, skim off and discard any fat that floats to the surface. Heat another teaspoon oil in the pan. Add the scallions, shallots, and celery and cook over moderately high heat, stirring, until the shallots are translucent, about 4 minutes. Stir in the garlic and cook for 2 minutes more. Add 1¼ cups of the stock and bring to a boil, stirring. Transfer to a bowl.

5. In the pan, heat the remaining teaspoon of oil over high heat. Add the mushrooms and cook, stirring, until browned, about 5 minutes. Add the remaining 1¼ cups stock and the wine; boil, skimming, for 5 minutes. Add the shallot mixture and the carrots to the pan. Continue cooking until the liquid is reduced to about ½ cup, about 5 minutes longer. Meanwhile, in a small bowl, combine the arrowroot and water. Stir the arrowroot mixture into the mushrooms, reduce the heat, and simmer until the liquid thickens, about 4 minutes. Add the chicken, peas, parsley, and thyme. Season with salt and pepper.

6. Heat the oven to 450°. Spoon the chicken mixture into four 1½-cup ramekins or small onion-soup bowls. Mound the mashed potatoes on top, covering the chicken mixture completely. Sprinkle with the Parmesan. Put the ramekins on a baking sheet.

7. Bake the pies until the potatoes are browned, about 35 minutes.

—Bob Chambers

You can make the recipe through step five a day in advance. Cover and refrigerate the chicken mixture and potatoes separately. Let both come to room temperature before proceeding with the recipe.

FRIED TURKEY CUTLETS WITH THREE-MUSHROOM GRAVY

Fried cutlets with gravy ought to register off the fat meter, but not these—they're fried in a nonstick pan with just a trace of oil, and the chicken stock used to make the gravy is skimmed of all fat. The cutlets are good on their own without the gravy, while the gravy pairs equally well with roasted meats, poultry, pasta, or polenta. Herbed Spaetzle, page 224, is a delicious partner for both.

WINE RECOMMENDATION
Turkey, like chicken, often goes with both red and white wine. Something fruity—a full-bodied chardonnay, a merlot, or a red from the northern Rhône region—will stand up best to the mushroom gravy.

4 SERVINGS

1⅓ cups 1-percent buttermilk
1¼ teaspoons Worcestershire sauce
1¼ teaspoons dry mustard
¼ teaspoon cayenne
¼ onion, cut into thin slices
1 small clove garlic, cut into thin slices
1 pound turkey cutlets
½ cup fresh bread crumbs
   Salt and fresh-ground black pepper
   Three-Mushroom Gravy, next page (optional)

1. In a large shallow glass dish or stainless-steel pan, combine the buttermilk, Worcestershire, mustard, and cayenne. Stir in the onion and garlic. Add the turkey cutlets and turn to coat. Cover and refrigerate for at least 4 hours, or overnight.

2. Heat the oven to 350°. Put the bread crumbs on a baking sheet and toast until golden, about 5 minutes. Transfer to a plate and season with salt and pepper.

3. Drain the turkey cutlets and discard the marinade. Coat the cutlets with the bread crumbs and shake off any excess.

4. Coat a large nonstick frying pan with vegetable-oil cooking spray and heat over moderately high heat. Add half of the cutlets and spray them lightly with cooking spray. Cook the cutlets, turning once, until just done, about 6 minutes. Remove and keep warm. Wipe out the pan. Repeat with more cooking spray and the remaining cutlets. Serve the cutlets topped with the gravy, if using.

—GRACE PARISI

PER SERVING: CALORIES 351 kcal TOTAL FAT 5.6 gm SATURATED FAT 1.5 gm
CARBOHYDRATE 26 gm PROTEIN 51 gm CHOLESTEROL 108 mg

THREE-MUSHROOM GRAVY

MAKES ABOUT ²/₃ CUP

⅓ ounce dried wild mushrooms, such as shiitake, porcini, or morels

⅔ cup boiling water

⅔ pound chicken wings

¼ pound fresh shiitake mushrooms, stems chopped, caps cut into ⅛-inch slices

3 ounces white mushrooms, stems chopped, caps cut into ⅛-inch slices

5 teaspoons brandy

1⅓ cups plus 2 teaspoons water

1 carrot, chopped

1 shallot, chopped

¼ teaspoon dried thyme

1 small bay leaf

3 peppercorns

¼ teaspoon olive oil

¼ plus ⅛ teaspoon arrowroot

Salt and fresh-ground black pepper

2 teaspoons minced chives or scallion tops

1. Put the dried mushrooms in a small bowl; pour the boiling water over them. Soak until softened, about 20 minutes. Strain the liquid and rinse the mushrooms well. Chop the mushrooms fine.

2. Heat a medium deep frying pan over high heat. Add the chicken wings; cook, turning once, until well browned, about 15 minutes. Remove; pour off all the fat from the pan. Add the chopped dried mushrooms and the chopped mushroom stems; cook, stirring occasionally, until beginning to brown, about 4 minutes. Add the brandy; boil until it evaporates. Pour in the reserved mushroom-soaking liquid. Bring to a boil, scraping the bottom of the pan. Add the 1⅓ cups water, chicken wings, carrot, shallot, thyme, bay leaf, and peppercorns and bring to a boil. Reduce the heat; simmer, partially covered, for 1½ hours.

3. Strain the stock; press the bones and vegetables to get all the liquid. Skim off any fat. Wipe out the pan; pour in the stock. Boil the stock over high heat until reduced to ½ cup, about 5 minutes.

4. Meanwhile, in a medium nonstick frying pan, heat the oil over high heat. Add the sliced mushroom caps; cook, stirring occasionally, until well browned, about 12 minutes. Stir the sliced mushrooms into the reduced stock; bring to a simmer over moderate heat. In a small bowl, mix the arrowroot with the 2 teaspoons water; stir the mixture into the gravy. Cook, stirring, just until thickened, about 3 minutes. Do not let boil. Season with salt and pepper. Stir in the chives.

PER 2½-TABLESPOON SERVING: CALORIES 30 kcal TOTAL FAT 1.3 gm SATURATED FAT .32 gm CARBOHYDRATE 4.8 gm PROTEIN 2.4 gm CHOLESTEROL 0 mg

DUCK STEAKS GRILLED OVER THYME

Here's a great low-fat alternative to a juicy beef steak—skinless duck breasts, cooked rare. Preparation time is minimal, but you'll need to allow at least four hours to marinate the duck.

WINE RECOMMENDATION
Duck deserves a full-bodied red. Cabernet sauvignon and Barolo are both good alternatives.

4 SERVINGS

- 1 teaspoon salt
- ¾ teaspoon coarse-ground black pepper
- ¼ teaspoon sugar
- 4 boneless, skinless duck breasts (about 1 pound in all)
- 1 bunch fresh thyme
- 1 teaspoon olive oil

1. In a small bowl, combine the salt, pepper, and sugar. Put the duck on a plate and rub this mixture over the breasts. Cover and refrigerate for at least 4 hours, or overnight.

2. Prepare a hardwood or charcoal fire in the grill. Put the bunch of thyme in a bowl. Add cold water to cover and let soak.

3. About 20 minutes before cooking, remove the duck from the refrigerator. Dry with paper towels; brush all over with the oil.

4. When the coals are white hot, remove the thyme from the water and shake dry. Scatter half of the thyme sprigs over the coals. Grill the duck, turning once, until cooked to rare, 6 to 8 minutes. While the duck cooks, feed the remaining thyme sprigs through the spaces in the grill as the first ones burn.

5. Transfer the duck steaks to a carving board. Let rest for 5 minutes and then cut them diagonally into thin slices.

—SALLY SCHNEIDER

PER SERVING: CALORIES 125 kcal TOTAL FAT 1.7 gm SATURATED FAT .15 gm CARBOHYDRATE 4 gm PROTEIN 22.7 gm CHOLESTEROL 119 mg

QUAIL AND SKEWERED VEGETABLES WITH ASIAN PRESERVED-PRUNE SAUCE

When you bite into an Asian preserved prune, the taste is a commingling of salty, sweet, and intensely tart sensations. Simmered with cinnamon, sherry, and hoisin, preserved prunes make a sauce that is especially good with grilled fowl—and appealingly low in fat.

WINE RECOMMENDATION
Here are two possibilities for this classically Asian combination of sweet and tart elements: a wine with matching sweet and tangy characteristics—a dry riesling or gewürztraminer, for example—or a bracing, fresh-tasting beverage such as a sparkling wine or a gamay Beaujolais.

4 SERVINGS

- 4 cloves garlic, minced
- 4 shallots, minced
- 2 teaspoons sugar
- 2 teaspoons Asian fish sauce (nuoc mam or nam pla)*
- 3 teaspoons medium-dry sherry
- 2 teaspoons cooking oil
- ¼ teaspoon fresh-ground black pepper
- 8 quail, butterflied
- 4 whole preserved prunes*
- 1 cup plus ¾ teaspoon water
- 1 small cinnamon stick
- 2 teaspoons hoisin sauce
- Small pinch dried red-pepper flakes
- ¼ plus ⅛ teaspoon cornstarch
- 1 large zucchini, cut diagonally into thick slices
- 1 large yellow summer squash, cut diagonally into thick slices
- 1 small onion, cut into quarters
- 4 mushrooms

*Available at Asian markets

1. In a small bowl, combine the garlic, shallots, sugar, fish sauce, 2 teaspoons of the sherry, the oil, and black pepper. Put the quail in a single layer in a large shallow glass dish or stainless-steel pan. Add the garlic mixture and turn to coat. Let marinate at room temperature for 2 hours.

2. In a small saucepan, combine the prunes, the 1 cup water, and the cinnamon stick. Bring to a boil over high heat. Reduce the heat and simmer until the prunes are soft, about 12 minutes. Remove the prunes and pit them. Mince the prunes and return them to the saucepan. Stir in the hoisin sauce, red-pepper flakes, and the remaining

PER SERVING: CALORIES 530 kcal   TOTAL FAT 29 gm   SATURATED FAT 7.7 gm
CARBOHYDRATE 19 gm   PROTEIN 45.6 gm   CHOLESTEROL 165.7 mg

1 teaspoon sherry and simmer for about 3 minutes. In a small bowl, combine the cornstarch with the remaining ¾ teaspoon water and add to the pan. Bring to a boil, stirring; cook until the sauce is thickened, about 2 minutes. Remove from the heat.

3. Heat the broiler. Thread the zucchini, summer squash, onion, and mushrooms onto four skewers. Put them on a baking sheet and brush on all sides with some of the prune sauce.

4. Put the quail, skin-side down, on another baking sheet. Broil about 5 inches from the heat for 1 minute. Turn and cook until the skin is brown and crisp and the meat is just done, about 3 minutes. Let sit in a warm spot.

5. Broil the skewered vegetables, turning, until the vegetables are browned and softened, about 6 minutes.

6. Put the quail and vegetable skewers on four plates. Pour about 1 tablespoon of the warm prune sauce over each of the quail.

—MARCIA KIESEL

TO BUTTERFLY QUAIL

Put the quail, breast-side down, on a work surface. Using poultry shears or Joyce Chen scissors, cut along the sides of the back bone and remove it. Turn the quail over and press firmly on the breast bone to break the bone and flatten the bird. You can use this method for other small birds, such as Cornish hens, or for chicken.

PORK-TENDERLOIN TOSTADAS WITH RED-ONION MARMALADE

The achiote called for here are musky-flavored seeds from the annatto tree; you may find them called annatto seed rather than achiote. They're optional, but they do add an authentic flavor to the pork tenderloin—which, unlike some other cuts of pork, is low in fat.

WINE RECOMMENDATION
A grenache rosé from California or France would be a good match for the onion marmalade. Or choose a simple red that's low in tannins, such as Valpolicella or Beaujolais.

4 SERVINGS

2 ancho chiles

¼ teaspoon cumin seeds

1 large clove garlic

1¼ teaspoons achiote* (optional)

Salt

Pinch ground allspice

4¼ teaspoons orange juice

4 teaspoons white-wine vinegar

¾ teaspoon olive oil

⅔ pound pork tenderloin

1 small green bell pepper

1 small red bell pepper

1 small yellow bell pepper

Fresh-ground black pepper

4 6-inch corn tortillas

½ head romaine lettuce, shredded

⅔ cup plain nonfat yogurt

⅓ cup drained and rinsed canned black beans

¼ cup Red-Onion Marmalade, next page

4 lime wedges, for serving

*Available at Latin American and Asian markets

1. In a medium frying pan, toast the chiles over moderately high heat, turning, until fragrant, about 3 minutes. Let cool. Tear into pieces; discard the stems and seeds.

2. Add the cumin seeds to the pan; toast over moderately high heat, tossing, until fragrant, about 2 minutes. Transfer to a blender and add the toasted chiles, garlic, achiote, if using, ¼ teaspoon salt, and the allspice. Blend until chopped fine. Add the orange juice, vinegar, and oil; puree. Put the pork tenderloin in a shallow glass dish or stainless-steel pan and rub with the chile paste. Let marinate at room temperature for 2 to 4 hours. ➤

PER SERVING: CALORIES 305 kcal   TOTAL FAT 7.2 gm   SATURATED FAT 2 gm   CARBOHYDRATE 37 gm   PROTEIN 23 gm   CHOLESTEROL 51 mg

3. Roast the bell peppers over a gas flame or grill or broil, turning with tongs until charred all over, about 10 minutes. When the peppers are cool enough to handle, pull off the skin. Remove the stems, seeds, and ribs. Cut the peppers into ¼-inch strips. Put in a bowl; season with salt and pepper.

4. Heat the oven to 400°. Bake the tortillas on a baking sheet until crisp, about 4 minutes.

5. Put the pork tenderloin in a roasting pan and season with salt and pepper. Roast the tenderloin until cooked to medium, about 12 minutes. Transfer to a carving board and leave to rest in a warm spot for about 10 minutes.

6. To serve, cut the pork diagonally into thin slices. Put a tortilla on each of four plates and top with the lettuce, yogurt, beans, and pepper strips. Mound the pork slices on the peppers and top with 1 tablespoon of the onion marmalade. Serve with the lime wedges.

—CHARLES WILEY

RED-ONION MARMALADE

Use any leftover marmalade to top a hamburger or as an accompaniment to grilled meat or poultry. Sweet red onions are nice here, but you can use any type you have on hand.

MAKES ABOUT 1 CUP

- 1 large red onion, cut into thin slices
- 1 clove garlic, minced
- 1 cup port
- 1 cup full-bodied red wine, such as Burgundy
- 1 teaspoon grated orange zest
- ½ cup orange juice (from about 1 orange)
- ⅓ cup honey
- ¼ cup balsamic vinegar
- ½ teaspoon salt

1. Coat a medium nonstick frying pan with vegetable-oil cooking spray. Add the onion and cook over moderate heat until browned, about 6 minutes. Add the garlic and stir for 1 minute. Add the port and simmer, stirring, for 10 minutes.

2. Add the wine, orange zest, orange juice, honey, vinegar, and salt and simmer until the liquid is reduced and the onions are very soft, about 15 minutes. Let cool. Refrigerate overnight, if possible. Serve at room temperature.

SPICED-PORK TORTILLAS

Slices of lean pork are grilled to perfection, topped with tomatillo salsa, and rolled into tortillas. The tomatillo salsa would also be delicious with other grilled meats, poultry, or seafood.

WINE RECOMMENDATION
A sparkling wine from California or France will stand up to the powerful flavors in these tortillas.

4 SERVINGS

½ pound tomatillos, husked, rinsed, and halved

½ onion, quartered

3 large cloves garlic

2 serrano chiles, halved and seeded

⅔ cup water

½ cup cilantro with tough stems removed

1 tablespoon lime juice

Salt

1 teaspoon ground cumin

1 teaspoon dried oregano

½ teaspoon fresh-ground black pepper

1 pork tenderloin (about ¾ pound), cut diagonally into 4 slices and pounded ½ inch thick

4 8-inch flour tortillas

2 scallions including green tops, sliced thin

1. Light a grill or heat the broiler. In a small stainless-steel saucepan, combine the tomatillos, onion, two of the garlic cloves, one of the chiles, and the water. Bring to a boil over moderately high heat. Reduce the heat and simmer until the tomatillos are soft, about 5 minutes. Reserve 2 tablespoons of the cooking liquid, and drain.

2. In a food processor, combine the remaining garlic clove and chile with the cilantro, lime juice, and ½ teaspoon salt. Pulse to chop. Add the tomatillo mixture and the reserved cooking liquid and pulse until the mixture is a coarse puree. Let sit for up to 1 hour.

3. In a small bowl, combine the cumin, oregano, ½ teaspoon salt, and the pepper. Rub the mixture on both sides of the pork slices. Grill or broil the pork, turning once, until cooked to medium, about 8 minutes. Let sit in a warm spot for about 5 minutes. Grill or broil the tortillas until golden, about 30 seconds.

4. Cut the pork into ½-inch-wide strips; divide among the tortillas. Spoon a little of the salsa on the pork and roll up. Top with the remaining salsa and the scallions.

—JEAN GALTON

PER SERVING: CALORIES 274 kcal   TOTAL FAT 7.1 gm   SATURATED FAT 1.8 gm
CARBOHYDRATE 27 gm   PROTEIN 25 gm   CHOLESTEROL 60 mg

CHILE CITRUS PORK WITH SAUTÉED PEARS

Enhancing flavor is the key to light cooking. Here, mild pork loin is brushed with a pungent chile paste, and sautéed pears provide a hint of sweetness.

WINE RECOMMENDATION

A white wine with floral notes will emphasize the fruity flavors here. Try a pinot gris or pinot blanc from Alsace, or a flowery viognier from California, Virginia, or the northern Rhône Valley in France.

4 SERVINGS

3   ancho chiles, seeded

2   reconstituted dry-packed sun-dried tomatoes

1½   teaspoons cooking oil

1   small onion, chopped

¼   cup orange juice

2   tablespoons lemon juice

2   tablespoons tomato paste

1   tablespoon grated orange zest

1½   teaspoons chopped fresh tarragon

½   teaspoon dried oregano

Salt

1¼   pounds boneless center-cut pork loin, fat removed

Fresh-ground black pepper

2   pears, peeled, cored, and cut lengthwise into ⅓-inch slices

3   cups watercress, tough stems removed

1. Put the chiles and tomatoes in two small bowls and add boiling water to cover. Let soak until softened, about 20 minutes. Drain. Chop the chiles.

2. In a frying pan, heat the oil over moderate heat. Cook the onion, chiles, and tomatoes until softened, about 6 minutes. Puree in a blender with the juices, tomato paste, zest, tarragon, oregano, and 2 teaspoons salt.

3. Heat the oven to 450°. Put the pork in a roasting pan and cook for 15 minutes. Spread 3 tablespoons of the chile paste on the pork. Reduce the oven temperature to 375° and cook for 10 minutes. Spread one more tablespoon of the chile paste on the pork and cook until medium (145°), about 30 minutes longer. Let sit for 10 minutes. Season with salt and pepper.

4. Meanwhile, in a nonstick frying pan, cook the pears over moderately high heat, without stirring, until golden, about 4 minutes. To serve, put the watercress and pears on four plates. Cut the pork into thin slices and arrange on top.

—CHARLIE PALMER

PER SERVING: CALORIES 332 kcal   **TOTAL FAT** 11 gm   **SATURATED FAT** 3 gm
CARBOHYDRATE 26 gm   **PROTEIN** 34.5 gm   **CHOLESTEROL** 89 mg

FIVE MEATY TIPS

These principles apply to all cuts of meat, but are most important for cuts that have less fat to tenderize them.

• Get more flavor from oil-based marinades by first sautéing onions, chiles, or spices in oil.

• Don't let meat sit too long in a highly acidic marinade or it will get chewy.

• Salt meat lightly or not at all before cooking, so juices won't be drawn out.

• Sear steaks over high heat. Low-fat roasts should also be cooked at a high temperature.

• Keep the heat low when braising or stewing; if the meat boils, it toughens.

COMPARING CHICKEN, BEEF, AND PORK

With just three grams of fat per three-ounce serving, chicken is usually thought to be the best meat for a low-fat diet. But today, you can get cuts of beef and pork that come close in fat content to skinless chicken breasts. Pork tenderloin, beef eye of round, and beef top round all weigh in at only four grams of fat per three-ounce serving. As far as dietary cholesterol goes, you'll generally get twenty to twenty-five milligrams per ounce whether you choose beef, pork, or chicken. Beef is a bit higher in iron, zinc, and B_{12} than pork or chicken; chicken has the most niacin; and pork is richest in thiamine. But, says Phoenix-based nutrition consultant Robyn DeBell, R.D., "If you're eating a balanced diet, these differences aren't worth worrying about."

—JULIA CALIFANO

PORK MEDALLIONS
WITH CURRY HONEY GLAZE

To accompany these satisfying hot, sweet, and tart pork medallions, you might try steamed basmati rice and sautéed chayote or cucumber slices.

WINE RECOMMENDATION
The volatile flavors of curry often overwhelm white wines and make reds taste sour or metallic. Two wines that work well are Champagne and riesling.

4 SERVINGS

2   teaspoons curry powder

2   tablespoons honey

2   tablespoons Worcestershire sauce

1   clove garlic, minced

2   pork tenderloins (about 10 ounces each), cut crosswise into 1¼-inch medallions

½   cup Chicken Stock, page 61, or canned chicken broth

3   tablespoons whole milk

1   teaspoon flour

4   lime wedges, for serving

1. In a small frying pan, stir the curry powder over high heat until fragrant, about 2 minutes. Transfer to a large shallow bowl and stir in the honey, Worcestershire, and garlic. Add the pork and turn to coat. Let marinate for at least 1 hour and up to 3 hours.

2. Coat a large nonstick grill pan or nonstick frying pan with vegetable-oil cooking spray and heat over moderately high heat. Remove the meat from the marinade and pat dry. Reserve the marinade. Put the pork in the pan. Cook, turning once, until browned and cooked to medium, about 6 minutes. Remove.

3. If using canned chicken broth, skim off and discard any fat that floats to the surface. Add the reserved marinade and the stock to the pan and simmer, scraping the bottom of the pan to dislodge any browned bits. In a small bowl, gradually stir the milk into the flour until smooth. Add this mixture to the pan and cook, stirring, until the sauce is thickened, about 2 minutes. Strain the sauce. Serve the pork with the sauce over it and the lime wedges alongside.

—GRACE PARISI

PER SERVING: CALORIES 477 kcal TOTAL FAT 7.3 gm SATURATED FAT 2.2 gm
CARBOHYDRATE 66 gm PROTEIN 41 gm CHOLESTEROL 103 mg

BALSAMIC-GLAZED RACK OF VENISON

You can substitute another venison cut, such as tenderloin or leg, for the racks. You'll need to roast the tenderloin for less time and the leg for more.

WINE RECOMMENDATION
This robust red meat is perfectly suited to any cabernet-based wine, to full-bodied zinfandels, and to Barolo, Barbaresco, or wines from the northern Rhône in France.

4 SERVINGS

¼ cup balsamic vinegar

2 tablespoons olive oil

1½ tablespoons ketchup

1 tablespoon Worcestershire sauce

Salt

Coarse-ground black pepper

1 tablespoon cooking oil

2 venison racks (about 1¼ pounds each), 4 chops each, chine bones and excess fat removed

1. In a small glass or stainless-steel bowl, combine the vinegar, olive oil, ketchup, Worcestershire, ¾ teaspoon salt, and 1½ teaspoons pepper.

2. Heat the oven to 450°. In a stainless-steel ovenproof frying pan or a roasting pan, heat the cooking oil over high heat. Put the venison racks, bone-side up, in the pan. Cook, turning once, until browned, about 3 minutes. Put the pan in the oven and cook the meat, brushing the racks three times with the balsamic glaze, until done to taste, about 20 minutes for rare (125°). Transfer the racks to a carving board. Cover loosely with aluminum foil and let rest in a warm spot for about 10 minutes. Season with salt and pepper.

3. Add the remaining glaze to the pan and bring to a boil over high heat, scraping the bottom of the pan to dislodge any browned bits. Cut the venison into chops and serve with the pan sauce.

—CHARLIE PALMER

FAT IN GAME

Wild game tends to be lower in total fat than domesticated meats because the fat is concentrated on the back or under the spine, rather than being dispersed as marbling. Farm-raised game often contains more fat but is still leaner than beef, pork, and some poultry.

—JULIA CALIFANO

PER SERVING: CALORIES 340 kcal TOTAL FAT 14.9 gm SATURATED FAT 3 gm
CARBOHYDRATE 3 gm PROTEIN 46 gm CHOLESTEROL 169 mg

ROSEMARY FLANK STEAK WITH ROASTED POTATOES

Flank steak, one of the leaner cuts of beef, is marinated here with rosemary, garlic, cumin, and cayenne for intense flavor. The potatoes roasted with onions, balsamic vinegar, and a little olive oil are fine companions to the steak. Add a steamed green vegetable to round out the meal.

WINE RECOMMENDATION

Steak is best with a robust red. You can't miss with a Bordeaux or Bordeaux blend from California, Italy, or Australia. Other possibilities include zinfandel, Côtes-du-Rhône, and pinotage, a dark South African red.

4 SERVINGS

   3 tablespoons cooking oil

1½ medium Spanish onions, the whole one cut into thin wedges attached at the root end, the half cut into thin slices

   1 large clove garlic, cut into thin slices

   1 shallot, cut into thin slices

2½ tablespoons minced fresh rosemary

   1 tablespoon red-wine vinegar

 ½ teaspoon ground cumin

 ¼ teaspoon cayenne

 14 ounces flank steak, fat removed

   1 pound small new potatoes, quartered

   1 tablespoon balsamic vinegar

1½ teaspoons olive oil

   Salt and fresh-ground black pepper

1. In a large stainless-steel frying pan, heat the cooking oil over moderately low heat. Add the sliced onion, garlic, and shallot; cook, stirring, until softened, about 5 minutes. Add the rosemary and cook for 1 minute longer. Add the vinegar, cumin, and cayenne. Remove and let cool. Scrape into a large resealable plastic bag, add the steak, and distribute the marinade over it. Seal the bag; refrigerate for 1 to 4 hours, turning once.

2. Heat the oven to 400°. In a large bowl, toss the potatoes, onion wedges, balsamic vinegar, and olive oil and season with salt and pepper. Spread the vegetables in a large nonstick roasting pan and roast, stirring once, until tender, about 40 minutes.

3. Light a grill or heat the broiler. Scrape the excess marinade from the steak and grill or broil, turning once, until done to your taste, about 15 minutes for medium-rare. Transfer to a carving board and let rest in a warm spot for about 5 minutes. Cut into thin slices; serve with the potatoes.

—CHARLIE PALMER

PER SERVING: CALORIES 348 kcal TOTAL FAT 14.6 gm SATURATED FAT 3.8 gm CARBOHYDRATE 30 gm PROTEIN 24 gm CHOLESTEROL 50 mg

New England Boiled Dinner

Brined beef surrounded by boiled winter vegetables is a New England specialty perfect for casual gatherings. For a simple low-fat version of the creamy horseradish sauce that often goes with boiled dinners, mix bottled or grated fresh horseradish with yogurt.

WINE RECOMMENDATION
The slightly sweet and briny flavors of the home-cured meat would overpower a delicate white wine, while a robust red would be too strong. Something in between is called for: a big oaky chardonnay for white-wine fans or a fruity merlot for those who love red.

8 SERVINGS

Brined Beef, opposite page

1/4 cup stout, such as Guinness

1 onion, peeled and stuck with 2 cloves

1 clove garlic

1 1/2 teaspoons sugar

10 peppercorns

3 juniper berries, crushed

3 sprigs fresh thyme, or 1/2 teaspoon dried

1 large bay leaf

5 quarts water

1 pound small red new potatoes

3/4 pound small beets, tops removed, scrubbed

1 3/4 pounds small white boiling onions or shallots

3/4 pound baby carrots, 1/2 inch of tops left on, or large carrots, cut diagonally into 1/2-inch slices

3/4 pound parsnips, peeled and cut into 1/2-inch slices

3/4 pound Savoy cabbage, cut into 1-inch wedges

1. Put the beef in a large pot and add enough cold water to cover the meat by about 4 inches. Bring the water to a boil over moderate heat. Reduce the heat to moderately low and simmer for 1 1/2 hours. Remove the beef and discard the cooking liquid.

2. Add the stout, onion, garlic, sugar, peppercorns, juniper berries, thyme, and bay leaf to the pot. Pour in the water and bring to a boil over high heat. Boil for 5 minutes. Return the beef to the pot and bring the water back to a simmer. Reduce the heat to moderately low and cook, uncovered, until the meat is very tender when pierced with a fork, about 1 3/4 hours.

3. Add the potatoes to the pot and, if necessary, add a little water to cover. Continue cooking for 15 minutes longer. Remove

PER SERVING: CALORIES 397 kcal   TOTAL FAT 9.7 gm   SATURATED FAT 3.3 gm   CARBOHYDRATE 52 gm   PROTEIN 26.6 gm   CHOLESTEROL 67.6 mg

the beef and put it on a plate. Cover loosely with aluminum foil; let sit in a warm spot.

4. Meanwhile, put the beets in a medium saucepan; add enough water to cover by about 2 inches. Bring to a boil over high heat. Reduce the heat and simmer the beets until tender, about 25 minutes.

5. Add the onions to the potatoes and simmer for 5 minutes. Add the carrots and parsnips and simmer for 5 minutes longer; if necessary, add water during cooking to cover the vegetables. Add the cabbage and simmer until all the vegetables are very tender, about 10 minutes longer.

6. Using a slotted spoon, remove the cabbage wedges from the pot and arrange them around the edge of a large platter. Repeat with the other vegetables in the pot. Drain the beets well and put them on the platter. Cover and keep warm.

7. Return the beef to the pot and simmer until warmed through, about 1 minute. Transfer the beef to a carving board and cut into thin slices. Put the slices in the center of the platter. Spoon several tablespoons of the broth over the meat and vegetables.

—SALLY SCHNEIDER

BRINED BEEF

Because the brine is made without the nitrites that are usually added to preserve the rosy color of corned beef, the meat will look more like traditional boiled beef. Plan on at least four days for brining.

3½ quarts water
1 quart stout, such as Guinness
2¼ cups dark-brown sugar
1½ cups coarse salt
15 juniper berries, crushed
15 peppercorns, crushed
5 allspice berries
3 sprigs fresh thyme or ½ teaspoon dried
1 large bay leaf
2½ pounds beef brisket, fat removed

1. In a large stainless-steel pot, combine all the ingredients except the beef brisket. Bring to a boil over moderate heat and boil for 5 minutes. Let cool.

2. Add the beef to the brine and put a plate on top to keep the meat submerged. Cover the pot and refrigerate for at least 4 days and up to 1 week.

3. Before cooking, rinse the meat with cool water to remove some of the salt. Discard the brine.

chapter 7

VEGETABLES

Roasted Fennel with Olives, page 189

ZUCCHINI AND CARROTS PARMESAN

Grated vegetables cook in a snap. Rather than butter or oil, here the medium for "sautéing" is chicken stock, boiled down to intensify its flavor.

4 SERVINGS

½ cup Chicken Stock, page 61, or canned chicken broth

2 zucchini (about 1 pound), grated

2 carrots, grated

Salt and fresh-ground black pepper

1 tablespoon grated Parmesan cheese

1. If using canned chicken broth, skim off and discard any fat that floats to the surface. In a large frying pan, bring the stock to a boil over moderately high heat. Boil until reduced to approximately ¼ cup, about 2 minutes.

2. Add the zucchini and carrots to the pan. Cook, stirring occasionally, until the vegetables are just tender, about 4 minutes. Season with salt and pepper. Sprinkle the Parmesan over the vegetables.

—MICHELE SCICOLONE

VARIATIONS

Many different vegetables will work well in this recipe. You might try:
• Asparagus, cut diagonally into ¼-inch pieces
• Artichoke hearts, slivered
• Snow peas, cut diagonally into thin strips
• Yellow summer squash, grated

PER SERVING: CALORIES 42 kcal TOTAL FAT .8 gm SATURATED FAT .4 gm CARBOHYDRATE 7 gm PROTEIN 3 gm CHOLESTEROL 1.2 mg

SKILLET-STEAMED BROCCOLI WITH LEMON

Simple steamed broccoli is one of the most basic low-fat side dishes, but it can be boring. In our swift skillet-steaming method, you sauté shallots and then add the broccoli and lemon zest and steam everything briefly with the shallots. While the fat used in this method is minimal, the improvement in flavor is significant.

4 SERVINGS

- 1 teaspoon olive oil
- 2 shallots, minced
- 1 large bunch broccoli (about 1½ pounds), cut into florets
- ¼ cup water
- ½ teaspoon grated lemon zest
- 2 tablespoons lemon juice

  Salt and fresh-ground black pepper

> ## VARIATIONS
>
> • Cauliflower is a good substitute for the broccoli. Add a tablespoon of chopped fresh parsley before serving.
> • Slivered reconstituted sun-dried tomato halves are a fine addition to either steamed broccoli or cauliflower.

1. In a medium nonstick frying pan, heat the oil over moderately high heat. Add the shallots and cook, stirring occasionally, until starting to soften, about 1 minute.

2. Add the broccoli, water, and lemon zest. Cover the pan. Reduce the heat and simmer, shaking the pan occasionally, until the broccoli is just tender, 3 to 4 minutes. Stir in the lemon juice and season with salt and pepper.

—GEORGIA CHAN DOWNARD

PER SERVING: CALORIES 49 kcal TOTAL FAT 1.4 gm SATURATED FAT .2 gm CARBOHYDRATE 8 gm PROTEIN 4 gm CHOLESTEROL 0 mg

SAUTÉED WILD MUSHROOMS WITH RADICCHIO

Radicchio leaves, tossed with mint, basil, and two types of vinegar, make a delicious bed for sautéed mushrooms. The wine and stock in which the mushrooms are simmered before they're sautéed give them loads of low-fat flavor.

4 SERVINGS

- 1 cup plus 2 tablespoons Chicken Stock, page 61, or canned chicken broth
- 1½ pounds wild mushrooms, such as shiitake (stems removed), cremini, or morels, or a combination, cut into ¼-inch slices
- ¾ cup dry white wine
- 2¼ teaspoons balsamic vinegar
- ¾ teaspoon sherry vinegar
- Salt
- 1 tablespoon plus 1½ teaspoons olive oil
- 1 head radicchio (about 4½ ounces), leaves separated
- 1 teaspoon chopped fresh mint
- 1 teaspoon chopped fresh basil
- 2 shallots, minced
- 5 cloves garlic, minced
- ¾ cup chopped fresh parsley
- Fresh-ground black pepper

1. If using canned chicken broth, skim off and discard any fat that floats to the surface. In a large stainless-steel frying pan, combine the mushrooms, stock, and ½ cup of the wine. Bring to a boil over moderately high heat, cover, and cook, stirring occasionally, for 4 minutes. Uncover the pan. Cook, stirring, until the liquid evaporates and the mushrooms are soft, about 5 minutes longer. Add the remaining ¼ cup wine and boil until it evaporates, about 2 minutes.

2. Meanwhile, in a medium bowl, combine ¾ teaspoon of the balsamic vinegar, the sherry vinegar, and a pinch of salt. Stir in the 1½ teaspoons oil. Add the radicchio, mint, and basil. Toss and put on four plates.

3. Add the remaining 1 tablespoon oil to the mushrooms. Stir in the shallots, garlic, and parsley. Cook, stirring, until the garlic and shallots start to soften, 2 to 3 minutes. Stir in the remaining 1½ teaspoons balsamic vinegar and season with salt and pepper. Spoon the mushroom mixture over the radicchio leaves.

—SALLY SCHNEIDER

PER SERVING: CALORIES 112 kcal TOTAL FAT 5.2 gm SATURATED FAT .7 gm CARBOHYDRATE 12.8 gm PROTEIN 6 gm CHOLESTEROL 0 mg

FIRE-ROASTED CORN WITH SPICY RED-PEPPER PUREE

With a palate-teasing blend of bell peppers, sun-dried tomatoes, and chipotle chile coating these roasted ears of corn, who needs melted butter? Be sure to remove the corn silk before roasting so that nothing stands between the corn and the peppy puree.

4 SERVINGS

2 red bell peppers

2 reconstituted dry-packed or rinsed oil-packed sun-dried tomatoes, chopped

1 canned chipotle chile *en adobo**

1 shallot, chopped

1 clove garlic, chopped

1 tablespoon light-brown sugar

4 large ears of corn, in their husks

Salt and fresh-ground black pepper

*Available at Latin American markets and specialty-food stores

1. Roast the bell peppers over a gas flame or grill or broil them, turning with tongs until charred all over, about 10 minutes. When the peppers are cool enough to handle, pull off the skin. Remove the stems, seeds, and ribs. Chop the peppers.

2. In a blender or food processor, combine the roasted peppers with the tomatoes, chipotle, shallot, garlic, and brown sugar. Puree until smooth.

3. Light the grill or heat the oven to 500°. Pull the husks of the corn back and remove the silks.

4. Spray four pieces of aluminum foil with vegetable-oil cooking spray. Spread the red-pepper puree over the corn; season with salt and pepper. Wrap the corn in the prepared foil. Grill over a low fire or roast in the middle of the oven, turning occasionally, until the corn is tender, about 30 minutes.

—CHARLES WILEY

PER SERVING: CALORIES 194 kcal   TOTAL FAT 5.6 gm   SATURATED FAT .8 gm   CARBOHYDRATE 36.1 gm   PROTEIN 5.4 gm   CHOLESTEROL 0 mg

LEMON-AND-GARLIC-ROASTED BEETS

The sweet, earthy flavor of beets is intensified by roasting. For an additional treat, shred the beet greens, steam or sauté them with some garlic and just a touch of olive oil, and serve alongside the beets.

4 SERVINGS

¾ pound beets, peeled, halved, and cut into ¼-inch slices

3 cloves garlic, sliced

¼ teaspoon grated lemon zest

1½ tablespoons lemon juice

½ teaspoon olive oil

¼ teaspoon sugar

Salt and fresh-ground black pepper

1. Heat the oven to 375°. In an 8-inch square glass or stainless-steel baking dish, toss the beets with the garlic, lemon zest, lemon juice, oil, and sugar. Season with salt and pepper. Spread the beets out in a single layer.

2. Spray an 8-inch square of parchment paper with vegetable-oil cooking spray and put it, oiled-side down, on top of the beets. Cover the dish with aluminum foil and cook, shaking occasionally, until the beets are tender, about 40 minutes.

—GRACE PARISI

MAKE IT AHEAD

Prepare the beets several days ahead, cover, and refrigerate. Reheat the beets and serve either hot or warm.

VARIATION

Toss the roasted beets with some chopped fresh tarragon or chives.

PER SERVING: CALORIES 37 kcal **TOTAL FAT** .7 gm **SATURATED FAT** .1 gm **CARBOHYDRATE** 7.4 gm **PROTEIN** 1.1 gm **CHOLESTEROL** 0 mg

ROASTED FENNEL WITH OLIVES

Olives and sun-dried tomatoes lend their sharp flavors to tender roasted fennel in a memorable combination. Though the olives are relatively high in fat, they have such a distinctive, pungent taste that only a few are needed.

4 SERVINGS

2 medium fennel bulbs, each cut into 8 wedges

Salt and fresh-ground black pepper

½ cup Chicken Stock, page 61, or canned chicken broth

1½ teaspoons butter

1 small onion, cut into thin slices

8 black olives, such as Kalamata, pitted and quartered

8 reconstituted dry-packed or rinsed oil-packed sun-dried tomatoes, cut into thin slices

2 tablespoons shredded fresh basil

1. Heat the oven to 450°. Coat a large nonstick baking sheet with vegetable-oil cooking spray. Put the fennel wedges on the baking sheet; season with salt and pepper. Roast for 20 minutes. Remove the fennel from the oven; transfer it to a large baking dish. Reduce the oven temperature to 375°.

2. If using canned chicken broth, skim off and discard any fat that floats to the surface. In a small frying pan, melt the butter over moderately high heat. Add the onion and cook, stirring, until starting to brown, about 7 minutes. Add the stock and bring to a simmer. Pour the mixture over the fennel, cover the baking dish with aluminum foil, and bake for 10 minutes. Uncover and bake until the fennel is tender, about 30 minutes longer. Stir in the olives, tomatoes, and basil.

—BOB CHAMBERS

PER SERVING: CALORIES 99 kcal   TOTAL FAT 4.6 gm   SATURATED FAT 1.2 gm
CARBOHYDRATE 11.5 gm   PROTEIN 3.7 gm   CHOLESTEROL 3.9 mg

Oven-Roasted Parsnips with Onions and Chestnuts

Chances are, parsnips aren't high on your list of favorite vegetables. But that may change after you try this warming winter side dish. The oft-neglected roots have a wonderful nuttiness and subtle sweetness that are enhanced by roasting. Chestnuts and pearl onions prove to be ideal companions.

4 SERVINGS

¾ pound fresh chestnuts

½ pound pearl onions

1½ teaspoons butter

1½ teaspoons cooking oil

1¼ pounds parsnips, peeled and cut into ½-inch pieces

Salt and fresh-ground black pepper

1½ cups Chicken Stock, page 61, or canned chicken broth

1 teaspoon minced fresh thyme

1 tablespoon chopped fresh parsley

1. Heat the oven to 350°. Cut an X through the shell on the flat end of each of the chestnuts. Put the chestnuts on a baking sheet. Bake until the shell at each X lifts away from the chestnut, 10 to 15 minutes. Peel the chestnuts while they are still warm and break them into ½-inch pieces. Increase the oven temperature to 450°.

2. Bring a medium saucepan of salted water to a boil. Add the onions and cook for 4 minutes. Drain and rinse the onions. Trim the root end from each onion and slip off the skin.

3. On a large rimmed baking sheet, melt the butter with the oil in the oven, about 3 minutes. Remove the pan from the oven and tilt it to spread the melted butter and oil over the bottom. Add the onions and parsnips and season with salt and pepper. Roast the vegetables, stirring occasionally, until tender and browned, about 25 minutes.

4. Meanwhile, if using canned chicken broth, skim off and discard any fat that floats to the surface. In a medium saucepan, combine the chestnuts with the stock and thyme. Season with salt and pepper. Bring to a boil over high heat and cook until the liquid is reduced to approximately ½ cup, about 5 minutes.

5. In a bowl, combine the onions and parsnips with the chestnuts and their liquid. Serve with the parsley sprinkled on top.

—Katherine Alford

PER SERVING: CALORIES 358 kcal TOTAL FAT 6.3 gm SATURATED FAT 1.7 gm CARBOHYDRATE 71 gm PROTEIN 6 gm CHOLESTEROL 4 mg

MASHED ACORN SQUASH WITH APPLES

Two fall favorites—mellow acorn squash and sweet Golden Delicious apples—are featured in this cinnamon-spiced dish. The squash is roasted, mashed, and mixed with a bit of butter for a rich, comforting taste and texture.

4 SERVINGS

- 2 acorn squash (about 1½ pounds each), halved lengthwise and seeds removed
- Salt and fresh-ground black pepper
- 2 Golden Delicious apples
- 1 tablespoon sugar
- ⅛ teaspoon cinnamon
- 2 tablespoons honey
- 1 tablespoon butter

1. Heat the oven to 450°. Coat a nonstick baking sheet with vegetable-oil cooking spray. Sprinkle the cut sides of the squash with salt and pepper and put them, cut-side down, on the baking sheet. Bake until the flesh is tender and caramelized, about 1 hour. Let the squash cool on the baking sheet.

2. Meanwhile, peel and core the apples and cut each one in eight wedges. Cut each wedge crosswise into ¼-inch pieces. Put the apples in a bowl and toss with the sugar and cinnamon. Spray a second nonstick baking sheet with vegetable-oil cooking spray and spread the apples on it in a single layer. Cook until the apples are tender and brown, about 30 minutes.

3. Scoop the flesh from the squash. In a large saucepan, bring the honey and butter just to a simmer. Stir in the squash, along with any caramelized bits from the baking sheet, and mash. Fold in the baked apples. Heat until just warmed through, 2 to 3 minutes. Season with salt and pepper.

—BOB CHAMBERS

MAKE IT AHEAD

Prepare the dish a day ahead and warm over moderate heat before serving.

PER SERVING: CALORIES 224 kcal TOTAL FAT 3.4 gm SATURATED FAT 1.9 gm
CARBOHYDRATE 52 gm PROTEIN 2.3 gm CHOLESTEROL 7.8 mg

EGGPLANT IN SMOKY TOMATO SAUCE

Broiling gives vegetables a charred, smoky taste that's complemented here by the Indian spices cumin and turmeric. If you have a gas broiler that doesn't allow you to cook very far from the heat source, go ahead and broil the tomatoes and eggplant close to the flame—but watch carefully so they don't burn.

4 SERVINGS

2 large eggplants, halved lengthwise

1½ pounds plum tomatoes (about 7), halved lengthwise

1 tablespoon olive oil

1 onion, chopped

4 teaspoons ground cumin

1 teaspoon turmeric

1 teaspoon sugar

Salt

Cayenne

Chopped cilantro, for serving

Lemon wedges, for serving

1. Heat the broiler. Line a large baking sheet with aluminum foil. Put the eggplant and tomato halves, cut-side down, on the baking sheet. Cook in the middle of the oven, as far from the heat as possible, until the tomato skins char, 8 to 10 minutes. Remove the tomatoes. Continue cooking the eggplant until the flesh is soft and the skin chars, about 15 minutes longer. Let the eggplant cool slightly.

2. Peel the tomatoes and puree in a blender or food processor. Scrape the pulp from the skin of the eggplant and chop.

3. In a large stainless-steel frying pan, heat the oil over moderately high heat. Add the onion and cook, stirring, until translucent, about 5 minutes. Stir in the cumin and turmeric. Add the tomato puree, reduce the heat, and simmer, covered, until thickened, 12 to 15 minutes. Stir in a little water if the sauce is too thick. Add the eggplant, sugar, 1 teaspoon salt, and a pinch of cayenne. Simmer, covered, for 10 minutes. Season with additional salt and cayenne to taste. Serve with chopped cilantro and lemon wedges.

—BHARTI KIRCHNER

PER SERVING: CALORIES 178 kcal TOTAL FAT 4.8 gm SATURATED FAT .6 gm
CARBOHYDRATE 34 gm PROTEIN 6 gm CHOLESTEROL 0 mg

CHICKPEA AND RED-PEPPER MEDLEY

The creaminess of this hearty Indian-inspired dish comes not from fat—there's only one tablespoon of oil in the whole recipe—but from pureed chickpeas.

4 SERVINGS

3   cups canned chickpeas (from two 15-ounce cans), with their liquid

1   tablespoon olive oil

1   large onion, chopped fine

6   cloves garlic

1   teaspoon turmeric

2   red bell peppers, cut into approximately 2-by-⅛-inch strips

2   jalapeño peppers, seeded and minced

    Salt

1. Drain the chickpeas, reserving 1 cup of their liquid. In a blender or food processor, puree 1 cup of the chickpeas with the liquid until smooth.

2. In a large frying pan, heat the oil over moderately high heat. Add the onion and garlic and cook, stirring frequently, until the onion is translucent and the garlic is just golden, about 5 minutes. Stir in the turmeric. Add the chickpea puree, the bell peppers, the jalapeños, and 1 teaspoon salt. Reduce the heat and simmer, covered, for 5 minutes. Add the remaining chickpeas and simmer, covered, until the bell peppers are just tender, about 5 minutes longer. If the stew seems too thick, stir in a little water. Season with additional salt.

—BHARTI KIRCHNER

MAKE IT AHEAD

Make the medley several days before serving and refrigerate. Stir in a little water when reheating.

PER SERVING: CALORIES 287 kcal   TOTAL FAT 6.9 gm   SATURATED FAT .8 gm   CARBOHYDRATE 46 gm   PROTEIN 13 gm   CHOLESTEROL 0 mg

WARM SMOKY GREENS

Wilted greens can be enjoyed at any time of the year. If curly endive isn't available, substitute escarole, spinach, dandelion greens, bok choy, or young collard or mustard greens.

4 SERVINGS

1 ounce smoked ham, trimmed of fat

¾ cup water

1 tablespoon olive oil

1 shallot, minced

1 clove garlic, minced

2 tablespoons balsamic vinegar

2 quarts curly endive torn into approximately 2-inch pieces (about 1 pound)

   Salt and fresh-ground black pepper

KITCHEN TIP

If you keep the leaves in the hot pot for too long, they'll cook. The effect you want is greens that have just wilted. Toss them quickly with the hot liquid and then pile them onto plates.

---

1. Put the ham and water in a small saucepan. Bring to a simmer and cook until the liquid is reduced to about 2 tablespoons, 20 to 25 minutes. Discard the ham.

2. In a large stainless-steel saucepan, heat the oil over moderately low heat. Add the shallot and garlic; cook, stirring frequently, until the shallot is translucent, about 5 minutes. Stir in the ham liquid and the vinegar. Bring to a boil. Add the endive and turn off the heat. Toss the greens until completely coated with the dressing and slightly wilted. Season with salt and pepper.

—SALLY SCHNEIDER

PER SERVING: CALORIES 57 kcal   TOTAL FAT 3.8 gm   SATURATED FAT .6 gm
CARBOHYDRATE 4.7 gm   PROTEIN 2.2 gm   CHOLESTEROL 1.7 mg

WILTED WINTER GREENS

Napa cabbage, arugula, radicchio, and escarole wilt in a warm bath of chicken stock. A drizzle of walnut oil adds a luxurious, nutty note to the finished dish.

4 SERVINGS

½ cup Chicken Stock, page 61, canned chicken broth, or water

2 cloves garlic, minced

½ pound napa cabbage, torn into approximately 2-inch pieces (about 7 cups)

1½ quarts radicchio torn into approximately 2-inch pieces (about ½ pound)

1½ quarts escarole torn into approximately 2-inch pieces (about ½ pound)

5 cups arugula stems removed and leaves torn in half (about ½ pound)

Salt and fresh-ground black pepper

1 teaspoon walnut oil

VARIATION

Add a teaspoon of grated fresh ginger and a pinch of dried red-pepper flakes to the simmering stock. Drizzle the greens with sesame oil instead of walnut oil.

---

1. In a large saucepan, bring the stock and garlic to a simmer over moderately high heat. Cover; cook until the garlic is softened, about 1 minute.

2. Add the cabbage, radicchio, escarole, and arugula. Season with salt and pepper. Cover and cook until the greens just wilt, about 2 minutes. Transfer to a serving dish and drizzle the walnut oil over the greens.

—KATHERINE ALFORD

PER SERVING: CALORIES 51 kcal TOTAL FAT 1.8 gm SATURATED FAT .2 gm
CARBOHYDRATE 7 gm PROTEIN 4 gm CHOLESTEROL 0 mg

STIR-FRIED CABBAGE WITH RED AND GREEN PEPPERS

Fresh ginger and sesame oil give cabbage an Eastern accent in this straightforward stir-fry. Bok choy and Chinese cabbage are good alternatives to green cabbage.

4 SERVINGS

½ teaspoon peanut oil

½ teaspoon Asian sesame oil

1½ teaspoons grated fresh ginger

Salt

1 pound green cabbage, cored and cut into approximately 3-by-¼-inch strips (about 1 quart)

1 tablespoon dry white wine

½ red bell pepper, cut into ⅛-inch strips

½ green bell pepper, cut into ⅛-inch strips

3 tablespoons Chicken Stock, page 61, or canned chicken broth, more if needed

more stock during cooking if the vegetables look dry. Season the stir-fry with additional salt to taste.

—EILEEN YIN-FEI LO

VARIATION

Substitute one carrot, cut diagonally into thin slices, for the green bell pepper. Add it to the pan along with the cabbage.

1. In a large frying pan or wok, heat the peanut and sesame oils over high heat. Add the ginger and ½ teaspoon salt. Stir-fry for 10 seconds. Add the cabbage; stir-fry for 30 seconds. Stir in the wine and bell peppers. Stir-fry for 1 minute.

2. Add the stock to the pan. Cook, stirring frequently, until the cabbage and peppers are just tender, about 7 minutes. Add

PER SERVING: CALORIES 49 kcal TOTAL FAT 1.4 gm SATURATED FAT .2 gm
CARBOHYDRATE 8 gm PROTEIN 2 gm CHOLESTEROL 0 mg

Sautéed Cabbage with Prosciutto

A couple of ounces of prosciutto go a long way. Here the sharp, salty ham makes plain ol' cabbage taste luscious.

4 SERVINGS

½ cup Chicken Stock, page 61, or canned chicken broth

1½ teaspoons butter

1 large carrot, cut into ⅓-inch slices

1 onion, chopped

1½ pounds Savoy cabbage, shredded (about 1½ quarts)

1 teaspoon sugar

Salt and fresh-ground black pepper

2 ounces thin-sliced prosciutto, cut into ⅓-inch strips

1 tablespoon chopped fresh parsley

¼ teaspoon chopped fresh thyme, or a pinch of dried

1. If using canned chicken broth, skim off and discard any fat that floats to the surface. In a medium pot, melt the butter over moderately high heat. Add the carrot and onion and cook, stirring, until the onion is starting to brown, about 8 minutes. Add the cabbage, stock, and sugar and toss to coat. Season with salt and pepper. Cover, reduce the heat to low, and cook, stirring occasionally, until the cabbage is tender, about 15 minutes.

2. Uncover the pot and increase the heat to high. Cook, stirring, until most of the liquid evaporates, about 5 minutes. Stir in the prosciutto, parsley, and thyme and cook until just heated through, about 1 minute longer.

—Bob Chambers

PER SERVING: CALORIES 125 kcal   TOTAL FAT 3.7 gm   SATURATED FAT 1.4 gm   CARBOHYDRATE 17.9 gm   PROTEIN 8.6 gm   CHOLESTEROL 15.4 mg

THREE CABBAGES WITH CARAWAY

The kale in this medley makes it perfect for the winter months, when this mild-mannered member of the cabbage family is at its peak. At other times of year, you can replace it with additional green cabbage.

4 SERVINGS

- 1 tablespoon olive oil
- 1 red onion, chopped
- ½ pound red cabbage, cored and sliced thin (about 2 cups)
- ½ pound kale, sliced thin (about 4 cups)
- 1 pound green cabbage, cored and sliced thin (about 4 cups)
- 1 teaspoon caraway seeds
  Salt and fresh-ground black pepper

KITCHEN TIP

Cabbage takes up considerably more room in the pot when it's raw than when it's cooked. If you can't fit all of the ten cups called for in this recipe in your pot at first, start with the red and green cabbage and cook them for five minutes. Remove the lid, press down on the cabbage to condense it, and put the kale on top. Continue cooking until everything is wilted.

---

1. In a large pot, combine the oil and onion. Top with the red cabbage, kale, and green cabbage. Cover and cook over moderately low heat until the cabbage is wilted, about 15 minutes.

2. Stir in the caraway seeds. Cover and cook until the cabbage is tender and the onion is starting to caramelize, about 12 minutes. Season with salt and pepper.

—DIANA STURGIS

PER SERVING: CALORIES 111 kcal **TOTAL FAT** 4.5 gm **SATURATED FAT** .6 gm **CARBOHYDRATE** 18 gm **PROTEIN** 4.5 gm **CHOLESTEROL** 0 mg

chapter *8*

POTATOES, RICE &
OTHER SIDE DISHES

Marie's Potato Gratin, page 203

MARIE'S POTATO GRATIN

Inspiration for this rich-tasting dish comes from gratins made in France during World War II. Since luxuries such as cream were in short supply, they were replaced with more readily available ingredients like chicken stock.

4 SERVINGS

1¼ cups Chicken Stock, page 61, or canned chicken broth

1 shallot, sliced (about ¼ cup)

1¼ pounds baking potatoes (about 3), peeled and cut into ⅛-inch slices

Salt and fresh-ground black pepper

2 tablespoons grated Parmesan cheese

2 tablespoons chopped fresh chives or scallion tops

1 ounce Gruyère cheese, grated (about ¼ cup)

1. If using canned chicken broth, skim off and discard any fat that floats to the surface. Heat the oven to 400°. Bring the stock to a boil in a medium saucepan. Add the shallot, reduce the heat, and simmer, partially covered, until tender, about 5 minutes. Strain the stock into a bowl and spread the shallot over the bottom of a large gratin dish or a shallow baking dish.

2. Layer a quarter of the potato slices over the shallot. Season with salt and pepper. Put another quarter of the potato slices on top and sprinkle with 1 tablespoon each of the Parmesan and chives. Season with salt and pepper. Make two more layers with the remaining potatoes, seasoning each layer with salt and pepper.

3. Pour enough stock over the potatoes so that the top layer of potatoes is just above the liquid. Sprinkle the remaining tablespoon each of the Parmesan and chives over the top. Spread the Gruyère in an even layer over all. Bake until the potatoes are tender and the top is brown, about 1¼ hours. Let the gratin sit for 10 minutes before serving.

—BOB CHAMBERS

PER SERVING: CALORIES 142 kcal TOTAL FAT 3.2 gm SATURATED FAT 1.8 gm CARBOHYDRATE 22 gm PROTEIN 6.7 gm CHOLESTEROL 9.8 mg

CUMIN-SPICED POTATOES

Indian spices, such as cumin, are most flavorful when they're toasted whole and then ground, as in this recipe. The addition of both fresh and dried chiles makes the potatoes particularly pungent.

4 SERVINGS

1½ pounds all-purpose potatoes, such as Yukon Gold (about 5), cut into 1-inch pieces

1½ teaspoons cumin seeds

4 teaspoons cooking oil

2 small dried red chile peppers

1 jalapeño pepper, seeded and minced

½ teaspoon salt

1. In a steamer basket set over boiling water, cook the potatoes until tender, about 15 minutes.

2. In a small heavy frying pan, toast the cumin seeds over moderate heat, shaking the pan, until fragrant, about 1 minute. Grind the seeds in a mortar with a pestle or in a spice grinder.

3. In a large frying pan, heat the oil over moderate heat. Add the dried chiles and cook until they start to darken, about 10 seconds. Add the potatoes, jalapeño, ground cumin, and salt. Cook, stirring occasionally, until the potatoes brown, about 15 minutes. Discard the dried chiles before serving.

—BHARTI KIRCHNER

VARIATIONS

• Substitute fennel seeds for the cumin seeds; toast and grind as directed. Sprinkle the potatoes with half a teaspoon of grated orange zest before serving.

• Use coriander seeds instead of the cumin seeds; toast and grind them as directed.

• Eliminate the cumin seeds and add one-and-a-half teaspoons chili powder to the pan along with the potatoes.

• Eliminate the cumin seeds. Toss three tablespoons chopped fresh cilantro or parsley with the potatoes before serving.

PER SERVING: CALORIES 179 kcal **TOTAL FAT** 4.7 gm **SATURATED FAT** .4 gm **CARBOHYDRATE** 32 gm **PROTEIN** 4 gm **CHOLESTEROL** 0 mg

ROASTED POTATO STICKS

The secret here is potato starch. A light coating makes potato wedges come out crusty, crunchy, crispy, and downright irresistible—all at less than half a gram of fat per serving.

4 SERVINGS

2½   tablespoons potato starch

2½   teaspoons dried thyme

2½   teaspoons salt

1¼   teaspoons fresh-ground black pepper

1½   pounds baking potatoes (about 3), each cut lengthwise into 12 wedges

1. Heat the oven to 450°. Line a baking sheet with parchment paper.

2. In a small bowl, combine the potato starch, thyme, salt, and pepper. In a large resealable plastic bag, shake one third of the potato wedges with one third of the seasonings until coated. Put the seasoned potatoes, skin-side down, in a single layer on the prepared baking sheet. Repeat with the remaining potatoes and seasonings. Bake until golden brown and tender, about 45 minutes.

—BOB CHAMBERS

VARIATIONS

• Replace the thyme with hot or sweet paprika, according to your taste.

• For a Greek variation, substitute dried oregano for the thyme. Add a sprinkling of grated lemon zest at the end for an even more authentic flavor.

PER SERVING: CALORIES 143 kcal   TOTAL FAT .4 gm   SATURATED FAT .1 gm   CARBOHYDRATE 32 gm   PROTEIN 3 gm   CHOLESTEROL 0 mg

GARLIC MASHED POTATOES

Low-fat comfort food? Believe it. Five cloves of garlic and just a touch of olive oil give these smashed spuds an enticing flavor. If you're not a garlic lover, give our yogurt-and-scallion variation a try.

4 SERVINGS

1½ pounds boiling or baking potatoes, peeled and cut into 1-inch pieces

5 cloves garlic, peeled and quartered

½ cup 1-percent milk

Salt and fresh-ground black pepper

1½ teaspoons olive oil

1. Put the potatoes and garlic in a medium saucepan of salted water. Bring to a boil, reduce the heat, and simmer until the potatoes are tender, 20 to 25 minutes.

2. Drain the potatoes and garlic and put them back into the saucepan. Mash over very low heat, gradually incorporating the milk. Season with salt and pepper. Serve the potatoes drizzled with the oil.

—GEORGIA CHAN DOWNARD

VARIATIONS

• Eliminate the garlic; chop two scallions including the green tops. Save two tablespoons of the potato-cooking water before draining. Use half a cup of plain yogurt in place of the milk and add the potato water. Stir the scallions in at the end.

• Add three tablespoons chopped fresh herbs, such as basil, tarragon, or chives, to the mashed potatoes.

• Add two tablespoons of grated Parmesan or another hard grating cheese and one teaspoon chopped fresh parsley to the finished mashed potatoes.

PER SERVING: CALORIES 160 kcal TOTAL FAT 2.4 gm SATURATED FAT .4 gm
CARBOHYDRATE 31 gm PROTEIN 4 gm CHOLESTEROL 1.2 mg

BOURBON-SPIKED SWEET-POTATO PUREE

Traditional candied sweet potatoes may lose their place on your holiday table to this delectable alternative. The sweet potatoes are roasted, pureed, and then laced with a little bourbon. The result: full flavor with very little fat.

4 SERVINGS

2½ pounds sweet potatoes or yams (about 4)

¼ teaspoon grated lemon zest

1½ teaspoons lemon juice

Salt and fresh-ground black pepper

2 tablespoons bourbon

2 tablespoons dark-brown sugar

MAKE IT AHEAD

The puree can be made a day in advance. Keep it covered in the refrigerator until ready to use and then warm over low heat.

---

1. Heat the oven to 450°. Prick the sweet potatoes a few times with a fork and put them in a large nonstick roasting pan. Cook the potatoes until soft and brown on the bottom, about 1 hour. When they are cool enough to handle, remove the skins, leaving as much caramelized sweet-potato flesh as possible. Cut the potatoes into chunks and put in a food processor. Add the lemon zest and lemon juice and puree until smooth. Season with salt and pepper.

2. In a large stainless-steel saucepan, combine the bourbon and brown sugar. Bring just to a boil. Stir in the puree. Cook over low heat until just warmed through.

—BOB CHAMBERS

PER SERVING: CALORIES 258 kcal TOTAL FAT .6 gm SATURATED FAT .1 gm CARBOHYDRATE 56 gm PROTEIN 3.4 gm CHOLESTEROL 0 mg

Fried Rice with Asparagus

Authentic fried rice is made with rice that's been steamed and then cooled before frying. Rinsing and soaking the rice before cooking ensures perfectly cooked grains. If you have leftover rice, you can use it instead. You'll need four cups.

4 SERVINGS

1½ cups long-grain rice

1½ cups water

¾ teaspoon salt

1 egg

1 egg white

1 tablespoon peanut oil

4 tablespoons Chicken Stock, page 61, or canned chicken broth

2 tablespoons oyster sauce

1½ teaspoons soy sauce

2 teaspoons dry white wine

1 teaspoon sugar

½ teaspoon Asian sesame oil

Fresh-ground black pepper

2 cloves garlic, minced

12 asparagus spears, trimmed, stalks cut into ½-inch pieces

6 drained and rinsed canned water chestnuts, cut into ¼-inch pieces

3 scallions including green tops, sliced thin

3 tablespoons minced cilantro

1. Rinse the rice in several changes of cold water. Drain. Put the rice and the 1½ cups water in a medium saucepan. Let the rice soak for 1 hour.

2. Add the salt to the rice and bring to a boil over high heat. Boil, stirring occasionally, until most of the water evaporates, about 5 minutes. Cover the pan and reduce the heat to low. Cook the rice until tender, about 10 minutes. Remove the pan from the heat and fluff the rice with a fork. Spread the rice out on a plate to cool completely.

3. In a small bowl, beat the egg with the egg white. Heat 1 teaspoon of the peanut oil in a large frying pan or wok. Pour the eggs into the pan and cook them, stirring, until set, 2 to 3 minutes. Remove the eggs from the pan and cut into ½-inch cubes.

4. If using canned chicken broth, skim off and discard any fat that floats to the surface. In a small bowl, combine 2 tablespoons of the stock with the oyster sauce, soy sauce, wine, sugar, sesame oil, and a pinch of pepper.

5. Heat the remaining 2 teaspoons peanut oil in the frying pan or wok over high heat. Add the garlic and cook until

PER SERVING: CALORIES 369 kcal TOTAL FAT 5.8 gm SATURATED FAT 1.2 gm
CARBOHYDRATE 67 gm PROTEIN 11 gm CHOLESTEROL 53 mg

fragrant, about 30 seconds. Add the aspara-gus and stir-fry for 1 minute. Add the water chestnuts and the remaining 2 tablespoons stock. Stir-fry for 2 minutes. Add the rice; stir-fry until hot, 2 to 3 minutes.

6. Add the oyster-sauce mixture and stir until the rice is thoroughly coated. Stir in the eggs, scallions, and cilantro.

—Eileen Yin-Fei Lo

MAKE IT AHEAD

The rice can be boiled several days in advance and refrigerated until ready to use. In fact, completely chilled rice makes the best fried rice. The grains stay separate when fried rather than clumping together.

VARIATION

Use half a pound of green beans or Chinese long beans instead of the aspara-gus. Trim the ends and cut the beans into half-inch pieces. Stir-fry the beans for one minute. Add the remaining ingredients as directed.

FRIED RICE WITH PEAS AND SUN-DRIED TOMATOES

Though not exactly a traditional Asian ingredient, sun-dried tomatoes bring a surprising burst of flavor to fried rice. To keep it low-fat, be sure to rinse oil-packed tomatoes before you add them.

4 SERVINGS

1½ cups long-grain rice

1½ cups water

    Salt

 3 eggs

    Fresh-ground black pepper

 1 tablespoon plus 1 teaspoon peanut oil

1½ tablespoons oyster sauce

 1 tablespoon Chicken Stock, page 61, or canned chicken broth

 2 teaspoons soy sauce

 1 teaspoon dry white wine

 ¾ teaspoon sugar

 ½ teaspoon Asian sesame oil

1½ teaspoons minced fresh ginger

1¼ cups fresh shelled or thawed frozen peas

 4 reconstituted dry-packed or rinsed oil-packed sun-dried tomato halves, cut into ½-inch pieces

 4 scallions including green tops, sliced thin

 3 tablespoons chopped cilantro

1. Rinse the rice in several changes of cold water. Drain. Put the rice and the 1½ cups water in a medium saucepan. Let the rice soak for 1 hour.

2. Add ¾ teaspoon salt to the rice and bring to a boil over high heat. Boil, stirring occasionally, until most of the water evaporates, about 5 minutes. Cover the pan and reduce the heat to low. Cook until tender, about 10 minutes. Remove the pan from the heat; fluff the rice with a fork. Spread the rice out on a plate to cool completely.

3. In a small bowl, beat the eggs with a pinch each of salt and pepper. Heat the 1 teaspoon peanut oil in a large frying pan or wok. Pour the eggs into the pan and cook, stirring, until set, 2 to 3 minutes. Remove the eggs from the pan and cut into ½-inch cubes.

4. In a small bowl, combine the oyster sauce, stock, soy sauce, wine, sugar, sesame oil, and a pinch of pepper.

5. Heat the remaining 1 tablespoon peanut oil in the frying pan or wok over high

PER SERVING: CALORIES 426 kcal TOTAL FAT 9.7 gm SATURATED FAT 2.2 gm CARBOHYDRATE 70 gm PROTEIN 14 gm CHOLESTEROL 159 mg

heat. Add the ginger and stir-fry for 20 seconds. Add the peas; stir-fry for 20 seconds. Stir in the rice and stir-fry until hot, 2 to 3 minutes.

6. Add the oyster-sauce mixture and stir until the rice is thoroughly coated. Stir in the eggs, tomatoes, scallions, and cilantro.

—Eileen Yin-Fei Lo

Make It Ahead

The rice can be boiled several days in advance and kept refrigerated until ready to use. Or, use four cups of leftover cooked rice.

Stir-Fry Ingredient Exchange

You can do a lot of mixing and matching of ingredients when you make a stir-fry. If you don't like a certain ingredient or you don't have it on hand, try a new combination. Many of the ingredients below, because of their similar flavors, textures, or cooking times, can be used interchangeably.

- **Firm vegetables:** broccoli, bell peppers, green beans, asparagus, carrots, cauliflower, eggplant
- **Medium-firm vegetables:** bok choy, napa cabbage, green cabbage, Savoy cabbage, mushrooms, snow peas, sugar snap peas, zucchini, escarole, Swiss chard
- **Leafy vegetables:** watercress, spinach, Belgian endive, various lettuces

BAKED RICE WITH CHICKPEAS

Substitute vegetable stock for the chicken stock, and this hearty casserole can be the centerpiece of a vegetarian dinner. Multiply the ingredient quantities by one-and-a-half to serve it as a main dish.

4 SERVINGS

4½ cups Chicken Stock, page 61, or canned chicken broth

1½ tablespoons olive oil

3 cloves garlic, chopped

3 tomatoes, peeled, seeded, and chopped

1½ cups drained and rinsed canned chickpeas

1½ teaspoons paprika

Pinch saffron threads

1½ cups rice, preferably medium grain

Salt and fresh-ground black pepper

1. If using canned chicken broth, skim off and discard any fat that floats to the surface. Heat the oven to 400°. In a small saucepan, bring the stock just to a boil over moderately high heat. Reduce the heat and keep the stock warm.

2. In a medium ovenproof pot, heat the oil over moderate heat. Add the garlic and cook until fragrant, about 30 seconds. Add the tomatoes, chickpeas, paprika, and saffron. Bring to a simmer.

3. Stir in the rice, ¾ teaspoon salt, and ¼ teaspoon pepper. Add the hot stock and bring to a simmer over moderate heat. Cover and bake until most of the liquid is absorbed and the rice is almost tender, about 15 minutes. Remove the pot from the oven and let stand, covered, until the rice is tender, about 10 minutes. Fluff the rice with a fork and season with salt and pepper.

—MICHELE SCICOLONE

PER SERVING: CALORIES 433 kcal TOTAL FAT 7.6 gm SATURATED FAT .9 gm CARBOHYDRATE 76 gm PROTEIN 13.4 gm CHOLESTEROL 0 mg

CORN PILAF

Whole cardamom pods and a cinnamon stick help to make this Indian-inspired pilaf especially fragrant and flavorful. Remove them either before serving the side dish or as you eat it.

4 SERVINGS

1 cup basmati or long-grain white rice

2¼ cups Vegetable Stock, page 61, Chicken Stock, page 61, or canned broth

2 teaspoons olive oil

½ teaspoon cumin seeds

1 2-inch cinnamon stick

4 to 5 cardamom pods (optional)

Salt

¾ cup fresh (cut from about 2 ears) or thawed frozen corn kernels

1. Rinse the rice in several changes of cold water. Drain.

2. If using canned chicken broth, skim off and discard any fat that floats to the surface. In a medium saucepan, heat the oil over moderate heat. Add the cumin, cinnamon stick, and cardamom pods, if using, and cook, stirring, until the cumin is brown, about 1 minute. Add the rice, stock, and ¾ teaspoon salt; cover and bring to a boil. Reduce the heat and simmer, covered, until all the liquid is absorbed and the rice is tender, about 15 minutes. Add the corn, cover, and cook until heated through, about 2 minutes longer. Fluff the rice with a fork and season with salt if needed.

—BHARTI KIRCHNER

VARIATION

Instead of corn, use three quarters of a cup fresh or thawed frozen petite peas. They'll need to steam with the rice for about four minutes.

PER SERVING: CALORIES 216 kcal   TOTAL FAT 3.9 gm   SATURATED FAT .3 gm   CARBOHYDRATE 44 gm   PROTEIN 6 gm   CHOLESTEROL 0 mg

CREAMY WILD RICE WITH MUSHROOMS

A rich-tasting sauce made from our version of half-and-half (skim and whole milk) gives this rice dish a creamy texture without the cream. The mushrooms and shallots are oven roasted to intensify their flavor.

4 SERVINGS

6 ounces wild rice (about ⅞ cup)

¾ teaspoon butter

¾ teaspoon cooking oil

1 shallot, minced (about ¼ cup)

1½ teaspoons minced fresh thyme

Salt and fresh-ground black pepper

½ pound white mushrooms, cut into ¼-inch slices

6 ounces shiitake mushrooms, stems removed and caps cut into ¼-inch slices

¾ cup skim milk

1 tablespoon arrowroot

¾ cup whole milk

1 tablespoon chopped flat-leaf parsley

1½ teaspoons minced fresh chives or scallion tops

1. Rinse the rice in several changes of cold water. Drain. In a medium pot of boiling, salted water, cook the rice until very tender, about 45 minutes. Drain.

2. Heat the oven to 475°. Heat the butter and oil in a medium ovenproof pot. Add the shallot and thyme, season with salt and pepper, and cook over high heat, stirring, for 2 minutes. Stir in the white and shiitake mushrooms. Bake until the mushrooms soften, about 15 minutes. Stir the mushrooms and bake until they absorb the liquid in the pot, about 10 minutes longer.

3. In a bowl, gradually whisk 2 tablespoons of the skim milk into the arrowroot until smooth.

4. Remove the pot from the oven and put over high heat. Add the remaining skim milk and the whole milk and bring to a boil. Stir in the arrowroot mixture and cook until thickened, about 1 minute. Add the rice and cook, stirring, until heated through. Season with salt and pepper. Sprinkle the parsley and chives over the top.

—BOB CHAMBERS

PER SERVING: CALORIES 247 kcal TOTAL FAT 3.9 gm SATURATED FAT 1.6 gm CARBOHYDRATE 44 gm PROTEIN 12 gm CHOLESTEROL 9.2 mg

RICE AND RED BEANS

The combination of red beans and rice—a staple of Caribbean cuisine—is both low in fat and high in fiber. It's often served as a mild contrast to a spicy main dish.

4 SERVINGS

1½ cups long-grain rice

2 cups water

Salt

1¾ cups drained and rinsed canned red kidney beans (from one 19-ounce can)

Fresh-ground black pepper

2 scallions including green tops, sliced thin

1. Rinse the rice in several changes of cold water. Drain.

2. In a medium saucepan, combine the rice, water, and ¾ teaspoon salt. Bring to a boil over high heat. Cover, reduce the heat, and simmer until all the liquid is absorbed and the rice is nearly tender, 12 to 15 minutes. Remove the pan from the heat and let stand, covered, until the rice is tender, about 10 minutes. Uncover and fluff the rice with a fork.

3. In a colander, rinse the beans under very hot water to warm them. Fold into the hot rice and season with salt and pepper as needed. Sprinkle with the scallions.

—MARCIA KIESEL

VARIATIONS

• Toss three tablespoons of chopped cilantro into the rice with the beans.
• Dice one red or green bell pepper and toss it into the finished dish. This would be particularly good in combination with the cilantro variation above.
• Use canned black beans in place of the kidney beans.

PER SERVING: CALORIES 319 kcal **TOTAL FAT** 1 gm **SATURATED FAT** .2 gm
CARBOHYDRATE 67 gm **PROTEIN** 9 gm **CHOLESTEROL** 0 mg

REFRIED BLACK BEANS

This variation on refried beans adds something new—a sprinkling of chopped fresh mint—and deletes something old—the lard that's often used to give refried beans their creamy consistency. Here, the beans are cooked in a small amount of oil and then mashed into a smooth puree.

4 SERVINGS

1   poblano chile

2   teaspoons cooking oil

1   onion, chopped

2   cups cooked black beans, plus 3 tablespoons of the cooking liquid

    Salt and fresh-ground black pepper

1   tablespoon chopped fresh mint

1. Roast the poblano over a gas flame or grill or broil it, turning with tongs until charred all over, about 10 minutes. When the chile is cool enough to handle, pull off the skin. Remove the stem, seeds, and ribs. Chop the chile.

2. In a medium nonstick frying pan, heat the cooking oil over moderately high heat. Add the onion and cook, stirring occasionally, until starting to brown, about 5 minutes.

3. Reduce the heat to low and stir in the beans and their liquid. Using a potato masher, mash the beans to a thick puree. Add the poblano and stir until the mixture is heated through, about 3 minutes. Season with salt and pepper. Sprinkle the chopped mint over the beans.

—JEAN GALTON

USING CANNED BEANS

You can substitute canned beans for the cooked black beans without sacrificing quality. Drain and rinse the beans before putting them in the frying pan; use three tablespoons of chicken stock or water in place of the cooking liquid.

PER SERVING: CALORIES 140 kcal   TOTAL FAT 2.7 gm   SATURATED FAT .3 gm
CARBOHYDRATE 23 gm   PROTEIN 7 gm   CHOLESTEROL 0 mg

FIRESIDE PINTO-BEAN AND CHILE STEW

Nopal cactus pads add an appropriate trailside touch to this spicy Southwestern stew, but green beans make a surprisingly good substitute. If you're serving the stew as a main dish instead of a side, serve it over boiled white rice.

4 SERVINGS

¾ cup dried pinto beans (about ¼ pound)

1 cup full-bodied beer

3⅓ cups water

1 teaspoon olive oil

1 rib celery, cut into ¾-inch pieces

1 small red onion, diced

1 carrot, cut into ¾-inch pieces

1 clove garlic, minced

1 dried ancho chile, seeded and crumbled

⅔ cup dry white wine

½ teaspoon cumin seeds

1 Anaheim chile, preferably red, or poblano chile, seeded and cut into ½-inch pieces

½ green bell pepper, cut into ¾-inch pieces

½ yellow bell pepper, cut into ¾-inch pieces

1 large pad of nopal cactus, thorns removed, pad cut into ¾-inch pieces, or 3 ounces green beans, cut into ¾-inch lengths

1 tomato, seeded and diced

1½ tablespoons cider vinegar

2 teaspoons tomato paste

2 teaspoons molasses

Salt

3 tablespoons chopped cilantro

1. In a medium pot, combine the pinto beans, beer, and water. Bring to a boil over moderately high heat. Reduce the heat and simmer until the beans are tender, about 1½ hours.

2. In a large pot, heat the oil over moderately high heat. Add the celery, onion, and carrot and cook, stirring, until starting to brown, about 5 minutes. Stir in the garlic and ancho chile and cook for 1 minute. Add the wine and cook, stirring, until the liquid is reduced by half, about 5 minutes.

3. Meanwhile, in a small frying pan, toast the cumin seeds over moderately high heat, shaking the pan, until fragrant, about 30 seconds. Grind the seeds in a mortar with a pestle or in a spice grinder.

4. Stir the ground cumin seeds into the vegetables. Add the Anaheim chile, bell peppers, cactus, tomato, vinegar, tomato paste, and molasses. Stir in the beans with their cooking liquid and ¾ teaspoon salt. Cook,

PER SERVING: CALORIES 182 kcal TOTAL FAT 2.3 gm SATURATED FAT .3 gm CARBOHYDRATE 35 gm PROTEIN 8 gm CHOLESTEROL 0 mg

stirring occasionally, until the vegetables are tender and the stew is slightly thickened, 20 to 30 minutes. Season with salt and sprinkle the cilantro over the stew.

—CHARLES WILEY

FIVE LOW-FAT TIPS

• **Intensify flavor** by using techniques such as marinating low-fat cuts of meat (such as pork tenderloin) or poultry (like skinless chicken or turkey breasts); pickling ordinary vegetables; or roasting.

• **If the recipe calls for cheese,** use small amounts of an aged or hard variety. Its concentrated flavor means you won't need to use as much.

• **Instead of the usual butter and cream,** thicken sauces with crumbled baked tortillas, pureed roasted vegetables, or a combination of bread crumbs and wine or stock.

• **Make use of vegetable-oil cooking sprays** and nonstick pans.

• **Toast spices, then grind them** for maximum impact. Choose pure chile powder when buying it already ground, and grind dried chiles for chile powder yourself whenever possible.

BASIC COOKED LENTILS

Toss these lentils with greens for a salad. Stir them into rice or pasta. Or eat them all by themselves. You can use typical brown lentils, the firm French green lentils, or Indian red lentils here.

4 SERVINGS

1⅓ cups green, brown, or red lentils (about ½ pound)

1 small onion, stuck with 2 whole cloves

2 cloves garlic, smashed

½ serrano or jalapeño chile, ribs and seeds removed

5 sprigs fresh parsley

3 to 4 sprigs fresh thyme, or ½ teaspoon dried

1 bay leaf

4 cups water

¾ teaspoon salt

1. Rinse the lentils in several changes of cold water and drain. Put the lentils in a medium saucepan with the onion, garlic, chile, parsley, thyme, bay leaf, and water. Bring to a boil over moderate heat. Reduce the heat and simmer until the lentils are tender, about 8 minutes for red lentils, 20 for brown or green. Add the salt halfway through the cooking time.

2. Drain the lentils, reserving the cooking liquid. Discard the onion, garlic, chile, parsley, fresh thyme, if using, and bay leaf.

Serve immediately, or reheat the lentils in their liquid.

—SALLY SCHNEIDER

LENTIL LARGESSE

When properly prepared, lentils not only are delicious but offer extraordinary nutritional value as well. These little gems are an inexpensive source of protein and have just a trace of fat. They're also high in carbohydrates, fiber, B vitamins, and minerals. Lentils can be used at a moment's notice; they need no soaking and cook very quickly.

PER SERVING: CALORIES 198 kcal TOTAL FAT .6 gm SATURATED FAT .1 gm
CARBOHYDRATE 34 gm PROTEIN 16 gm CHOLESTEROL 0 mg

LENTILS WITH FRAGRANT RICE

Red lentils, which are typically used in Indian recipes, cook more quickly and have a milder flavor and softer texture than brown or green lentils. You can use any type here, but red lentils seem particularly appropriate with the fragrant basmati rice.

4 SERVINGS

1 tablespoon cooking oil

½ teaspoon cumin seeds

1 onion, chopped

4 cloves garlic, chopped

½ teaspoon minced jalapeño or serrano chile

¼ teaspoon saffron threads, crushed (optional)

1 cup basmati rice

1⅛ teaspoons *garam masala**

1½ tablespoons grated fresh ginger

1 cup water

¾ cup Chicken Stock, page 61, or canned chicken broth

½ teaspoon salt

Basic Cooked Lentils, page 221, preferably red, plus ½ cup of their cooking liquid

1 teaspoon balsamic vinegar

½ cup chopped fresh cilantro

¾ cup plain low-fat yogurt

*Available at Indian markets and many supermarkets

1. In a medium saucepan, heat the oil over moderate heat. Add the cumin seeds and cook until fragrant, about 1 minute. Add the onion and cook, stirring frequently, until translucent, about 5 minutes. Add the garlic, chile, and saffron, if using, and cook for 1 minute. Stir in the rice and *garam masala* and stir until the rice is coated with the spices and oil. Add the ginger and cook for 30 seconds.

2. Add the water, stock, and salt and bring to a boil over high heat. Reduce the heat, cover, and simmer until the rice is nearly tender, 12 to 15 minutes. Remove from the heat and let stand, covered, until the rice is tender, about 10 minutes.

3. Put the lentils and their cooking liquid in a medium stainless-steel saucepan. Heat over moderate heat, covered, until the lentils are hot, about 8 minutes. Toss with the vinegar and ¼ cup of the cilantro.

4. Spoon the rice and the lentils into four bowls, mixing them together slightly. Serve topped with the yogurt and the remaining ¼ cup cilantro.

—SALLY SCHNEIDER

PER SERVING: CALORIES 449 kcal TOTAL FAT 5 gm SATURATED FAT 1 gm
CARBOHYDRATE 78 gm PROTEIN 23 gm CHOLESTEROL 3 mg

ORZO WITH LEMON AND HERBS

Rice-shaped orzo pasta is popular in Greece as well as Italy. This lightened version of a Greek dish includes lemon juice, chicken stock, and loads of fresh herbs.

4 SERVINGS

3½ cups Chicken Stock, page 61, or canned chicken broth

½ pound orzo

1½ teaspoons olive oil

2 tablespoons lemon juice

¼ cup plus 2 tablespoons chopped fresh parsley, chervil, or basil, or a combination

Salt and fresh-ground black pepper

VARIATION

Try using orange juice instead of lemon. Either variation would be delicious in combination with chopped fresh tarragon in place of the suggested herbs.

1. If using canned chicken broth, skim off and discard any fat that floats to the surface. In a large stainless-steel saucepan, bring the stock to a boil over moderate heat. Add the orzo and cook, stirring often, until most of the stock is absorbed and the orzo is tender, about 10 minutes.

2. Remove the pan from the heat. Stir in the oil, lemon juice, and herbs. Season with salt and pepper.

—MARTHA ROSE SHULMAN

PER SERVING: CALORIES 243 kcal TOTAL FAT 3 gm SATURATED FAT .4 gm CARBOHYDRATE 44 gm PROTEIN 9 gm CHOLESTEROL 0 mg

HERBED SPAETZLE

The dumpling-like noodles known as *spaetzle* are usually made with flour, eggs, milk, and salt. We've replaced one of the whole eggs with an egg white, used water instead of milk, and stirred fresh herbs into the dough for a slimmer updated version of this German specialty.

4 SERVINGS

1 egg

1 egg white

¾ cup water

2¼ cups flour

1 tablespoon chopped fresh chives

1 tablespoon chopped fresh parsley

½ teaspoon chopped fresh thyme

1¼ teaspoons salt

½ recipe warm Three-Mushroom Gravy, page 164

1. In a medium bowl, whisk together the egg, egg white, and water. Add the flour, chives, parsley, thyme, and salt and stir just until a sticky dough forms.

2. Bring a large pot of salted water to a simmer. Pat one third of the dough into a 3-inch square on a small cutting board or on the back of a square cake pan. Holding the board over the pot and working quickly, scrape ¼-inch strips of dough into the water. Working quickly over the pot, slice the remaining dough into the simmering water. Moisten the knife if it sticks to the dough.

3. Stir the spaetzle and cook over moderate heat until the dumplings float to the surface and are just cooked through, about 2 minutes. Using a slotted spoon, transfer the spaetzle to a bowl and keep warm. Repeat with the rest of the dough.

4. Add the gravy to the cooked spaetzle and toss to combine.

—GRACE PARISI

VARIATIONS

Instead of the gravy, toss the spaetzle with some warm chicken stock or with a bit of tomato sauce and a sprinkling of Parmesan cheese.

PER SERVING: CALORIES 326 kcal TOTAL FAT 3.9 gm SATURATED FAT .1 gm CARBOHYDRATE 62 gm PROTEIN 14 gm CHOLESTEROL 53 mg

Quinoa and Vegetable Pilaf

Nutty-tasting quinoa is packed with protein. Most varieties have a bitter coating that's removed during processing. Any small amount that remains will wash away under running water, so be sure to rinse the grain before cooking it.

4 SERVINGS

⅔ cup quinoa

1¼ cups Chicken Stock, page 61, or canned chicken broth

Salt

1½ teaspoons olive oil

3 tablespoons diced red bell pepper

3 tablespoons diced yellow bell pepper

1 leek, white part only, chopped and washed well

1 carrot, diced

1 rib celery, diced

1 clove garlic, minced

2 teaspoons grated Parmesan cheese

Fresh-ground black pepper

3 tablespoons chopped flat-leaf parsley

1. Rinse the quinoa well. Drain. If using canned chicken broth, skim off and discard any fat that floats to the surface.

2. In a medium saucepan, combine the quinoa, stock, and ½ teaspoon salt and bring to a boil over moderately high heat. Reduce the heat, cover, and simmer until all the liquid has been absorbed and the quinoa is tender, about 15 minutes.

3. Meanwhile, heat the oil in a medium frying pan over moderate heat. Add the bell peppers, leek, carrot, and celery. Cook, stirring occasionally, until the vegetables are starting to soften, about 7 minutes. Stir in the garlic and cook 1 minute longer.

4. Stir the vegetables into the quinoa. Add the Parmesan and season with salt and pepper. Sprinkle the chopped parsley over the pilaf.

—Laurie Burrows Grad

PER SERVING: CALORIES 144 kcal **TOTAL FAT** 4 gm **SATURATED FAT** .7 gm
CARBOHYDRATE 23 gm **PROTEIN** 5 gm **CHOLESTEROL** .8 mg

Baked Mushroom Polenta with Mozzarella

Packed with peppers and Parmesan, mushrooms and mozzarella, and crushed tomatoes and fresh herbs, this low-fat layered polenta makes a great side dish for Grilled Chicken Breasts with Caramelized-Onion Marmalade, page 154.

4 SERVINGS

- 1 red bell pepper
- 1 yellow bell pepper
- ½ pound mushrooms, cut into thick slices
- 2 cups Chicken Stock, page 61, or canned chicken broth
- ¾ cup water
- ¾ cup coarse or medium yellow cornmeal
- 3 tablespoons grated Parmesan cheese
  Salt and fresh-ground black pepper
- 2 shallots, chopped
- 1 clove garlic, minced
- ½ cup dry white wine
- 1½ cups canned crushed tomatoes with their juice
- 1 tablespoon chopped flat-leaf parsley
- ½ teaspoon minced fresh thyme, or ¼ teaspoon dried
  Pinch sugar
- ¼ pound part-skim mozzarella, grated (about ¾ cup)

1. Roast the peppers over a gas flame or grill or broil them, turning with tongs until charred all over, about 10 minutes. When the peppers are cool enough to handle, pull off the skin. Remove the stems, seeds, and ribs. Cut the peppers into approximately 1-by-¼-inch strips.

2. Coat a large nonstick frying pan with vegetable-oil cooking spray. Heat the pan over moderately high heat. Add the mushrooms and cook, stirring, until browned, about 10 minutes.

3. If using canned chicken broth, skim off and discard any fat that floats to the surface. In a medium saucepan, bring the stock and the water to a boil. Add the cornmeal in a slow stream, whisking constantly. Reduce the heat; simmer, stirring frequently with a wooden spoon, until the polenta is very thick, about 20 minutes. Stir in the mushrooms, 1 tablespoon of the Parmesan, ¾ teaspoon salt, and ¼ teaspoon pepper. Spread the polenta about ½ inch thick in a jelly-roll pan. Cool until set. Cut into rectangles.

4. In a stainless-steel saucepan, simmer the shallots and garlic in the wine until

PER SERVING: CALORIES 255 kcal   TOTAL FAT 6.7 gm   SATURATED FAT 3.8 gm
CARBOHYDRATE 33 gm   PROTEIN 17 gm   CHOLESTEROL 20 mg

almost all of the liquid has evaporated, about 4 minutes. Add the tomatoes, parsley, thyme, and sugar. Season with salt and pepper. Cook, stirring, until the sauce is thickened, about 10 minutes.

5. Heat the oven to 375°. Spread one third of the tomato sauce in a large glass or stainless-steel baking dish. Put half of the polenta rectangles on top, overlapping if necessary. Sprinkle with half of the mozzarella, peppers, remaining sauce, and Parmesan. Put the rest of the polenta on top. Cover with the remaining mozzarella, peppers, sauce, and Parmesan. Bake until bubbling and brown on top, about 30 minutes.

—BOB CHAMBERS

CHEESE Q & A

Q: What is the role of fat in cheese?

A: Fat is what gives cheese its voluptuousness, what builds and carries its flavors. With a few exceptions (mascarpone, some goat cheeses, and cream cheese), the blander the cheese, the lower its fat content. For example, an ounce of low-fat cottage cheese averages less than a third of a gram of fat and twenty-two calories.

Q: Does cheese have any redeeming nutritional virtues?

A: Plenty. It's a powerhouse of calcium, protein, phosphorous, and vitamin A. But many cheeses are also loaded with sodium. If you're sensitive to salt, scrutinize the labels.

Q: Which is the easiest cheese to digest: goat, cow, or sheep?

A: Because of their protein makeups, cheeses made from goat or sheep milk (Roquefort is the best-known sheep cheese) are more digestible than cow cheeses. But, for people with lactose (milk sugar) intolerance, goat- and sheep-milk cheeses are no better than cow's-milk cheese. All three varieties contain similar amounts of lactose.

—JEAN ANDERSON

chapter 9

BREAKFAST &
BRUNCH DISHES

Warm Blueberry-and-Mango Compote, page 243; Herbed Turkey-Sausage
Patties, page 232; and Caramelized-Apple French Toast, page 231

CARAMELIZED-APPLE FRENCH TOAST

Instead of being fried in butter, our French toast is baked in the oven until it is deliciously caramelized. For an extra treat, top the French toast with Warm Blueberry-and-Mango Compote, page 243, and serve Herbed Turkey-Sausage Patties, page 232, alongside.

4 SERVINGS

1 teaspoon unsalted butter

¼ cup dark-brown sugar

1 cup 1-percent milk

2 large eggs

¼ cup plus 2 tablespoons unsweetened applesauce

¼ cup granulated sugar

2 tablespoons rum, preferably dark

1 teaspoon vanilla extract

¼ teaspoon ground cardamom

Pinch salt

8 ½-inch slices white bread

1. Heat the oven to 375°. Coat a large nonstick baking sheet with the butter. Press the brown sugar through a sieve to remove any lumps and sprinkle 2 tablespoons of the sugar evenly over the prepared baking sheet.

2. In a shallow bowl, whisk the milk with the eggs, applesauce, granulated sugar, rum, vanilla, cardamom, and salt. Dip the bread slices into the mixture one at a time, turning to coat, until thoroughly moistened. Arrange the slices on the prepared baking sheet and sprinkle evenly with the remaining 2 tablespoons brown sugar.

3. Bake the toast, turning once, until the sugar is caramelized, about 20 minutes.

—GRACE PARISI

VARIATION

In place of the cardamom, use half a teaspoon of cinnamon.

PER SERVING: CALORIES 352 kcal **TOTAL FAT** 6.9 gm **SATURATED FAT** 2.8 gm **CARBOHYDRATE** 59 gm **PROTEIN** 9.3 gm **CHOLESTEROL** 114 mg

HERBED TURKEY-SAUSAGE PATTIES

When buying ground turkey for these sausage patties (pictured on page 230), make sure you're getting just turkey breast, not a combination of light and dark meat. The mixed type may look similar, but it has substantially more fat. If you can't find ground turkey breast, buy breast meat and chop it yourself; the instructions are in the recipe.

4 SERVINGS

1 large red potato

2 teaspoons vegetable oil

¼ pound shiitake mushrooms, stems removed and caps chopped fine

1 small onion, chopped fine

2 cloves garlic, minced

1 pound ground turkey breast, or 1 pound skinless turkey breast cut into 1-inch cubes

2 ounces cured ham, such as prosciutto, trimmed of fat and chopped fine

1 tablespoon 1-percent milk

1 tablespoon chopped flat-leaf parsley

1 teaspoon chopped fresh sage

½ teaspoon chopped fresh thyme, or ⅛ teaspoon dried

1 teaspoon salt

¼ teaspoon fresh-ground black pepper

1. In a steamer basket set over 1 inch of simmering water, steam the potato until it is tender when pierced with a fork, about 18 minutes. When it is cool enough to handle, peel and grate the potato.

2. In a large nonstick frying pan, heat 1 teaspoon of the oil over high heat. Add the mushrooms and cook, stirring occasionally, until beginning to brown, about 4 minutes. Add the onion and garlic and cook, stirring, until translucent, about 3 minutes. Transfer to a bowl and let cool.

3. If using cubed turkey breast, whir it in a food processor until chopped to a course grind. Add the turkey to the mushroom mixture along with the potato, ham, milk, parsley, sage, thyme, salt, and pepper and stir until thoroughly combined. Shape the mixture into eight 3-inch patties.

4. In a large nonstick frying pan, heat the remaining 1 teaspoon oil over moderately high heat. Cook the patties, turning once, until they are well browned and cooked through, about 6 minutes.

—GRACE PARISI

PER SERVING: CALORIES 229 kcal   TOTAL FAT 5.3 gm   SATURATED FAT 1.1 gm   CARBOHYDRATE 11 gm   PROTEIN 34 gm   CHOLESTEROL 82 mg

CORNMEAL PANCAKES WITH BANANA YOGURT FILLING

Because draining the yogurt takes time, you'll have to start the night before, but these pancakes layered with maple-flavored banana filling are worth the advance planning. Pineapple Kiwi Compote, page 244, is a delicious accompaniment.

4 SERVINGS

3 cups plain nonfat yogurt

1 banana, cut into ¼-inch dice

¼ cup plus 3 tablespoons maple syrup

½ cup cornmeal

1 cup flour

¼ cup light-brown sugar

1 teaspoon baking soda

Salt

¾ cup water

2 egg whites

1 teaspoon cooking oil

1. Set a strainer over a medium bowl and line it with a double layer of cheesecloth. Put the yogurt in the strainer and cover it. Let the yogurt drain in the refrigerator overnight.

2. Discard the liquid that has accumulated in the bowl. Wipe out the bowl and put the drained yogurt into it. Stir the diced banana and the 3 tablespoons maple syrup into the yogurt.

3. In a large bowl, whisk together the cornmeal, flour, brown sugar, baking soda, and a pinch of salt. Stir in the water. In a medium bowl, beat the egg whites with a pinch of salt until they hold firm peaks when the beaters are lifted. Fold into the cornmeal mixture until just combined.

4. Heat the oven to 250°. Heat a large nonstick frying pan over moderately high heat. Add ¼ teaspoon of the oil; tilt the pan to coat the bottom. For each pancake, drop a rounded tablespoon of batter into the pan; allow room for the cakes to spread. Cook until bubbles appear on the surface and the bottom is golden; turn and cook until the second side is golden, about 1 minute per side. Keep warm in the oven. Repeat with the remaining oil and batter.

5. Put one pancake on each of four plates. Spread 2½ tablespoons of the banana filling on top of each. Continue layering, using three more pancakes and two more layers of filling for each serving. Drizzle the remaining syrup over the stacks.

—MARCIA KIESEL

PER SERVING: CALORIES 423 kcal **TOTAL FAT** 2.2 gm **SATURATED FAT** .3 gm **CARBOHYDRATE** 87 gm **PROTEIN** 13 gm **CHOLESTEROL** 0 mg

POTATO AND RED-PEPPER FRITTATA

The ingredients in this Italian omelet—six eggs, fried potatoes, prosciutto—may seem rich, but look again. Egg whites replace most of the whole eggs, the potatoes are cooked in a tiny amount of oil, and the prosciutto is trimmed of fat.

4 SERVINGS

- 1 pound red potatoes (about 3), peeled and cut into thin slices
- 2 teaspoons olive oil
- 1 red onion, cut into thin slices
- 2 large cloves garlic, cut into thin slices
- 1 large red bell pepper, cut into thin slices
- 2 large jalapeño peppers, seeds and ribs removed, minced
- 1 ounce prosciutto or country ham, trimmed of fat and chopped fine
- ¼ cup chopped cilantro
  Salt and fresh-ground black pepper
- 2 large eggs
- 4 large egg whites

1. Rinse the potato slices in a bowl of cold water. Drain and rinse again. Pat the slices dry with paper towels.

2. In a large heavy nonstick ovenproof pan, heat the oil over moderate heat. Add the potato slices and cook, shaking the pan occasionally, for 15 minutes. Using a wide spatula, turn the potatoes and cook until the potatoes are just tender and some slices are golden, about 5 minutes. Add the onion and garlic, turn the potatoes, and cook for 5 minutes longer.

3. Add the bell pepper and jalapeños to the potatoes, turn the mixture, and cook, stirring once, until the peppers are tender, about 10 minutes. Sprinkle the prosciutto and 3 tablespoons of the cilantro on top and season with salt and pepper.

4. Heat the broiler. In a medium bowl, whisk the eggs and egg whites. Pour the eggs over the potatoes in the pan and cook, without stirring, until the eggs are firm at the edges but still slightly runny on top, about 6 minutes.

5. Broil the frittata until golden and set, about 2 minutes. Top with the remaining tablespoon of cilantro.

—DIANA STURGIS

PER SERVING: CALORIES 204 kcal TOTAL FAT 6.1 gm SATURATED FAT 1.3 gm CARBOHYDRATE 26 gm PROTEIN 12 gm CHOLESTEROL 112 mg

GINGERBREAD LOAF

Chunks of candied ginger stand out in a classic dark gingerbread made with skim milk, a single egg, and just two tablespoons of butter.

16 SERVINGS

- 1   cup dark-brown sugar
- ½   cup molasses
- 2   tablespoons unsalted butter
- 1   large egg
- ½   cup skim milk
- 2½ cups flour
- 1   tablespoon ground ginger
- 1   teaspoon baking soda
- ⅓   cup chopped candied ginger

1. Heat the oven to 325°. Coat a 9-by-4½-inch loaf pan with vegetable-oil cooking spray. Line the bottom of the pan with a piece of parchment or wax paper.

2. In a medium saucepan, combine the sugar, molasses, and butter. Cook over moderate heat, stirring occasionally, until the butter melts, about 2 minutes.

3. In a small bowl, beat the egg with the milk. In a large bowl, whisk together the flour, ground ginger, and baking soda. Stir in the brown-sugar mixture and the beaten egg until smooth. Stir in the candied ginger. Scrape the gingerbread batter into the prepared pan.

4. Bake the gingerbread in the lower third of the oven until a toothpick stuck in the center comes out clean, about 1 hour and 20 minutes. Run a knife around the sides of the gingerbread. Invert the loaf onto a rack and then turn it over again. Let cool.

—DIANA STURGIS

MAKE IT AHEAD

Make the gingerbread a day in advance and store it in an airtight container.

PER SERVING: CALORIES 181 kcal **TOTAL FAT** 2 gm **SATURATED FAT** 1 gm **CARBOHYDRATE** 39 gm **PROTEIN** 3 gm **CHOLESTEROL** 17 mg

CRANBERRY SPICE BREAD

Here's a bread that's worth waking up for. Cranberries, dates, and bran cereal give it plenty of nutritional value, applesauce takes the place of much of the fat, and maple syrup serves as a sweetener. Buttermilk, a great low-fat liquid for baking, gives the bread extra lightness.

12 SERVINGS

1¼ cups flour, more for dusting

1 teaspoon baking powder

¾ teaspoon cinnamon

½ teaspoon ground cardamom

½ teaspoon grated nutmeg

½ teaspoon baking soda

½ teaspoon salt

½ cup shredded bran cereal

½ cup pitted dates, chopped

¾ cup 1-percent buttermilk

⅓ cup maple syrup

1 large egg

2 tablespoons unsweetened applesauce

2 tablespoons cooking oil

½ cup fresh or frozen cranberries

1. Heat the oven to 400°. Coat an 8-by-3-inch nonstick loaf pan with vegetable-oil cooking spray and dust with flour.

2. In a large bowl, whisk together the flour, baking powder, cinnamon, cardamom, nutmeg, baking soda, and salt. Stir in the bran cereal and dates.

3. In another large bowl, whisk the buttermilk with the maple syrup, egg, applesauce, and oil. Stir in the cranberries. Fold in the dry ingredients. Scrape the batter into the prepared loaf pan.

4. Bake the bread in the middle of the oven until golden and a toothpick stuck in the center comes out clean, about 50 minutes. Let cool in the pan for 5 minutes. Invert onto a rack, turn over, and let cool.

—MARY CARROLL

MAKE IT AHEAD

The bread can be kept in an airtight container for a day, or frozen for up to one month.

PER SERVING: CALORIES 137 kcal   TOTAL FAT 3.2 gm   SATURATED FAT .4 gm
CARBOHYDRATE 26 gm   PROTEIN 3 gm   CHOLESTEROL 18 mg

ORANGE DATE MUFFINS

Many muffins get their moistness from lots of oil and eggs. Not these: The important ingredients here are low-fat buttermilk, unsweetened applesauce, dates, and pureed orange sections. For tender muffins, do not overmix.

MAKES 12 MUFFINS

  2   large oranges

½   cup 1-percent buttermilk

  1   large egg

  3   tablespoons honey

  2   tablespoons unsweetened applesauce

  2   tablespoons cooking oil

½   cup pitted dates, chopped

1½   cups flour

  1   teaspoon baking powder

  1   teaspoon baking soda

1. Heat the oven to 400°. Coat a 12-cup nonstick muffin tin with vegetable-oil cooking spray.

2. Grate the zest from both oranges into the food processor. Using a stainless-steel knife, peel one of the oranges down to the flesh, removing all of the white pith. Cut the sections away from the membranes and add them to the food processor.

3. Add the buttermilk, egg, honey, applesauce, and oil and puree. Add the dates and pulse until just combined.

4. In a large bowl, whisk together the flour, baking powder, and baking soda. Stir in the orange mixture until just combined. Scrape the batter into the prepared muffin cups, filling them about three-quarters full.

5. Bake the muffins in the middle of the oven until the tops are golden and the centers spring back when touched lightly, about 15 minutes. Let cool in the pan for 5 minutes. Unmold the muffins onto a rack to cool slightly. Serve warm or room temperature.

—MARY CARROLL

MAKE IT AHEAD

The muffins can be kept in an airtight container for one day, or frozen for up to a month. Reheat them in a 350° oven before serving.

PER MUFFIN: CALORIES 132 kcal   TOTAL FAT 3.2 gm   SATURATED FAT .4 gm   CARBOHYDRATE 24 gm   PROTEIN 2.8 gm   CHOLESTEROL 18 mg

BUTTERMILK SCALLION BISCUITS

For a homier look, bake these biscuits in a ten-inch Dutch oven or a cast-iron frying pan instead of on a baking sheet; the baking time will be the same. The biscuits may run together but will pull apart easily.

MAKES 6 BISCUITS

1¼ cups flour

¼ cup cornmeal

2 teaspoons baking powder

2 teaspoons sugar

½ teaspoon salt

1½ teaspoons unsalted butter

4 scallions including green tops, chopped fine

1 cup 1.5-percent buttermilk

VARIATION

Use one quarter cup of chopped mixed fresh herbs, such as thyme, rosemary, and parsley, in place of—or in addition to—the scallions.

---

1. Heat the oven to 375°. Coat a baking sheet with vegetable-oil cooking spray.

2. In a large bowl, whisk together the flour, cornmeal, baking powder, sugar, and salt. Cut or rub in the butter until combined. Add the scallions. Stir in the buttermilk until the dough just comes together.

3. Spoon the dough onto the prepared baking sheet in six equal mounds about 2 inches apart. Bake until the biscuits are golden, about 25 minutes.

—CHARLES WILEY

PER BISCUIT: CALORIES 155 kcal **TOTAL FAT** 2.1 gm **SATURATED FAT** 1 gm **CARBOHYDRATE** 29 gm **PROTEIN** 4.9 gm **CHOLESTEROL** 5 mg

CINNAMON RAISIN STICKY BUNS

Orange juice, maple syrup, and a little bit of butter make up the mouthwatering glaze on these gratifyingly gooey cinnamon rolls. Served straight out of the oven, they're irresistible.

MAKES 9 BUNS

- ¾ cup lukewarm 1-percent milk
- 1 package dry yeast (about 2¼ teaspoons)
- 2 tablespoons dark-brown sugar
- 1¾ cups flour
- ¾ cup raisins
- 2 tablespoons fine-chopped walnuts
- ⅓ cup plus 2 tablespoons maple syrup
- 1 teaspoon grated orange zest
- 3 tablespoons orange juice
- 1 tablespoon cinnamon
- ½ teaspoon ground cardamom
- 2 tablespoons unsalted butter

1. In a medium bowl, combine the milk, yeast, and sugar. Set aside in a warm place until the mixture bubbles, about 10 minutes.

2. Stir 1 cup of the flour into the yeast mixture. Cover the bowl and set aside in a warm place for 30 minutes.

3. Coat a large bowl and a 9-inch square pan with vegetable-oil cooking spray. Stir the remaining ¾ cup flour into the dough.

On a lightly floured surface, knead the dough until smooth and elastic, about 7 minutes. Transfer to the prepared bowl, cover with a dish towel, and let rise in a warm place for 1 hour.

4. In a small bowl, combine the raisins and walnuts. In another small bowl, combine the maple syrup, orange zest, orange juice, cinnamon, and cardamom. Pour all but 3 tablespoons of the maple-syrup mixture into the prepared pan and tilt to coat the bottom evenly.

5. On a lightly floured surface, gently knead the dough to knock out the excess air. Roll the dough to a 10-by-12-inch rectangle. Sprinkle the raisins and walnuts evenly on top of the dough to within ¼ inch of the edge. Starting from a short end, roll into a tight cylinder. Cut into nine slices and put the slices, cut-side down, in the prepared pan. Cover and let the buns rise in a warm place until almost doubled in bulk, about 30 minutes.

6. Heat the oven to 350°. In a small saucepan, melt the butter with the reserved 3 tablespoons of maple-syrup mixture over

PER BUN: CALORIES 228 kcal TOTAL FAT 4.1 gm SATURATED FAT 1.8 gm
CARBOHYDRATE 45 gm PROTEIN 4.5 gm CHOLESTEROL 7.3 mg

moderate heat. Drizzle the mixture over the cinnamon buns.

7. Bake the buns until the tops brown and the centers spring back when touched lightly, about 25 minutes. Let cool in the pan for 5 minutes. Invert the buns onto a plate and separate them. Drizzle any remaining maple-syrup mixture from the pan over the buns and serve warm.

—MARY CARROLL

MAKE IT AHEAD

Rather than let the buns rise at room temperature (as in step five), you can cover the pan with plastic wrap and let them rise in the refrigerator overnight. The next day, let the pan sit at room temperature while you heat the oven. You may need to add five or ten minutes to the baking time.

VARIATIONS

• Use another kind of nut, such as pecans, in place of the walnuts.
• Replace the raisins with chopped dried cherries, dried strawberries, or dried blueberries.

WARM BLUEBERRY-AND-MANGO COMPOTE

This sweet-tangy fruit compote (pictured on page 230) is especially good with pancakes, waffles, or Caramelized-Apple French Toast, page 231. You can also serve it with angel food cake for a wonderful low-fat dessert.

4 SERVINGS

- 1 mango, peeled and cut into ½-inch dice
- ½ cup blueberries
- 3 tablespoons sugar
- ¼ cup water
- ¼ teaspoon grated lemon zest
- 1 teaspoon lemon juice
- ½ teaspoon finely chopped candied ginger

1. In a small stainless-steel saucepan, combine the mango, blueberries, sugar, water, lemon zest, lemon juice, and ginger. Bring to a boil over high heat.

2. Reduce the heat and simmer until the fruit is softened and the liquid thickened, about 15 minutes. Let cool slightly. Serve warm.

—GRACE PARISI

MAKE IT AHEAD

Make the compote up to three days in advance and keep it, covered, in the refrigerator. Reheat before serving.

SEASON'S BEST

For best flavor, make the compote in the summer, when mangoes and blueberries are at their peak.

PER SERVING: CALORIES 88 kcal **TOTAL FAT** .2 gm **SATURATED FAT** .1 gm **CARBOHYDRATE** 23 gm **PROTEIN** .4 gm **CHOLESTEROL** 0 mg

PINEAPPLE KIWI COMPOTE

Add a tropical touch to breakfast or brunch with this simple compote of pineapple pieces simmered in maple syrup, flavored with vanilla, and mixed with kiwis. We like it alongside Cornmeal Pancakes with Banana Yogurt Filling, page 233.

4 SERVINGS

1 large pineapple (about 3 pounds), peeled, cored, and cut into 1-inch pieces

3 tablespoons maple syrup

1 teaspoon vanilla extract

2 kiwis, peeled and cut into 1-inch pieces

1. In a large stainless-steel frying pan, combine the pineapple and maple syrup. Cover and cook over low heat until the pineapple is almost tender, about 8 minutes. Raise the heat to high. Boil, uncovered, until the juices are slightly thickened, about 3 minutes. Transfer the pineapple and juices to a medium glass or stainless-steel bowl; let cool to room temperature. Add the vanilla.

2. Just before serving, stir the kiwis into the pineapple mixture. Serve the compote at room temperature.

—Marcia Kiesel

MAKE IT AHEAD

You can make the compote through step one and keep it, covered, in the refrigerator for up to three days. Let the compote come to room temperature before serving, and wait until the last minute to peel, cut, and add the kiwis.

PER SERVING: CALORIES 140 kcal   TOTAL FAT 1 gm   SATURATED FAT 0 gm   CARBOHYDRATE 35 gm   PROTEIN 1 gm   CHOLESTEROL 0 mg

PEACHY ORANGE SHAKE

It may taste like a thick, frosty milk shake, but this mixture of peaches, orange juice, and buttermilk is missing most of the fat. Garnished with a peach and orange slice and a sprig of mint, it's perfect for a sunny summertime brunch.

4 SERVINGS

2 pounds peaches (about 6)

8 medium ice cubes

2 cups nonfat buttermilk

¾ cup orange juice (from about 2 oranges)

¼ cup superfine sugar

½ teaspoon vanilla extract

4 thin orange slices

4 mint sprigs, for garnish

1. Pit and peel the peaches. Cut four thin slices and then cut the rest into chunks.

2. Put the peach chunks in a blender and add the ice cubes, buttermilk, orange juice, sugar, and vanilla. Blend until smooth. Pour the shakes into four chilled tall glasses and top each glass with a slice each of peach and orange and a mint sprig.

—ANDREA CHESMAN

BUTTERMILK BASICS

Despite its name, buttermilk contains no butter. In the past, it was a by-product of butter-making and often had a buttery flavor. Today's product is made from fermented pasteurized low-fat or skim milk. You can find nonfat, one-percent, and one-and-a-half-percent buttermilk; all are good low-fat alternatives to whole milk and cream.

Buttermilk doesn't work as a replacement for milk or cream in all recipes because it separates when heated and the flavor is tangy. But it is ideal for drinks, such as this Peachy Orange Shake, where the tanginess is balanced by sweet ingredients. It's also great in pancakes and baked goods and makes a delicious base for cold vegetable soups.

PER SERVING: CALORIES 173 kcal **TOTAL FAT** 1.3 gm **SATURATED FAT** .7 gm **CARBOHYDRATE** 37 gm **PROTEIN** 5 gm **CHOLESTEROL** 5 mg

chapter *10*

FRUIT DESSERTS

Fruit Soup with Champagne, page 249

FRUIT SOUP WITH CHAMPAGNE

Berries and apple in anise-spiced fruit juices, topped with a scoop of sorbet, a splash of Champagne, and a sprinkling of shredded basil, make an impressive, exotic dessert. The pineapple and orange juices should be fresh, but store-bought is fine for the strawberry-orange-banana juice, and any banana-berry combination will do. So will any sparkling wine.

4 SERVINGS

⅔ cup fresh pineapple juice, see box at right

⅔ cup strawberry-orange-banana juice

5 tablespoons orange juice (from about 1 orange)

4 teaspoons lime juice

1 tart apple, such as Granny Smith, peeled, cored, and cut into ½-inch balls or dice

1 small star-anise pod

1⅓ cups mixed berries, such as raspberries, strawberries, blueberries, and blackberries

1⅓ cups lemon sorbet

½ cup Champagne

2 teaspoons shredded basil leaves

1. In a medium stainless-steel saucepan, combine the pineapple juice, strawberry juice, orange juice, lime juice, the apple, and star anise and bring to a boil. Reduce the heat to low and simmer until the apple is just tender, about 12 minutes. Transfer the mixture to a large bowl and refrigerate until chilled, about 2 hours.

2. Discard the star anise; stir the berries into the soup. To serve, divide the fruit soup among four bowls. Add a scoop of lemon sorbet and 2 tablespoons of Champagne to each bowl. Top with the basil.

—HANS RÖCKENWAGNER

PINEAPPLE JUICE

To make fresh pineapple juice, peel, core, and cut one quarter of a pineapple into about one-inch chunks. Puree the chunks in a food processor or blender and strain through a fine-mesh sieve, pressing on the fruit to get all the juice. You should have about two thirds of a cup of pineapple juice.

PER SERVING: CALORIES 170 kcal   TOTAL FAT .3 gm   SATURATED FAT 0 gm   CARBOHYDRATE 38 gm   PROTEIN 1 gm   CHOLESTEROL 0 mg

FRESH PEARS, KIWIS, AND ORANGES WITH ROSEMARY SYRUP

Red-tinged pears, such as red Bartletts, will make this cool-weather compote especially colorful. Rosemary adds an enticing herbal flavor.

4 SERVINGS

6   tablespoons sugar

6   tablespoons dry white wine

2½ tablespoons water

1½ tablespoons balsamic vinegar

2   tablespoons fresh rosemary leaves, plus 4 sprigs, for garnish

1   bay leaf

¼   teaspoon peppercorns

2   pears, halved, cored, and cut into wedges

1   kiwi, peeled and sliced

2   navel oranges, peeled and sliced crosswise

MAKE IT AHEAD

You can make the rosemary syrup up to one week in advance. Keep it in a covered jar in the refrigerator.

1. In a small stainless-steel saucepan, combine the sugar, wine, water, vinegar, the rosemary leaves, bay leaf, and peppercorns. Bring to a boil over moderately high heat. Reduce the heat and simmer for 5 minutes. Strain the syrup and let cool to room temperature. Refrigerate for at least 1 hour.

2. To serve, arrange the pears, kiwi, and oranges on a plate. Drizzle the rosemary syrup over the fruit. Top with the rosemary sprigs.

—JOHN ASH AND SID GOLDSTEIN

PER SERVING: CALORIES 210 kcal   TOTAL FAT .8 gm   SATURATED FAT 0 gm
CARBOHYDRATE 50 gm   PROTEIN 2 gm   CHOLESTEROL 0 mg

MELON WITH MINT LIME SYRUP AND JALAPEÑO

Cool melon and hot jalapeño meet in a fruit salad with a Southwestern kick. For a dessert that's spicy but not scorching, be sure to relieve the jalapeño of its ribs and seeds—the very hottest parts—before mincing.

4 SERVINGS

½ cup sugar

½ cup water

2 tablespoons lime juice (from about 1 lime)

¼ cup chopped fresh mint

1 small honeydew (about 2 pounds), peeled, seeded, and cut into 1-inch cubes

1 cantaloupe, peeled, seeded, and cut into 1-inch cubes

2 teaspoons minced jalapeño pepper (seeds and ribs removed)

1. In a small stainless-steel saucepan, bring the sugar and water to a boil over high heat, stirring until the sugar dissolves. Let cool. Stir in the lime juice and mint. Refrigerate for at least 1 hour.

2. In a large bowl, combine the honeydew and cantaloupe cubes. Add the chilled syrup and the jalapeño and toss to combine. Spoon into four bowls.

—JANET HAZEN DE JESUS

VARIATIONS

• Replace either the honeydew or the cantaloupe with watermelon.
• Instead of using two types of melon, use only cantaloupe or only honeydew.
• Cut the melons in half crosswise, cut the flesh into balls, and serve the fruit salad in the hollowed-out melon halves.
• Omit the jalapeño.
• Use lemon juice in place of lime.

PER SERVING: CALORIES 140 kcal TOTAL FAT .2 gm SATURATED FAT 0 gm
CARBOHYDRATE 36 gm PROTEIN .9 gm CHOLESTEROL 0 mg

PEACHES WITH CITRUS JUICE AND VANILLA YOGURT

Sometimes the simplest preparations are the best, as in this beautifully basic dessert of sliced fresh peaches and creamy vanilla yogurt.

4 SERVINGS

- 4 peaches
- 2 tablespoons orange juice
- 1 tablespoon lemon juice
- 1 cup nonfat vanilla yogurt
- 4 sprigs fresh mint, for garnish (optional)

VARIATIONS

- Use nectarines instead of peaches.
- Use another flavor of nonfat yogurt, such as caramel or any fruit.
- Substitute nonfat frozen for the nonfat regular yogurt.

---

1. Drop the peaches into a large pot of boiling water. Boil the peaches for 1 minute, drain, and then cool under cold water. Peel the peaches, remove the pits, and cut the fruit into thin slices.

2. In a medium glass or stainless-steel bowl, combine the peaches with the orange juice and lemon juice. Refrigerate for about 1 hour.

3. To serve, put the peach slices in four bowls. Top them with the yogurt and the mint sprigs, if using.

—LAURIE BURROWS GRAD

PER SERVING: CALORIES 111 kcal TOTAL FAT .1 gm SATURATED FAT 0 gm CARBOHYDRATE 25 gm PROTEIN 4 gm CHOLESTEROL 1.7 mg

FIGS IN RED-WINE SYRUP

Poaching dried figs in a red-wine syrup softens them and gives them a lovely ruby color and intense flavor. Use Calimyrna figs from California if you can find them—they're moister and more tender than most imported figs.

4 SERVINGS

- 2 cups red wine
- ½ cup sugar
- 1 3-inch strip orange zest
- 9 ounces dried figs (about 2¼ cups)
- ½ cup plain low-fat yogurt

1. In a medium stainless-steel saucepan, combine the wine, sugar, and orange zest. Bring to a boil and simmer for 10 minutes.

2. Add the figs, cover, and simmer until tender, about 20 minutes for small figs and 25 minutes for large ones. Remove the pan from the heat. Let the figs cool completely in the syrup.

3. Spoon the figs and syrup into four bowls and top with the yogurt.

—MICHELE SCICOLONE

VARIATIONS

- Add whole spices, such as a cinnamon stick and two or three cloves, to the pan with the wine.
- For a Provençal-inspired version, add a sprig of rosemary or thyme to the pan with the wine.
- If you happen to have a bottle of white wine open, by all means use it in place of the red.

PER SERVING: CALORIES 287 kcal TOTAL FAT 1.2 gm SATURATED FAT .4 gm CARBOHYDRATE 71 gm PROTEIN 4 gm CHOLESTEROL 1.7 mg

RHUBARB COMPOTE WITH STRAWBERRIES

Celebrate the coming of spring and the return of rhubarb with this classic combination. To temper its notorious tartness, the rhubarb is simmered in a sugar syrup and served with sweet strawberries.

4 SERVINGS

1½ cups water

½ cup sugar

¾ pound rhubarb, trimmed, cut into ¾-inch pieces

1 pint strawberries, sliced

½ cup low-fat vanilla yogurt

1. In a medium stainless-steel saucepan, bring the water and sugar to a boil over moderate heat, stirring occasionally, until the sugar is dissolved. Add the rhubarb and simmer until it is just tender when pierced with a knife, about 5 minutes. Transfer to a medium bowl and let cool slightly; the mixture should still be warm.

2. Gently stir the strawberries into the rhubarb compote. Cover and refrigerate until chilled, about 2 hours. Spoon the compote into four bowls and top each serving with a dollop of vanilla yogurt.

—Diana Sturgis

VARIATIONS

• Use thawed frozen rhubarb and strawberries instead of fresh.
• To make a spicier compote, add a cinnamon stick to the sugar-and-water mixture.

TEST-KITCHEN TIP

Rhubarb generally does not need to be peeled to remove the strings. Only toward the end of summer, when the stalks are older and the strings are tough, will peeling be necessary.

PER SERVING: CALORIES 163 kcal   TOTAL FAT .8 gm   SATURATED FAT .2 gm   CARBOHYDRATE 38 gm   PROTEIN 3 gm   CHOLESTEROL 1.4 mg

PINEAPPLE WITH GINGER SYRUP

Winter, when pineapples are at their peak, is the perfect time for this tropical treat. Slices of the fruit are topped with a ginger-infused white-wine syrup and garnished with chopped fresh mint.

4 SERVINGS

6	tablespoons sugar
12	nickel-size rounds of peeled fresh ginger
2	1-inch strips lemon zest
¾	cup water
3½	tablespoons dessert wine, such as late-harvest riesling
1	pineapple, peeled, quartered lengthwise, cored, and cut crosswise into ½-inch slices
1½	teaspoons chopped fresh mint

1. In a medium stainless-steel saucepan, combine the sugar, ginger, lemon zest, water, and 3 tablespoons of the wine and bring to a boil. Simmer until the liquid is reduced to ½ cup, about 4 minutes. Let cool for 20 minutes and then add the pineapple. Refrigerate for at least 1 hour.

2. Spoon the pineapple into four glasses, drizzle with the remaining 1½ teaspoons wine, and top with the mint.

—MATTHEW KENNEY

VARIATIONS

• Replace the pineapple with another type of fruit, such as four sliced peaches or four sliced oranges.
• Use brown sugar instead of white for a hint of caramel.
• Use one vanilla bean, split, in place of the fresh ginger, or flavor the cooled syrup with one-and-a-half teaspoons of vanilla extract.

PER SERVING: CALORIES 134 kcal   TOTAL FAT .5 gm   SATURATED FAT .1 gm
CARBOHYDRATE 32 gm   PROTEIN .5 gm   CHOLESTEROL 0 mg

CARAMELIZED PINEAPPLE WITH GRILLED BANANAS AND VANILLA SAUCE

We can't say enough about this glorious dessert, a low-fat indulgence perfect for company. Use slightly underripe bananas; they'll hold their shape as they cook.

8 SERVINGS

- 1 vanilla bean, split lengthwise, or 1½ teaspoons vanilla extract
- 1 cup 1-percent milk
- 1 1-inch strip lemon zest
- 2 large egg yolks
- ½ cup sugar, more if needed
- Pinch salt
- 1 pineapple (about 2 pounds)
- 4 bananas
- 2 tablespoons sugar-free pineapple jam or honey
- 2 tablespoons lemon juice
- 2 tablespoons safflower oil
- Mint sprigs and raspberries, for garnish (optional)

1. Scrape the seeds from the vanilla bean, if using, into a small heavy saucepan; add the bean. Add the milk and zest; cook over moderate heat until small bubbles form around the edge of the pan. Cover, remove from the heat, and let infuse for 15 minutes.

2. In a small bowl, beat the egg yolks and 3 tablespoons of the sugar until pale yellow, about 3 minutes. Bring the milk to a simmer, stirring. Add the hot milk to the beaten yolks in a thin stream, whisking. Pour the mixture back into the pan and cook over moderately low heat, stirring constantly, until it is just thick enough to coat a spoon, 2 to 3 minutes. Do not let the custard boil, or it may curdle. Strain and add the salt and the vanilla extract, if using. Refrigerate the custard to chill.

3. Cut the top and bottom off the pineapple and slice off the skin. Using the tip of a vegetable peeler, remove the eyes. Cut the pineapple into eight ½-inch-thick crosswise slices. Cut out the core with a pineapple or apple corer or a sharp knife.

4. Heat a large nonstick frying pan over high heat. Sprinkle two pineapple rings with 1 teaspoon of sugar each. Put the rings in the pan, sugared-side down, and cook until the edges begin to caramelize, 2 to 3 minutes. Sprinkle each ring with 1 teaspoon sugar, turn over, and cook until the other side is caramelized, about 2 minutes. Transfer to a large plate. Repeat with the remaining pineapple rings and sugar. Spoon the

PER SERVING: CALORIES 228 kcal   TOTAL FAT 5.8 gm   SATURATED FAT 1 gm
CARBOHYDRATE 44 gm   PROTEIN 2.7 gm   CHOLESTEROL 54 mg

caramelized juices from the pan over the pineapple and set aside at room temperature for up to 2 hours.

5. Light a grill or heat a large heavy frying pan. Cut the bananas in half lengthwise and then in half crosswise. In a small bowl, combine the jam and lemon juice. Brush the grill or pan lightly with the oil (if using a pan, you won't need as much oil). Add the bananas, cut-side down. Brush the bananas lightly with the jam mixture and cook until lightly browned, 2 to 3 minutes. Turn the bananas over and cook for 2 minutes longer.

6. To serve, arrange two banana quarters and a caramelized pineapple ring on each of four plates. Spoon any accumulated juices over the pineapple rings. Spoon the custard sauce around the pineapple slices. Top with the mint and berries, if using.

—Ann Chantal Altman

TIME SAVER

Buy a peeled and cored pineapple, so that all you have to do is cut slices. You will find prepared pineapple available in many supermarkets.

Mexican Oranges with Cinnamon, Cayenne, and Chocolate

The combination of cinnamon and chocolate is a common one in Mexico. Since only a very small amount is used in this dessert and the rest of the ingredients are utterly fat-free, the chocolate is an affordable luxury.

4 SERVINGS

- 4 navel oranges
- 1½ teaspoons sugar
- ¼ teaspoon cinnamon
- Pinch cayenne
- ½ ounce Mexican chocolate* or semisweet chocolate, shaved thin

  *Available at Latin American markets and specialty-food stores

1. Using a stainless-steel knife, peel the oranges down to the flesh, removing all of the white pith. Working over a medium glass or stainless-steel bowl to catch the juices, cut the sections away from the membranes. Put the orange sections in the bowl and squeeze the juice from the membranes into the bowl. Stir in the sugar, cinnamon, and cayenne. Refrigerate for about 2 hours.

2. Spoon the oranges and juice into four bowls and top with the chocolate.

—Jean Galton

Shaving Chocolate

You can shave chocolate with either a small sharp knife or a vegetable peeler. Hold the chocolate in one hand. With the other hand, scrape the blade of the knife or peeler away from you along the surface of the chocolate, letting the chocolate shavings fall into a shallow dish or onto wax paper.

Test-Kitchen Tip

Put the chocolate in a warm spot for about half an hour before you shave it. That way, you'll have longer, lovelier chocolate curls. Keep an eye on the chocolate, though; you don't want it to get so warm that it begins to melt.

PER SERVING: CALORIES 88 kcal   TOTAL FAT 1.2 gm   SATURATED FAT .6 gm   CARBOHYDRATE 20 gm   PROTEIN 2 gm   CHOLESTEROL 0 mg

Bananas in Orange Caramel Sauce

Here's a delicious, low-fat caramel sauce that uses neither cream nor butter. The secret ingredient? Fruit juice! We've used orange juice for this dessert of sliced bananas, but you can vary the flavor with apple juice, pineapple juice, or even red wine. A dollop of plain yogurt provides the finishing touch.

4 SERVINGS

½ cup sugar

3 tablespoons water

½ cup orange juice (from about 1 orange)

5 strips orange zest (from about 1 orange), cut into matchstick strips

4 bananas, cut into thin slices

1 cup plain low-fat yogurt

1. In a heavy medium stainless-steel saucepan, combine the sugar and water. Cook over moderate heat, stirring, until the sugar dissolves. Bring to a boil and cook without stirring until the sugar turns a medium amber color, about 5 minutes.

2. Remove the saucepan from the heat. Add the orange juice, pouring it slowly down the side of the pan so that the caramel does not boil over. Stir in the zest and cook the caramel over low heat, stirring, until smooth and melted, about 2 minutes. Let cool. Refrigerate the sauce for at least 1 hour.

3. To serve, gently combine the banana slices and the orange caramel sauce in a medium bowl. Spoon the mixture into four bowls and top with the yogurt.

—Michele Scicolone

Making the Perfect Caramel

The trickiest part of making a caramel sauce is cooking the sugar—and knowing when to stop. If you stop cooking when the syrup is too light in color, the sauce will lack flavor; if you wait until the color is too dark, the sauce will taste burned. Look for a rich golden brown; when the caramel reaches this stage, remove the pan from the heat and immediately proceed with the recipe.

PER SERVING: CALORIES 252 kcal   **TOTAL FAT** 1.5 gm   **SATURATED FAT** .8 gm   **CARBOHYDRATE** 59 gm   **PROTEIN** 4 gm   **CHOLESTEROL** 3.4 mg

BANANA BRÛLÉE WITH CITRUS-FRUIT SALSA

Rather than custard (as in crème brûlée), here it's the bananas that are brûléed—sprinkled with brown sugar and caramelized under the broiler. A mango, tangerine, and orange salsa, dotted with toasted almonds and tossed with honey and tea, lends a festive touch.

4 SERVINGS

1½ tablespoons slivered almonds

2 large tangerines

1 navel orange

1 small mango, peeled and cut into ½-inch dice

4 teaspoons honey

2 tablespoons brewed orange pekoe tea

2 teaspoons lime juice

⅛ teaspoon vanilla extract

6 finger bananas, or 4 medium bananas, peeled and halved lengthwise

2 tablespoons light-brown sugar

4 sprigs fresh mint, for garnish (optional)

1. In a small frying pan, toast the almonds over moderately low heat, stirring frequently, until golden brown, about 5 minutes. Or toast them in a 350° oven for about 8 minutes.

2. Using a stainless-steel knife, peel the tangerines and orange down to the flesh, removing all of the white pith. Cut the sec-tions away from the membranes and cut the sections into thirds; discard any seeds. Put the tangerine and orange pieces in a bowl and add the mango. In a small bowl, stir the honey into the tea until dissolved. Fold the tea mixture into the fruit; refrigerate to chill.

3. Heat the broiler. In a small bowl, combine the lime juice and vanilla extract. Arrange the halved bananas, cut-side up, in a single layer in a stainless-steel baking dish. Brush the bananas with the lime mixture and sprinkle with the brown sugar. Broil until caramelized, about 3 minutes. Let sit for 1 minute.

4. Fold the toasted almonds into the fruit salsa and spoon it into four shallow bowls. Arrange the bananas on the salsa and pour any liquid from the baking dish on top. Top with the mint, if using.

—ALLEN SUSSER

PER SERVING: CALORIES 226 kcal   TOTAL FAT 2 gm   SATURATED FAT .4 gm
CARBOHYDRATE 65 gm   PROTEIN 3 gm   CHOLESTEROL 0 mg

BANANA SOUFFLÉS WITH AMARETTI

Amaretti are crisp little Italian cookies with an intense almond flavor. They provide a delicious taste and texture contrast for the delicate banana soufflés.

4 SERVINGS

¼ teaspoon vegetable oil

3 tablespoons sugar, plus more for coating the ramekins

¼ cup brewed espresso or strong coffee

1 tablespoon marsala

4 amaretti cookies

3 ripe bananas

½ teaspoon lemon juice

2 large egg whites, at room temperature

Pinch salt

1. Heat the oven to 400°. Coat four 1-cup ramekins with the oil, spreading it evenly with a paper towel. Sprinkle the ramekins with sugar. Rotate the ramekins to coat the bottoms and sides. Turn the ramekins upside down and tap lightly to remove any sugar that does not cling.

2. In a small shallow bowl, combine the espresso and the marsala. Add the amaretti, flat-side down, and let sit until the bottoms soften, about 20 minutes.

3. In a medium bowl, mash the bananas with 2 tablespoons of the sugar to a coarse puree. Stir in the lemon juice. In a medium bowl, beat the egg whites at high speed with the salt until they hold soft peaks when the beaters are lifted. Add the remaining 1 tablespoon sugar and continue beating until the egg whites hold firm peaks when the beaters are lifted. Fold the egg whites into the banana puree until just combined.

4. Scrape the banana mixture into the prepared ramekins. Run your thumb around the inside edge of each ramekin, making a little trough. This encourages even rising.

5. Bake the soufflés in the middle of the oven for 5 minutes. Remove the amaretti from the soaking liquid and gently put one on each soufflé, soaked-side down. Continue baking the soufflés until puffed and barely set. Transfer the soufflés to four plates. If you like, break open each soufflé at the edge of the cookie and spoon a little of the amaretti-soaking liquid inside. Serve at once.

—MARCIA KIESEL

PER SERVING: CALORIES 144 kcal TOTAL FAT .6 gm SATURATED FAT .2 gm CARBOHYDRATE 33 gm PROTEIN 3 gm CHOLESTEROL 0 mg

GELATINA DI FRUTTA

You might have thought gelatin went out with TV dinners and maraschino cherries, but this pretty, refreshing dessert is right in step with current tastes. It's made with fresh orange juice, orange liqueur, and just enough gelatin for the liquid to set in beautiful individual molds.

4 SERVINGS

2   ¼-ounce envelopes unflavored gelatin

½   cup cold water

½   cup sugar

3   cups orange juice (from about 6 oranges)

2   tablespoons orange liqueur, such as Grand Marnier, or rum

1   navel orange

4   sprigs fresh mint, for garnish (optional)

1. In a medium stainless-steel saucepan, sprinkle the gelatin over the water. Let stand for 5 minutes to soften. Add the sugar. Heat the mixture over moderately low heat, stirring, until the gelatin is completely dissolved. Don't let it boil.

2. Stir in the orange juice and liqueur. Pour the mixture into four small bowls, ramekins, or wineglasses. Cover with plastic wrap. Refrigerate until set, at least 4 hours, or overnight.

3. Using a stainless-steel knife, peel the orange down to the flesh, removing all of the white pith. Cut the sections away from the membranes. Set the sections aside.

4. If using bowls or ramekins, dip the bottoms in warm water for 30 seconds. Run a small knife around the side of each mold and invert it onto a small plate. Top each dessert with the orange sections and the mint sprigs, if using.

—MICHELE SCICOLONE

PER SERVING: CALORIES 213 kcal   TOTAL FAT .4 gm   SATURATED FAT .1 gm   CARBOHYDRATE 47 gm   PROTEIN 4 gm   CHOLESTEROL 0 mg

PEAR AND HONEY NAPOLEONS WITH HAZELNUTS

Wonton wrappers, brushed sparingly with butter, coated with sugar, and baked until crisp and caramelized, replace the traditional puff pastry in these light napoleons. Layered with baked pears and hazelnut honey cream and served in a delicious strawberry sauce, they make a sublime dessert.

4 SERVINGS

1 cup strawberries

1½ teaspoons pear brandy, or more to taste

¼ cup plus 2 tablespoons sugar

12 wonton wrappers

1 tablespoon unsalted butter, melted

2 tablespoons hazelnuts

2 tablespoons *fromage blanc** or Whole-Milk Yogurt Cheese, next page

1½ tablespoons honey

1 teaspoon cinnamon

4 large pears, such as Bartlett

1½ tablespoons lemon juice

*Available at specialty-food stores

1.   Heat the oven to 375°. In a food processor or blender, puree the strawberries with the pear brandy. Strain the puree into a small bowl.

2.   Line a large baking sheet with parchment paper. Put the ¼ cup of the sugar in a shallow bowl. Lightly brush one side of each wonton wrapper with a little of the melted butter and press the buttered side into the sugar. Repeat with the other side. Put the sugared wonton wrappers on the prepared baking sheet and bake for 4 minutes. Turn the wrappers over and bake until golden brown and caramelized, 3 to 4 minutes longer. Transfer to a rack to cool.

3.   Put the hazelnuts in a small pan; toast in the oven until the skins crack and loosen and the nuts are golden brown, about 10 minutes. Reduce the oven temperature to 350°. Wrap the hot hazelnuts in a kitchen towel and firmly rub them together to loosen most of the skins. Discard the skins. Chop the nuts fine. In a small bowl, combine the nuts with the *fromage blanc* and honey.

4.   Line the baking sheet with fresh parchment paper. In a small bowl, combine the remaining 2 tablespoons sugar and the cinnamon.

5.   Peel, quarter, and core the pears. Put them in a medium bowl and sprinkle with

PER SERVING: CALORIES 361 kcal   TOTAL FAT 6.5 gm   SATURATED FAT 2 gm
CARBOHYDRATE 75.6 gm   PROTEIN 4.7 gm   CHOLESTEROL 10 mg

the lemon juice. Put the pear quarters on a work surface and cut each one lengthwise, almost to the top, into thin slices.

6. Put the pear quarters on the baking sheet and press lightly to spread the slices slightly. Sprinkle the pears with the cinnamon sugar. Bake in the middle of the oven until soft and lightly colored, about 18 minutes. Let cool for 3 minutes.

7. Put a caramelized wonton wrapper on each of four plates. Put a pear section on

each wonton and top with a slightly rounded teaspoon of the hazelnut honey cream. Cover with another wonton wrapper and put two pear quarters in opposite directions on top of each. Top each with another rounded teaspoon of the hazelnut mixture. Finish with a third wonton wrapper and top with the remaining pear quarter. Spoon the strawberry sauce around the napoleons.

—Ann Chantal Altman

Whole-Milk Yogurt Cheese

With a consistency comparable to that of sour cream and very little fat, yogurt cheese makes a healthy substitute for crème fraîche, sour cream, or whipped cream. Make the cheese up to four days ahead and keep it covered in the refrigerator.

MAKES ¼ CUP

½ cup plain whole-milk yogurt

Set a strainer over a small bowl and line it with a double layer of cheesecloth.

Alternatively, line a coffee cone with a coffee filter and set it over a cup. Put the yogurt in the strainer. Cover and let the yogurt drain in the refrigerator overnight. Discard the liquid that has accumulated in the bowl.

PER 1-TABLESPOON SERVING: CALORIES 21 kcal   TOTAL FAT 1.5 gm   SATURATED FAT 1 gm CARBOHYDRATE .6 gm   PROTEIN 1.4 gm   CHOLESTEROL 6 mg

PEACH AND BLACKBERRY CRISP

Here's a clever take on an American favorite. The buttery topping of oats and brown sugar remains, but there's less of it. It's baked separately from the fruit and sprinkled on top at the end. That way, you get just enough flavor and crunch without much fat.

6 SERVINGS

1¾ pounds peaches (about 5), peeled and cut into 1-inch chunks

1 pint blackberries

3 tablespoons honey

2 teaspoons grated lemon zest

1 teaspoon instant tapioca

2 tablespoons unsalted butter, cut into thin slices

1¾ cups old-fashioned rolled oats

⅓ cup light-brown sugar

1 teaspoon cinnamon

1. Heat the oven to 400°. In a medium baking dish, toss the peaches and the blackberries with the honey, zest, and tapioca. Cover with aluminum foil and bake for 20 minutes. Stir, cover, and bake until the fruit is tender and the juices are slightly thickened, about 10 minutes more.

2. In a medium bowl, combine the butter with the oats. Stir in the brown sugar and cinnamon. Pour the mixture into a large heavy frying pan and cook over moderate heat, stirring, until the oats are toasted and the sugar hardens into clumps, about 7 minutes. Remove from the heat; keep stirring for 3 minutes longer.

3. To serve, spoon the warm fruit into six bowls and sprinkle with the oat topping.

—CHARLES WILEY

VARIATIONS

• Use nectarines instead of peaches.
• Instead of blackberries, you can use blueberries or raspberries, or a mixture. If you want to use strawberries, you'll have the best result if you combine them with other berries, since they exude so much juice during cooking.

PER SERVING: CALORIES 274 kcal TOTAL FAT 5.6 gm SATURATED FAT 2.7 gm CARBOHYDRATE 54.5 gm PROTEIN 5 gm CHOLESTEROL 10 mg

Nectarine and Dried-Cherry Clafoutis

A traditional French dessert of fruit baked in a custard batter, *clafoutis* is easy to make. With just a couple of substitutions—egg whites for whole eggs, low-fat milk and yogurt for whole milk—the fat content comes tumbling down.

8 SERVINGS

- ½ cup dried sour cherries
- ½ cup very hot water
- 1 tablespoon plus 1 teaspoon unsalted butter
- ½ cup plus 1 tablespoon granulated sugar
- ⅓ cup whole blanched almonds
- ¼ cup plus 2 tablespoons flour
- ¼ teaspoon salt
- 1 large egg
- 3 large egg whites
- ¾ cup 1-percent milk
- ½ cup plain whole-milk yogurt
- 1 teaspoon vanilla extract
- 1½ pounds nectarines (about 4), halved, pitted, and cut into ½-inch wedges
- ¼ cup light-brown sugar
- ¼ teaspoon cinnamon
- 2 teaspoons confectioners' sugar

1. In a small bowl, soak the dried cherries in the hot water for 20 minutes. Drain the cherries and set aside.

2. Heat the oven to 400°. Coat a 10-inch glass or ceramic pie pan with the 1 teaspoon butter and sprinkle with 1 tablespoon of the granulated sugar. In a food processor, grind the almonds with the flour until the nuts are fine. Transfer to a medium bowl and stir in the salt. In another medium bowl, whisk the whole egg and egg whites until frothy. Stir in the milk, yogurt, the remaining ½ cup granulated sugar, and the vanilla. Gradually whisk the yogurt mixture into the almond flour until smooth. Let the batter sit for 10 minutes.

3. Meanwhile, melt the remaining 1 tablespoon butter in a large nonstick frying pan over moderately high heat. Add the nectarine wedges; cook, stirring, for 2 minutes. Stir in the drained sour cherries. Cook over moderate heat until the nectarines begin to exude juice, about 2 minutes. Stir in the light-brown sugar and the cinnamon. Cook, stirring occasionally, until the juices thicken and coat the fruit, 2 to 3 minutes.

4. Pour half of the batter into the prepared baking dish. Spoon the fruit over the

PER SERVING: CALORIES 251 kcal   TOTAL FAT 6.8 gm   SATURATED FAT 2 gm
CARBOHYDRATE 44 gm   PROTEIN 6 gm   CHOLESTEROL 34 mg

batter in an even layer and cover with the remaining batter. Bake the *clafoutis* until the batter puffs up and a knife stuck in the center comes out clean, about 45 minutes. Let cool for 20 minutes. Sift the confectioners' sugar over the *clafoutis* and serve warm.

—Ann Chantal Altman

Variations

• In place of the nectarines, use peaches or sweet plums, such as red plums.
• In place of the dried sour cherries, use chopped dried apricots.
• Use a different kind of nut, such as pecans, instead of the almonds.

PLUM COBBLER

There's just a bit of butter in the biscuit topping for this pleasing plum dessert.
Part-skim ricotta cheese and low-fat milk help hold the dough together.

8 SERVINGS

¾ cup flour

¾ cup sugar

1 teaspoon baking powder

Pinch salt

¼ cup cold part-skim ricotta

2 tablespoons cold 1-percent milk

3 tablespoons cold unsalted butter

2 drops almond extract

1 tablespoon corn syrup

2 tablespoons water

3 pounds red plums, halved, pitted, and cut into ¾-inch wedges

1. In a food processor, combine the flour, ¼ cup of the sugar, the baking powder, and the salt. Process for 10 seconds. Add the ricotta, milk, 2 tablespoons of the butter, and the almond extract and pulse until the dough just begins to come together in a ball. Pat the dough into a 5-inch disk, wrap well, and refrigerate for at least 1 hour.

2. In a heavy 10-inch ovenproof frying pan, combine the remaining ½ cup sugar with the corn syrup and water. Cook over high heat, without stirring, until the sugar mixture turns a deep brown caramel color, about 6 minutes. Add the remaining tablespoon of butter and the plums. Stir gently; the caramel may harden but it will melt again. Cook, stirring occasionally, until the plums are coated with caramel and their juices are syrupy, about 8 minutes.

3. Pour the plum mixture into a strainer set over a medium bowl. Let cool for 10 minutes. Return the syrup to the pan and cook over high heat until thickened, about 2 minutes.

4. Heat the oven to 375°. On a lightly floured surface, roll or pat the dough into a 10-inch round. Put the plums in the syrup in the pan, spreading them out evenly. Drape the dough carefully on top of the plums, tucking in the edges; cut six small vents in the dough. Or you can drop spoonfuls of the dough on top of the plums and spread them together. Don't worry about making this homey dessert look perfect.

5. Bake the cobbler until the topping is lightly browned, about 30 minutes. Let cool for 15 minutes.

—ANN CHANTAL ALTMAN

PER SERVING: CALORIES 261 kcal   TOTAL FAT 6 gm   SATURATED FAT 3 gm
CARBOHYDRATE 51 gm   PROTEIN 3.5 gm   CHOLESTEROL 14 mg

MIXED-BERRY SHORTCAKE

Buttermilk-biscuit wedges are split and filled with fresh berries and then topped with low-fat frozen yogurt for a scrumptious version of this classic. The berries get a flavor boost from grated orange zest and orange liqueur.

4 SERVINGS

1½   pints mixed berries, such as raspberries, blueberries, and strawberries, halved

4   tablespoons plus 1 teaspoon sugar

1   tablespoon orange liqueur, such as Grand Marnier

½   teaspoon grated orange zest

1   cup flour

1½   teaspoons baking powder

¼   teaspoon baking soda

Pinch salt

2   tablespoons cold vegetable shortening

½   cup low-fat buttermilk

1   egg white, beaten with 1 teaspoon water to mix

1   cup nonfat vanilla frozen yogurt (optional)

1. In a medium bowl, combine the berries, 2 tablespoons of the sugar, the orange liqueur, and the orange zest. Refrigerate for about 2 hours.

2. Heat the oven to 425°. Lightly coat a baking sheet with vegetable-oil cooking spray. In a large bowl, whisk together the flour, 2 tablespoons of the sugar, the baking powder, baking soda, and salt. Cut or rub in the shortening until the mixture is the texture of coarse meal. Using a fork, stir in the buttermilk to make a soft dough.

3. Put the dough on the prepared baking sheet and pat it into a 6-inch disk, about ½ inch thick. Lightly brush the dough with the egg-white mixture and sprinkle with the remaining 1 teaspoon sugar. Cut the dough into quarters. Bake the wedges until golden and cooked through, about 15 minutes. Transfer to a rack and let cool for 5 minutes.

4. Split each shortcake in half horizontally. Put the bottoms on four dessert plates. Top with the berry mixture and cover with the shortcake tops. Serve with the frozen yogurt, if using.

—GEORGIA CHAN DOWNARD

PER SERVING: CALORIES 351 kcal   TOTAL FAT 7.6 gm   SATURATED FAT 1.7 gm   CARBOHYDRATE 63 gm   PROTEIN 7 gm   CHOLESTEROL 1.9 mg

OATMEAL WEDGES WITH WINTER-FRUIT COMPOTE

Made with rolled oats and toasted almonds, these cookie wedges are thin, crumbly, buttery, and delicious. Spread the thick dried-fruit compote on top for a casual dessert or a healthy snack.

12 SERVINGS

  1 cup quick-cooking rolled oats

  ¼ cup sliced almonds

  10 dried apricots, minced

  10 pitted prunes, minced

  3 large dried figs, preferably Calimyrna, stemmed and minced

  1¼ cups unsweetened apple juice

  ½ cup flour

  3 tablespoons unsalted butter, at room temperature

  1 teaspoon cinnamon

  ½ teaspoon baking soda

  Pinch salt

  3 tablespoons molasses

  1 teaspoon vanilla extract

1. Heat the oven to 400°. Toast the oats and the almonds in the oven on separate baking sheets until golden, about 7 minutes. Let cool.

2. In a flameproof baking dish, bring the apricots, prunes, figs, and apple juice to a boil over high heat. Reduce the heat to low and simmer for 5 minutes. Transfer the saucepan to the oven and bake, stirring occasionally, until most of the liquid has evaporated, about 30 minutes. Let cool. Reduce the oven temperature to 350°.

3. In a medium bowl, combine the flour with the butter, cinnamon, baking soda, and salt. Add the oats and stir until the butter is evenly distributed. Add the molasses and vanilla and stir to make a dough.

4. Lightly coat a 10-inch springform pan with vegetable-oil cooking spray and line with parchment paper. Press the oatmeal dough into the bottom of the pan to a ¼-inch thickness. Bake until light brown, about 15 minutes. Let cool slightly and then remove the side of the pan. Invert the pastry onto a plate and peel off the paper. Cut into twelve wedges.

5. Spoon the compote into a bowl and sprinkle with the almonds. Serve with the oatmeal wedges.

—BOB CHAMBERS

PER SERVING: CALORIES 153 kcal   TOTAL FAT 4.6 gm   SATURATED FAT 2 gm
CARBOHYDRATE 26 gm   PROTEIN 3 gm   CHOLESTEROL 8 mg

Frozen Raspberry Yogurt with Chocolate Meringues

Whipped up from egg whites and sugar alone, meringues are light, luscious, and fat-free. Flavored with cocoa, they become the perfect finishing touch for frozen raspberry yogurt. The recipe makes more than enough, so you'll have leftovers to enjoy. These will keep for up to a week in an airtight container.

4 SERVINGS

- 2 large egg whites, at room temperature
- 1 cup plus 4½ tablespoons granulated sugar
- ¼ cup confectioners' sugar
- 1 tablespoon plus ¾ teaspoon unsweetened cocoa powder
- 2 pints raspberries, plus extra for garnish
- 2 cups plain low-fat yogurt

1. Heat the oven to 225°. Line a baking sheet with parchment paper. In a large bowl, using an electric mixer, beat the egg whites on medium speed until frothy, 2 to 3 minutes. Gradually add 1½ tablespoons of the granulated sugar and beat for 1 minute. On high speed, beat in 3 more tablespoons of the granulated sugar. Continue beating the egg whites until stiff, about 2 minutes.

2. Sift the confectioners' sugar with the cocoa powder into a medium bowl. Gently fold the cocoa mixture into the egg whites just until incorporated. Transfer the meringue to a pastry bag fitted with a large plain or star tip and pipe onto the prepared baking sheet two dozen 2½-inch-long swirls about 1 inch apart.

3. Bake the meringues in the middle of the oven until dry, about 1¼ hours. Turn off the heat but leave in the oven for 10 minutes. Let cool on the baking sheet and then remove from the paper.

4. In a blender or food processor, puree the raspberries with the remaining 1 cup granulated sugar. Strain the puree through a sieve, pressing the fruit to get all the juice.

5. Put a 1-quart container in the freezer to chill. In a medium bowl, whisk the raspberry puree into the yogurt. Pour the mixture into an ice-cream maker and freeze according to the manufacturer's instructions. Transfer the yogurt to the chilled container and freeze until hard enough to scoop, about 30 minutes. Scoop the yogurt into four glasses and top each with a meringue and extra raspberries.

—HUBERT KELLER

PER SERVING: CALORIES 421 kcal   TOTAL FAT 2.7 gm   SATURATED FAT 1.3 gm
CARBOHYDRATE 94.7 gm   PROTEIN 9 gm   CHOLESTEROL 6.8 mg

PINEAPPLE ORANGE SORBET

Strawberries, as specified here, make a tasty topping for this sunny sorbet, but you might also try blueberries or raspberries.

4 SERVINGS

¼ cup sugar

½ cup water

3 ½-inch strips orange zest

1 small pineapple (about 3 pounds), peeled, cored, and cut into ½-inch pieces

1 cup orange juice (from about 2 oranges)

1½ tablespoons lime juice

1 cup sliced strawberries

2 teaspoons orange liqueur, such as Grand Marnier

1. In a small saucepan, combine the sugar, water, and orange zest and bring to a boil over high heat. Reduce the heat and simmer until the syrup reduces to ¼ cup, about 5 minutes. Let cool.

2. In a food processor, puree two thirds of the pineapple pieces. Transfer the puree to a medium glass or stainless-steel bowl and stir in the orange juice and lime juice. Strain the sugar syrup into the puree and stir.

3. Put a 1-quart container in the freezer to chill. Pour the pineapple mixture into an ice-cream maker and freeze according to the manufacturer's instructions. Transfer the sorbet to the chilled container and store in the freezer until hard enough to scoop, about 30 minutes.

4. Meanwhile, in a medium bowl, combine the remaining pineapple, the strawberries, and the liqueur and let sit for at least 30 minutes. Scoop the sorbet into four bowls and top with the fruit.

—MARTHA ROSE SHULMAN

PER SERVING: CALORIES 82 kcal TOTAL FAT .4 gm SATURATED FAT 0 gm
CARBOHYDRATE 20 gm PROTEIN 1 gm CHOLESTEROL 0 mg

WATERMELON GRANITA

This simple, refreshing dessert is a case where beauty is more than skin deep. The redder the watermelon, the prettier *and* tastier the granita will be.

4 SERVINGS

¼ cup sugar

¼ cup water

3½ cups 1-inch watermelon cubes, seeds removed (from about 3 pounds watermelon), plus 4 thin wedges watermelon, for serving

4 teaspoons lime juice

1. In a small saucepan, combine the sugar and water. Bring to a boil over high heat, stirring until the sugar dissolves. Transfer the syrup to a blender or food processor. Add half of the watermelon cubes and the lime juice and pulse until smooth. Add the remaining watermelon cubes and blend until smooth.

2. Strain the puree, pressing the fruit to get all the liquid. Transfer the liquid to a 9-inch square or round pan and freeze, stirring every 30 minutes with a fork, until frozen, about 4 hours. Spoon into four glasses or bowls and top with the melon wedges.

—JIM ACKARD

PER SERVING: CALORIES 98 kcal TOTAL FAT .7 gm SATURATED FAT 0 gm CARBOHYDRATE 24 gm PROTEIN 1 gm CHOLESTEROL 0 mg

GINGER-BEER GRANITA

Jamaican ginger beer gives this super-simple granita a delicious spicy flavor. Look for it at specialty-food stores and some supermarkets.

4 SERVINGS

2 12-ounce bottles Jamaican ginger beer

4 lime wedges, for serving

1. Pour the ginger beer into a 9-inch square or round stainless-steel pan. Freeze until solid, at least 6 hours, or up to 1 day.

2. Using a large spoon, scrape the frozen ginger beer to form a granular ice. Spoon the granita into four bowls and top with the lime wedges.

—MARCIA KIESEL

PER SERVING: CALORIES 62 kcal TOTAL FAT 0 gm SATURATED FAT 0 gm CARBOHYDRATE 16 gm PROTEIN 0 gm CHOLESTEROL 0 mg

Ginger and Honeydew Sorbet

For big taste with no fat, spike sweet fruit with a strong flavoring like ginger. This sorbet gets a double dose, with grated fresh ginger in the frozen mixture and crystallized ginger sprinkled on top.

4 SERVINGS

- 1 small honeydew melon, seeded, peeled, and cut into 1-inch chunks (about 1 quart)
- 1 tablespoon grated fresh ginger
- 1 tablespoon light corn syrup
- 1 tablespoon lime juice
- 1 teaspoon superfine sugar
- 1 cup strawberries, hulled
- 1 mango, peeled and cut into slices
- 2 tablespoons thin-sliced crystallized ginger

> ## Variation
>
> In place of the honeydew melon, use cantaloupe. You'll need about one and a half cantaloupes to get one quart of chunks.

1. In a food processor, puree the melon. Add the fresh ginger, corn syrup, lime juice, and sugar; process until smooth. Pour into a bowl, cover, and refrigerate for about 1 hour.

2. Put a 1-quart container in the freezer to chill. Pour the honeydew mixture into an ice-cream maker and freeze according to the manufacturer's instructions. Transfer the sorbet to the chilled container. Store in the freezer until hard enough to scoop, about 30 minutes. Spoon into four bowls and top with the strawberries and mango. Sprinkle with the crystallized ginger.

—Sally Schneider

PER SERVING: CALORIES 152 kcal **TOTAL FAT** .5 gm **SATURATED FAT** 0 gm **CARBOHYDRATE** 39 gm **PROTEIN** 1 gm **CHOLESTEROL** 0 mg

STRAWBERRY SORBET

A dash of liqueur—whether raspberry (framboise) or black currant (crème de cassis)—is what makes this sorbet special. Of course, the strawberries are important, too; for the very best flavor, use local summer berries.

4 SERVINGS

½ cup sugar

⅓ cup water

2 pints strawberries, hulled, or
    4 cups thawed frozen strawberries

2 tablespoons lemon juice

1 tablespoon framboise or crème de cassis

1. In a small saucepan, bring the sugar and water to a boil over high heat, stirring until the sugar dissolves. Let cool.

2. In a food processor, puree the strawberries. With the machine running, pour in the sugar syrup, lemon juice, and framboise. Pour the strawberry mixture into a 9-inch square or round stainless-steel cake pan and freeze until solid, about 4 hours.

3. Break the sorbet into chunks with a fork and puree in the food processor until smooth. Serve at once.

—JEAN GALTON

VARIATIONS

• Instead of just strawberries, use a mixture of berries, such as blueberries, raspberries, and strawberries.

• Use a good orange liqueur, such as Grand Marnier, in place of the framboise or crème de cassis.

PER SERVING: CALORIES 157 kcal TOTAL FAT .6 gm SATURATED FAT .1 gm
CARBOHYDRATE 38 gm PROTEIN 1 gm CHOLESTEROL 0 mg

chapter *11*

CAKES, COOKIES
& OTHER DESSERTS

Banana Madeleines, page 305, and Mocha Mousse, page 309

ORANGE ANGEL FOOD CAKE WITH WARM BERRY COMPOTE

Angel food cake is an old favorite that has next to no fat. Keep it in the low-fat category by topping it with a tasty compote of fresh strawberries and blueberries in orange liqueur.

12 SERVINGS

1⅓ cups cake flour

2 cups sugar

2 cups egg whites (from about 16 large eggs), at room temperature

½ teaspoon cream of tartar

⅛ teaspoon salt

1 tablespoon grated orange zest

¼ teaspoon vanilla extract

Warm Berry Compote, next page

1. Heat the oven to 375°. Sift the flour with ¾ cup of the sugar three times into a large bowl.

2. In another large bowl, using an electric mixer, beat the egg whites at medium speed until foamy, about 1 minute. Add the cream of tartar and the salt and beat for 1 minute more. Increase the speed to high and gradually beat in the remaining 1¼ cups sugar until the egg whites hold stiff peaks when the beaters are lifted. Do not overbeat.

3. Scrape the egg whites onto the flour mixture and gently fold them in until just incorporated. Fold in the orange zest and vanilla. Gently pour the batter into a 10-inch tube pan with a removable bottom and smooth the top. Run a knife through the center of the batter to remove any large air bubbles.

4. Bake the cake in the middle of the oven until the top springs back when touched lightly and a toothpick inserted in the center comes out clean, about 45 minutes. Do not open the oven door during the first 35 minutes.

5. Invert the pan over a narrow-necked bottle and let cool completely. Run a thin sharp knife between the cake and the side and center of the pan and remove the side. Invert the cake onto a plate and remove the bottom of the pan in the same way as the side. Slice and serve topped with the Warm Berry Compote.

—CHARLES WILEY

PER SERVING: CALORIES 235 kcal TOTAL FAT .4 gm SATURATED FAT 0 gm CARBOHYDRATE 52 gm PROTEIN 6 gm CHOLESTEROL 0 mg

WARM BERRY COMPOTE

12 SERVINGS

1 teaspoon cornstarch

¼ cup water

2 pints strawberries, quartered

2 tablespoons orange liqueur, such as Grand Marnier

1 tablespoon sugar

1 pint blueberries

In a small bowl, dissolve the cornstarch in the water. Heat a medium stainless-steel frying pan over moderate heat. Add the strawberries, liqueur, and sugar. Stir in the cornstarch mixture and cook until slightly thickened, about 2 minutes. Stir in the blueberries. Serve warm.

TIPS FOR BEATING EGG WHITES

• Don't use eggs straight from the refrigerator. When they're at room temperature the whites are more elastic and expand better to incorporate more air.

• Even a small amount of fat on the bowl or beaters can reduce the volume of the beaten whites, so make sure all your equipment is scrupulously clean.

• Cream of tartar helps stabilize beaten egg whites, increasing their ability to incorporate air. Add it as soon as the eggs become foamy.

• Do not overbeat the whites. They should look shiny, not dry. Overbeating decreases the elasticity and weakens the structure of the egg whites so that when you fold them into another mixture, the trapped air bubbles pop easily. With fewer air bubbles, the whites won't be so light as they could be.

LEMON CLOUD CAKE WITH POPPY SEEDS

Luscious, lemony, and lighter than air, this heavenly creation is essentially an angel food cake flavored with lemon zest and poppy seeds. If you like, decorate each serving with a sprig of mint.

8 SERVINGS

- 1 cup granulated sugar
- ½ cup plus 1 tablespoon confectioners' sugar
- ⅔ cup flour
- ⅓ cup cornstarch
- 1¾ cups egg whites (from about 12 large eggs), at room temperature
- ¼ teaspoon salt
- 1 tablespoon grated lemon zest
- 1 tablespoon poppy seeds
- 1 teaspoon vanilla extract

1. Heat the oven to 350°. Sift the granulated sugar and the ½ cup confectioners' sugar twice into a medium bowl. Sift the flour with the cornstarch into another medium bowl. Add ½ cup of the sifted sugar mixture to the flour mixture and sift again.

2. In a large bowl, beat the egg whites at high speed with the salt until they hold stiff peaks when the beaters are lifted. Add the remaining sugar mixture, 2 tablespoons at a time, beating for 30 seconds after each addition. Beat until the egg whites are glossy, about 1 minute longer.

3. Gently fold the lemon zest, poppy seeds, and vanilla into the egg whites. Add one third of the flour mixture; fold gently until just combined. Fold in the remaining flour mixture ⅓ cup at a time, just until smooth. Gently pour the batter into a 10-inch tube pan with a removable bottom. Run a knife through the center of the batter to remove any large air bubbles.

4. Bake the cake in the middle of the oven until the top springs back when touched lightly, 35 to 40 minutes; do not open the oven during the first 35 minutes.

5. Invert the pan over a narrow-necked bottle and let cool completely. Run a thin sharp knife between the cake and the side and center of the pan and remove the side. Invert the cake onto a plate and remove the bottom of the pan in the same way as the side. Put the tablespoon of confectioners' sugar in a small sieve and dust over the cake.

—BOB CHAMBERS

PER SERVING: CALORIES 217 kcal TOTAL FAT .6 gm SATURATED FAT .1 gm
CARBOHYDRATE 46 gm PROTEIN 7 gm CHOLESTEROL 0 mg

RASPBERRY JELLY ROLL

Have your cake and eat it, too! There's no risk of excess fat with this jelly roll; the recipe uses less than half the usual number of egg yolks, but the cake remains moist and light. For the best texture, serve it on the day it's made.

12 SERVINGS

½   cup granulated sugar

2   large eggs

2   large egg whites

1   tablespoon vanilla extract

1   cup flour

⅔   cup seedless raspberry jam

1½   tablespoons confectioners' sugar

1. Heat the oven to 425°. Coat a 13-by-9½-inch jelly-roll pan with vegetable-oil cooking spray and line it with parchment or wax paper. Lightly spray the paper.

2. In a large stainless-steel bowl, combine the granulated sugar, eggs, and egg whites. Set the bowl over a medium saucepan filled with 1 inch of simmering water. Using an electric mixer, beat the eggs at high speed until tripled in volume, about 5 minutes. Beat in the vanilla. Remove from the heat.

3. Sift the flour over the egg mixture and gently fold it in until just combined. Do not overmix. Scrape the batter into the prepared pan and spread it evenly into the corners. Bake until golden brown, about 6 minutes.

4. Meanwhile, in a small bowl, stir the jam until smooth. Put a 15-inch-long sheet of parchment or wax paper on a work surface and evenly sift 1 tablespoon of the confectioners' sugar over it. As soon as the cake is done, turn it out onto the parchment. Peel off the paper.

5. Working quickly, trim ¼ inch from each side of the cake. Cut a lengthwise slit almost all of the way through the cake ½ inch in from the long edge nearest you (this will facilitate rolling the cake into a neat, tight log). Spread the jam in an even layer on the cake. Hold the paper in both hands and, starting from the side with the slit, push against the cake with your knuckles and roll it up. Wrap the parchment around the cake and let sit for 30 minutes, seam-side down. Remove the paper from the cake and sift the remaining 1½ teaspoons confectioners' sugar over the top.

—DIANA STURGIS

PER SERVING: CALORIES 148 kcal   TOTAL FAT 1 gm   SATURATED FAT .3 gm
CARBOHYDRATE 32 gm   PROTEIN 3 gm   CHOLESTEROL 35 mg

BANANA CAKE

Replacing fat with a fruit puree is a great way to slim down baked goods. This recipe is a fine example: Besides giving the cake an intense flavor and chunky texture, mashed bananas replace almost half of the usual amount of butter.

9 SERVINGS

- 4 tablespoons unsalted butter, at room temperature
- ¾ cup light-brown sugar
- ½ cup 1-percent buttermilk
- 2 large eggs
- 2 large egg whites
- 2 large overripe bananas, plus 1 large ripe banana
- 2 teaspoons grated lemon zest
- 2 tablespoons lemon juice
- 2 cups cake flour
- 1½ teaspoons baking soda
- 1 tablespoon granulated sugar

1. Heat the oven to 350°. Coat an 8-by-12-inch baking dish with vegetable-oil cooking spray. In a large bowl, using an electric mixer, beat the butter until fluffy, about 5 minutes. Beat in the brown sugar and buttermilk. Beat in the eggs and egg whites.

2. In a large measuring cup, mash the overripe bananas with a fork; you should have 1 cup of puree. Halve the ripe banana lengthwise and then cut it crosswise into ½-inch chunks; add it to the puree. Stir in the lemon zest and juice. Fold the banana mixture into the batter and then fold in the flour and baking soda just until no white streaks remain. Scrape the batter into the prepared baking dish and smooth the top. Sprinkle with the granulated sugar.

3. Bake the cake until the top is golden and springs back when touched lightly in the center, about 30 minutes. Let cool in the pan on a rack before cutting.

—DIANA STURGIS

TEST-KITCHEN TIP

The riper the fruit, the more intense the flavor. Whether you're making cakes, cookies, tarts, or sorbets, choose the ripest fruit available; you may even want to wait a few days to allow it to get really ripe. In some cases, as in this recipe, overripe fruit will give you the tastiest results.

PER SERVING: CALORIES 276 kcal TOTAL FAT 6.9 gm SATURATED FAT 3.8 gm CARBOHYDRATE 49 gm PROTEIN 5 gm CHOLESTEROL 62 mg

GINGER CAKE

For a decorative pattern on top of this spicy cake, put a store-bought or homemade doily on the cooled cake. Sift confectioners' sugar over it and then carefully lift off the doily.

8 SERVINGS

2 tablespoons plus ½ teaspoon unsalted butter, at room temperature

1½ cups sifted flour

2 tablespoons granulated sugar

1 large egg

6 tablespoons honey

2 tablespoons grated fresh ginger

1 teaspoon grated lemon zest

1 teaspoon vanilla extract

1 teaspoon baking soda

¾ teaspoon baking powder

½ teaspoon ground coriander

½ teaspoon cinnamon

⅛ teaspoon ground cardamom

Pinch salt

2 tablespoons minced crystallized ginger

½ cup buttermilk

Confectioners' sugar (optional)

1. Heat the oven to 350°. Coat the bottom and side of an 8-inch round cake pan with the ½ teaspoon butter. Sprinkle the bottom and side of the pan with 1 teaspoon of the flour.

2. In a large bowl, using an electric mixer, beat the remaining 2 tablespoons butter with the granulated sugar until fluffy. Beat in the egg, honey, fresh ginger, lemon zest, and vanilla. The mixture will look slightly curdled.

3. In a medium bowl, whisk the remaining flour with the baking soda and powder, coriander, cinnamon, cardamom, and salt. In a small bowl, toss the crystallized ginger with ½ teaspoon of the dry ingredients.

4. Add the dry ingredients and the buttermilk to the butter mixture alternately in three batches, beginning with the dry ingredients and beating well after each addition. Stir in the crystallized ginger. Scrape the batter into the prepared pan.

5. Bake the cake in the middle of the oven until a toothpick inserted in the center comes out clean, about 35 minutes. Let cool in the pan on a rack for about 10 minutes. Run a knife between the cake and the sides of the pan; invert the cake onto the rack, flip it over, and let cool. Sift the confectioners' sugar over the top, if using.

—SALLY SCHNEIDER

PER SERVING: CALORIES 201 kcal TOTAL FAT 4 gm SATURATED FAT 2 gm CARBOHYDRATE 38 gm PROTEIN 3.6 gm CHOLESTEROL 36 gm

FRESH-FRUIT CAKE

FOOD & WINE Test-Kitchen Director, Diana Sturgis, got her inspiration for this recipe from two sources: her mother-in-law's German apple kuchen and a fruit-cake from acclaimed pastry chef Jim Dodge. The cake is ideal for autumn, when apples and pears are at their peak.

10 SERVINGS

1 cup plus 2 tablespoons sugar, plus more for coating the pan

1 large, firm ripe pear, peeled, cored, and cut into ¾-inch dice

1 large tart apple, such as Granny Smith, peeled, cored, and cut into ¾-inch dice

6 ounces fresh or thawed frozen cranberries (about 1½ cups)

2 teaspoons cinnamon

5 tablespoons unsalted butter, at room temperature

⅓ cup 1-percent buttermilk

2 large eggs

2 large egg whites

2 cups cake flour

2 teaspoons baking powder

1. Heat the oven to 350°. Coat a 9-by-2-inch round cake pan with vegetable-oil cooking spray. Line the bottom of the pan with parchment or wax paper. Lightly spray the paper; sprinkle the side of the pan with sugar.

2. In a medium bowl, combine the diced pear and apple with the cranberries. Add 1 tablespoon of the sugar and the cinnamon and toss to coat.

3. In a large bowl, using an electric mixer, beat the butter until fluffy, about 5 minutes. Gradually beat in 1 cup of the sugar and the buttermilk. Beat in the eggs and egg whites until combined and then beat in the flour and the baking powder. Stir in the fruit. Scrape the batter into the prepared pan and sprinkle the top with the remaining 1 tablespoon sugar.

4. Bake the cake in the middle of the oven until golden and a toothpick inserted in the center comes out clean, about 1 hour. Let the cake cool in the pan on a rack for 20 minutes. Invert the cake onto a plate and peel off the paper. Invert the cake onto another plate and let cool.

—DIANA STURGIS

PER SERVING: CALORIES 276 kcal   TOTAL FAT 7.3 gm   SATURATED FAT 4 gm
CARBOHYDRATE 50 gm   PROTEIN 4.3 gm   CHOLESTEROL 59 mg

HONEY ORANGE CAKE

Olive oil may seem an odd ingredient for a cake recipe, but in fact it's often found in Italian baked goods, and here it adds a pleasing flavor that complements the honey and orange. Don't break out the extra-virgin oil; plain virgin and pure olive oil work just fine.

8 SERVINGS

- ⅔ cup orange juice (from about 2 oranges)
- ½ cup honey
- ¼ cup olive oil
- 2 large eggs, separated, at room temperature
- 2 teaspoons grated orange zest
- 1⅔ cups flour
- ½ cup granulated sugar
- 1 teaspoon baking powder
- ½ teaspoon salt
- 1 tablespoon confectioners' sugar

1. Heat the oven to 350°. Coat the bottom and side of an 8-inch springform pan with vegetable-oil cooking spray. Lightly flour the bottom and side of the pan.

2. In a medium bowl, combine the orange juice with the honey, oil, egg yolks, and orange zest. In a large bowl, whisk the flour with the granulated sugar, baking powder, and salt. In another medium bowl, beat the egg whites until they hold soft peaks when the beaters are lifted.

3. Stir the orange-juice mixture into the dry ingredients until just blended. Gently fold in the egg whites until just combined. Scrape the batter into the prepared pan and smooth the top.

4. Bake the cake in the middle of the oven until a toothpick inserted in the center comes out clean, about 50 minutes. Let the cake cool in the pan on a rack for 10 minutes. Carefully remove the side of the springform pan and allow the cake to cool completely. Remove the bottom of the pan and sift the confectioners' sugar over the top of the cake.

—MICHELE SCICOLONE

MAKE IT AHEAD

The cake will keep, well wrapped in an airtight container, for up to two days.

PER SERVING: **CALORIES** 308 kcal **TOTAL FAT** 8.8 gm **SATURATED FAT** 1.7 gm **CARBOHYDRATE** 54 gm **PROTEIN** 5 gm **CHOLESTEROL** 54 mg

COFFEE ALMOND LAYER CAKE WITH RASPBERRIES

Nuts are high in fat but, used judiciously, can be part of a low-fat diet. Here, ground almonds are folded into a fat-free meringue base for a springy, sweet, and nutty cake that's finished with low-fat buttercream (made with yogurt cheese) and fresh raspberries.

10 SERVINGS

¾ cup unblanched whole almonds

1¼ cups plus 2 tablespoons granulated sugar

2 tablespoons cornstarch

8 large egg whites, at room temperature

½ teaspoon cream of tartar, plus a pinch

¼ cup water

1 teaspoon light corn syrup

1 teaspoon unflavored gelatin

4 teaspoons instant espresso, dissolved in 2 tablespoons boiling water

½ teaspoon vanilla extract

½ cup Whole-Milk Yogurt Cheese, page 266

2 pints raspberries

2 tablespoons confectioners' sugar

1. Heat the oven to 350°. Coat a 15-by-10-inch jelly-roll pan with vegetable-oil cooking spray. Line the jelly-roll pan with parchment or wax paper, and then lightly spray the paper.

2. Put the almonds on a baking sheet and toast until golden brown, about 8 minutes. Let cool completely and then put the nuts in a food processor. Add ¾ cup of the granulated sugar and the cornstarch and process until the nuts are ground fine.

3. In a large bowl, beat six of the egg whites with the ½ teaspoon cream of tartar at high speed until they hold soft peaks when the beaters are lifted. Gradually beat in 2 tablespoons of the granulated sugar until the egg whites hold stiff peaks when the beaters are lifted, about 1 minute. Gently fold in the almond mixture. Scrape the batter into the prepared pan and spread it evenly. Bake the cake until the top is lightly browned and springs back slightly when touched, about 30 minutes. Cool on a rack for 2 minutes.

4. Invert the cake onto a work surface. Carefully peel off the paper. If the paper sticks to the cake, lightly brush the paper with a moistened pastry brush; wait 1 minute and try again. Trim ½ inch from each edge

PER SERVING: CALORIES 239 kcal TOTAL FAT 6.8 gm SATURATED FAT 1.2 gm CARBOHYDRATE 40 gm PROTEIN 6 gm CHOLESTEROL 5 gm

of the cake and cut crosswise into four 3½-by-9-inch rectangles.

5. In a small saucepan, combine the remaining ½ cup granulated sugar, the water, and the corn syrup and bring to a boil, stirring to dissolve the sugar. Brush the inside of the pan with a pastry brush dipped in water to dissolve any sugar crystals and continue to boil, without stirring, until the sugar reaches the soft-ball stage, about 4 minutes. A candy thermometer should register 240°. Remove from the heat.

6. Meanwhile, in a large bowl, using an electric mixer, beat the remaining 2 egg whites at high speed with the pinch of cream of tartar until the whites hold soft peaks when the beaters are lifted. In a small bowl, sprinkle the gelatin over the dissolved coffee. Let stand for 1 minute. Set the bowl over a small pan of simmering water and stir to melt the gelatin. Remove the bowl from the heat and beat the mixture into the egg whites.

7. Bring the sugar syrup back to a boil. Gradually beat the hot syrup into the egg whites and continue beating until the meringue is cool, about 5 minutes. Stir the vanilla into the yogurt cheese and then fold the yogurt mixture into the coffee mixture.

8. Put a cake layer on a rectangular plate and spread with a quarter of the coffee buttercream. Arrange ¾ cup of the raspberries on top. Cover with a second cake layer

and lightly press down. Repeat with the remaining coffee buttercream, raspberries, and cake layers, ending with a layer of buttercream. Arrange the remaining berries around the base of the cake. Sprinkle the cake with the confectioners' sugar just before serving.

—Ann Chantal Altman

MAKE IT AHEAD

Assemble the cake in advance and keep it refrigerated for up to eight hours. Let it stand at room temperature for about ten minutes before serving.

LOW-FAT TIP

Use vegetable-oil cooking spray to "butter" cake pans before baking. Most of the time, all you'll need is a light spray. For cakes that tend to stick, spray the pans, line them with parchment or wax paper, and then spray the paper. The first spray keeps the paper in place. Cooking spray doesn't work for all cakes, however; some, like the Ginger Cake on page 289, really do need a buttered and floured pan.

WARM SPICED CHOCOLATE SOUFFLÉ CAKE

Many soufflé cakes are made in a cake pan. This one's baked in a soufflé dish and served warm. It will sink as it begins to cool. You can cut it in wedges.

4 SERVINGS

2 ounces bittersweet chocolate, chopped

¼ cup plain nonfat yogurt

1 tablespoon vanilla extract

2 teaspoons instant espresso powder, dissolved in 1 tablespoon hot water

½ teaspoon paprika

½ teaspoon cinnamon

1 tablespoon unsweetened cocoa powder

1 tablespoon flour

4 large eggs, at room temperature

½ cup granulated sugar

½ teaspoon confectioners' sugar

1. Heat the oven to 375°. Coat a 1-quart soufflé dish with vegetable-oil cooking spray. In a small bowl set over a pan of simmering water, stir the chocolate until melted. Alternatively, melt the chocolate in a microwave oven. Let cool to tepid.

2. In a small bowl, combine the yogurt, vanilla, espresso, paprika, and cinnamon. In another small bowl, whisk together the cocoa and flour.

3. In a large bowl, beat the egg whites at medium speed until they hold soft peaks when the beaters are lifted. Gradually beat in the granulated sugar at high speed until the whites hold stiff peaks when the beaters are lifted. Gently fold in the melted chocolate. Fold in the yogurt mixture and then the dry ingredients just until combined. Scrape the batter into the prepared dish and smooth the top.

4. Bake the soufflé cake in the lower third of the oven until the top is just set and moist crumbs cling to a toothpick inserted in the center, about 30 minutes. Dust with the confectioners' sugar and serve warm.

—VINCENT GUERITHAULT

PER SERVING: CALORIES 218 kcal TOTAL FAT 5 gm SATURATED FAT 2.8 gm CARBOHYDRATE 38 gm PROTEIN 6 gm CHOLESTEROL .3 mg

CHOCOLATE CAKE

There's just a smidgen of high-fat chocolate in this quick-to-make cake. The big chocolate taste comes from unsweetened cocoa powder, which is far lower in fat. It's mixed into the batter and also sprinkled over the top of the finished cake, along with a little confectioners' sugar.

10 SERVINGS

1¼	cups cake flour
½	cup unsweetened cocoa powder, plus 1 teaspoon for dusting
1	teaspoon baking soda
1½	cups granulated sugar
½	ounce unsweetened chocolate, chopped
½	cup water
4	tablespoons unsalted butter
1	cup 1.5-percent buttermilk
1	tablespoon vanilla extract
2	large eggs
1	large egg white
1	teaspoon confectioners' sugar

1. Heat the oven to 350°. Coat a 9-by-2-inch round cake pan with vegetable-oil cooking spray and line the bottom with parchment or wax paper. In a bowl, whisk the cake flour with the ½ cup cocoa and the baking soda.

2. In a small saucepan, combine the granulated sugar, chocolate, and water. Cook over moderate heat, stirring occasionally, until the sugar dissolves and the chocolate melts, about 4 minutes. Transfer the mixture to a large bowl and stir in the butter until melted. Stir in the buttermilk and vanilla. Beat in the eggs and egg white and then the flour mixture until combined. Scrape the batter into the prepared pan.

3. Bake the cake in the middle of the oven until a toothpick inserted in the center comes out clean, about 35 minutes. Let cool in the pan on a rack for 20 minutes. Invert the cake onto a plate and let cool completely. Just before serving, sift the confectioners' sugar and the 1 teaspoon cocoa over the top.

—DIANA STURGIS

PER SERVING: CALORIES 258 kcal **TOTAL FAT** 7.8 gm **SATURATED FAT** 4.3 gm **CARBOHYDRATE** 45 gm **PROTEIN** 4.5 gm **CHOLESTEROL** 56 mg

COCOA CUPCAKES WITH WHITE FROSTING

These devil's-food cupcakes taste rich, but they're actually light as can be. Applesauce fools the palate into believing the cupcakes contain more butter than they really do. Each cake is topped with a little cloud of fluffy, fat-free frosting made from egg whites, sugar, and vanilla.

MAKES 12 CUPCAKES

1¼ cups flour

¼ cup plus 1 tablespoon unsweetened cocoa powder

1 teaspoon baking soda

½ teaspoon baking powder

Pinch salt

⅓ cup light-brown sugar

2 tablespoons unsalted butter, at room temperature

1 large egg

½ cup light corn syrup

¼ cup unsweetened applesauce

1 teaspoon vanilla extract

1 cup 1.5-percent buttermilk

White Frosting, next page

1. Heat the oven to 350°. Line a 12-cup muffin tin with paper liners. In a medium bowl, whisk the flour with the unsweetened cocoa powder, baking soda, baking powder, and salt.

2. In a large bowl, using an electric mixer, beat the brown sugar and butter until fluffy, about 5 minutes. Beat in the egg. Add the corn syrup, applesauce, and vanilla and beat well. Add the dry ingredients and the buttermilk alternately in three batches, beginning and ending with the dry ingredients, mixing until just combined.

3. Spoon the batter into the muffin cups. Bake the cupcakes in the middle of the oven until a toothpick inserted in the center of a cupcake comes out clean, about 18 minutes. Remove the cupcakes from the pan and let cool on a rack. Spread the frosting on the cupcakes.

—BOB CHAMBERS

MAKE IT AHEAD

The unfrosted cupcakes can be kept in an airtight container for up to two days. They also freeze well.

PER CUPCAKE: CALORIES 216 kcal TOTAL FAT 3 gm SATURATED FAT 1.7 gm CARBOHYDRATE 46 gm PROTEIN 3 gm CHOLESTEROL 24 mg

WHITE FROSTING

MAKES ABOUT 2 CUPS

1 cup sugar
½ cup water
1 large egg white
 Pinch salt
½ teaspoon vanilla extract

1. In a small heavy saucepan, combine the sugar and water. Bring to a boil, stirring to dissolve the sugar. Brush the inside of the pan with a pastry brush dipped in water to dissolve any sugar crystals and continue to boil, without stirring, until the sugar reaches the soft-ball stage. A candy thermometer should register 240°. Remove from the heat.

2. Meanwhile, using an electric mixer, beat the egg white with the salt until foamy. While beating, add the hot syrup in a thin steady stream. Add the vanilla and beat until the frosting is thick and cool, about 5 minutes.

VARIATIONS

• When making the cupcake batter, add a teaspoon of cinnamon to the dry ingredients.
• Sprinkle a teaspoon of unsweetened cocoa powder on top of the frosted cupcakes.
• Flavor the frosting with a different extract, such as almond, mint, or orange, in place of the vanilla. Start with a few drops and add more to taste.
• Add a quarter teaspoon of grated orange or lemon zest to the frosting along with the vanilla.

FUDGY CHOCOLATE BROWNIES

Like Cocoa Brownies, page 300, these chocolate squares use fruit puree and unsweetened cocoa powder to keep them low in fat. A single ounce of semi-sweet chocolate adds very little fat to the total, but it does make the brownies extra-fudgy and chewy.

MAKES 16 BROWNIES

- 3 tablespoons unsalted butter, at room temperature
- ¾ cup sifted flour
- ⅓ cup unsweetened cocoa powder
- ½ teaspoon baking powder
- ½ teaspoon salt
- 1 cup dark-brown sugar
- 1 large egg
- 1 teaspoon vanilla extract
- 1 ounce semisweet chocolate, melted
- ¼ cup unsweetened applesauce

1. Heat the oven to 350°. Coat a 9-inch square baking pan with ½ teaspoon of the butter. In a medium bowl, whisk the flour with the cocoa, baking powder, and salt.

2. In a large bowl, using an electric mixer, beat the brown sugar and the remaining butter for about 2 minutes. Add the egg and vanilla and beat until fluffy, about 5 minutes. Beat in the chocolate and then the applesauce.

3. Beat in the dry ingredients on low speed just until combined. Scrape the batter into the prepared pan and spread it evenly.

4. Bake the brownies in the middle of the oven until a toothpick inserted in the center comes out clean, about 25 minutes. Let cool in the pan on a rack. Cut the brownies into 16 squares.

—DIANA STURGIS

MAKE IT AHEAD

You can make the brownies up to two days in advance and keep them in an airtight container.

PER BROWNIE: CALORIES 113 kcal   TOTAL FAT 3.6 gm   SATURATED FAT 2 gm   CARBOHYDRATE 20 gm   PROTEIN 1.3 gm   CHOLESTEROL 20 mg

Cocoa Brownies

What's pumpkin puree doing in a recipe for brownies? Standing in for some of the fat. You won't taste the pumpkin, just dark, rich, delicious chocolate. At less than half a gram of saturated fat per brownie and less than half an hour of cooking time, these treats are the perfect way to satisfy a chocolate craving.

MAKES 48 BROWNIES

4 large eggs, at room temperature

2 cups sugar

1 cup canned unsweetened pumpkin puree

1 tablespoon vanilla extract

1 tablespoon vegetable oil

1¼ cups unsweetened cocoa powder

1 cup flour

1. Heat the oven to 350°. Coat a 9-by-13-inch baking pan with vegetable-oil cooking spray.

2. In a large bowl, using an electric mixer, beat the eggs and sugar until pale yellow, about 5 minutes. Beat in the pumpkin, vanilla, and oil.

3. Sift the cocoa and flour over the egg mixture and gently fold in until just combined. Scrape the batter into the prepared pan and spread it evenly.

4. Bake the brownies in the middle of the oven until they feel set when touched lightly in the center, about 25 minutes. Let cool in the pan on a rack and then cut into 48 squares.

—Diana Sturgis

Make It Ahead

You can bake the brownies up to two days ahead and keep them in an airtight container. You can also freeze them.

PER BROWNIE: CALORIES 59 kcal TOTAL FAT 1 gm SATURATED FAT .4 gm CARBOHYDRATE 12 gm PROTEIN 1 gm CHOLESTEROL 18 mg

DOUBLE-DATE BARS

Two helpings of dates—chopped dates and date puree—are twice as nice as one. The double dose makes these bars particularly chewy and satisfying. The walnuts provide an additional flavor bonus, although there are not enough of them to push the bars beyond the boundaries of a low-fat treat.

MAKES 20 BARS

1   cup flour
½   teaspoon baking powder
½   teaspoon baking soda
½   teaspoon cinnamon
½   teaspoon salt
     Pinch grated nutmeg
1½ cups pitted dates (about ½ pound)
⅓   cup water
⅔   cup dark-brown sugar
1   large egg
2   tablespoons vegetable oil
1   teaspoon vanilla extract
¼   cup chopped walnuts

1. Heat the oven to 350°. Coat an 8-inch square baking pan with vegetable-oil cooking spray. In a medium bowl, whisk together the flour, baking powder, baking soda, cinnamon, salt, and nutmeg.

2. Chop ¼ cup of the dates coarse. Put the remaining dates and the water in a food processor and puree. Add the brown sugar, egg, oil, and vanilla. Process until blended.

Fold the date-puree mixture into the dry ingredients. Fold in the chopped dates and nuts. Scrape the batter into the prepared pan and spread it evenly.

3. Bake the bars in the middle of the oven until the top springs back when touched lightly, about 25 minutes. Let cool in the pan on a rack. Cut into 20 bars.

—MICHELE SCICOLONE

MAKE IT AHEAD

You can store the bars in an airtight container for up to two days or freeze them for up to one month.

PER BAR: CALORIES 108 kcal   TOTAL FAT 2.7 gm   SATURATED FAT .3 gm
CARBOHYDRATE 21 gm   PROTEIN 1.3 gm   CHOLESTEROL 11 mg

CHEWY CHERRY FRUIT BARS

A dense whole-wheat cake wrapped around a chewy dried-cherry and orange center makes a delectable bar shaped something like a Fig Newton. Throw a few in a bag for a breakfast on the run or a between-meal snack.

MAKES 32 BARS

- 1 cup dried sour cherries (about 4 ounces), chopped coarse
- 1 3-inch strip orange zest
- ½ cup unsweetened apple juice
- 1½ tablespoons honey
- 1 cup all-purpose flour
- ½ cup whole-wheat flour
- 1 teaspoon baking powder
- ¼ teaspoon cinnamon
- ¼ teaspoon salt
- ⅔ cup light-brown sugar
- 2 tablespoons unsalted butter, at room temperature
- 1 large egg
- 2 tablespoons unsweetened applesauce
- 1 large egg white, beaten to mix
- 1 tablespoon coarse sugar (optional)

1. Heat the oven to 325°. In a small stainless-steel ovenproof saucepan, combine the dried cherries, orange zest, apple juice, and honey. Bring to a boil over moderate heat. Reduce the heat and simmer, stirring, for 5 minutes. Put the pan in the oven and bake, stirring occasionally, until the liquid is absorbed, about 30 minutes. Let cool slightly. Put the mixture in a food processor and chop fine. Refrigerate until cold.

2. In a medium bowl, whisk together the all-purpose and whole-wheat flours, baking powder, cinnamon, and salt. In a large bowl, using an electric mixer, beat the brown sugar and the butter until combined. Add the egg and beat on high speed until fluffy, about 5 minutes. Add the applesauce and the dry ingredients and beat on low speed until combined; the dough will be sticky. Divide the dough in half and place each on a piece of plastic. Shape each half into a 12-inch log, wrap in plastic, and refrigerate until firm.

3. Heat the oven to 350°. Unwrap one log and put it between two pieces of plastic wrap. Roll out the dough to a 13-by-5-inch rectangle, about ¼ inch thick. Remove the top piece of plastic. Spoon half of the cherry filling in a 1-inch-thick stripe lengthwise down the center of the dough, leaving a ½-inch border at each end. Using the plastic wrap, fold over one side of the dough to partially cover the filling. Pat down slightly. Lift the other side to cover the filling,

PER BAR: CALORIES 63 kcal   TOTAL FAT .9 gm   SATURATED FAT .5 gm   CARBOHYDRATE 13 gm   PROTEIN 1 gm   CHOLESTEROL 8.9 mg

slightly overlapping the first side, and pinch the edges together to seal. Tuck in the ends. Repeat the process with the remaining dough and filling.

4. Roll the filled logs onto a baking sheet, seam-side down, leaving about 3 inches between them. Flatten into 12-by-2-inch logs. Brush each with the egg white and sprinkle with the coarse sugar, if using.

5. Bake the logs until they are golden brown and the tops begin to crack, about 20 minutes. Let cool on the baking sheet for 5 minutes. Remove and, using a serrated knife, cut off the ends and slice each log into sixteen bars.

—GRACE PARISI

MAKE IT AHEAD

The fruit bars will keep in an airtight container for up to one week.

VARIATIONS

• Use chopped dried apricots in place of the dried sour cherries.
• Use orange juice instead of apple.
• Add an eighth of a teaspoon of ground cloves to the dry ingredients.

BANANA MADELEINES

Bananas and pecans update these delightful little French shell-shaped tea cakes immortalized by Marcel Proust. Be sure to use overripe bananas for a pronounced banana flavor, and to serve the madeleines on the day you make them.

MAKES 2 DOZEN MADELEINES

⅓ cup pecan halves

¾ cup cake flour

1 teaspoon baking powder

½ teaspoon salt

1 cup confectioners' sugar

2 overripe medium bananas

4 large egg whites

1 tablespoon unsalted butter, melted

1 teaspoon vanilla extract

1. Heat the oven to 375°. Coat two 12-mold madeleine pans with vegetable-oil cooking spray and dust lightly with flour.

2. Put the pecans on a baking sheet and toast in the oven until golden, about 8 minutes. Let cool and then chop fine.

3. In a medium bowl, whisk the flour with the baking powder, salt, and all but 2 tablespoons of the confectioners' sugar.

4. In a food processor, puree the bananas. Add the egg whites, butter, and vanilla and process until blended. Add the dry ingredients and pulse just until combined. Scrape the batter into a large bowl and gently fold in the pecans.

5. Divide the mixture among the madeleine molds. Bake until puffed and browned, about 12 minutes. Unmold onto a rack and let cool. Dust with the remaining 2 tablespoons confectioners' sugar.

—ANN CHANTAL ALTMAN

VARIATION

Can't find madeleine pans? Use nonstick mini-muffin pans instead.

PER MADELEINE: CALORIES 59 kcal TOTAL FAT 1.6 gm SATURATED FAT .4 gm
CARBOHYDRATE 10 gm PROTEIN 1 gm CHOLESTEROL 1.2 mg

CHOCOLATE CHERRY BISCOTTI

Though they seem light, biscotti can be fairly rich. These chocolatey, crisp, dried-cherry-studded cookies, however, cut fat to the bone. They're delicious as is or dunked in espresso.

MAKES ABOUT 3 DOZEN

1⅓ cups flour

½ cup unsweetened cocoa powder

1 teaspoon baking powder

½ teaspoon salt

2 large eggs

1 cup sugar

1 teaspoon vanilla extract

1 cup dried sour cherries (about 4 ounces)

1. Heat the oven to 350°. Line a large baking sheet with aluminum foil and lightly coat it with vegetable-oil cooking spray.

2. In a medium bowl, whisk the flour with the cocoa, baking powder, and salt. In a large bowl, using an electric mixer, beat the eggs, sugar, and vanilla until pale yellow and thick, about 3 minutes. Stir in the dry ingredients and then the cherries; the dough will be stiff. Divide the dough in half. With damp hands, shape each half into a smooth 12-inch log on the prepared baking sheet.

3. Bake the logs in the middle of the oven until the center springs back when touched lightly, about 30 minutes.

4. Carefully transfer the logs to a cutting board. Using a serrated knife and a gentle sawing motion, cut the logs into ¾-inch slices. Stand the biscotti on a baking sheet ½ inch apart. Bake until crisp, about 10 minutes. Transfer to a rack to cool.

—MICHELE SCICOLONE

MAKE IT AHEAD

You can keep the biscotti in an airtight container for a week or even longer.

PER COOKIE: CALORIES 60 kcal TOTAL FAT .7 gm SATURATED FAT .3 gm CARBOHYDRATE 13 gm PROTEIN 1 gm CHOLESTEROL 13 mg

HAZELNUT WAFERS

Use the best French nut oil you can find for these delectable rolled cookies. Our favorite: Huile de Noisettes from J. LeBlanc, imported by Select Vineyards, Ltd., and available at specialty-food stores. You can make the cookie dough in no time, but don't forget that it needs to chill for at least an hour before baking.

MAKES 32 COOKIES

- 1 cup plus 1½ tablespoons flour
- 3 tablespoons sugar
- ½ teaspoon baking powder
- ¼ teaspoon salt
- 2 tablespoons plus 2½ teaspoons hazelnut or walnut oil
- 2 tablespoons sour cream
- 1 teaspoon vanilla extract
- 1 teaspoon confectioners' sugar

1. In a medium bowl, whisk 1 cup of the flour with the sugar, baking powder, and salt. In a small bowl, whisk together the oil, sour cream, and vanilla. Pour the mixture into the dry ingredients. Using a fork, stir until thoroughly combined.

2. Lightly knead the dough in the bowl several times until smooth. Put on a work surface. Pat the dough into a 5- to 6-inch square. Wrap in plastic and refrigerate for at least 1 hour, or overnight.

3. Heat the oven to 350°. Let the dough sit for 10 minutes at room temperature. Cut the dough into quarters. Sprinkle a work surface with about 1 teaspoon of the remaining flour. Roll out one quarter of the dough to a 5-inch square, straightening the edges by pressing a metal spatula against the sides. Using a large knife, cut the square into quarters and then cut each quarter in half to make eight rectangles.

4. Using a metal spatula, transfer the rectangles to a large ungreased baking sheet, putting them about 1 inch apart. Repeat with the remaining flour and dough.

5. Bake the cookies in the middle of the oven until golden, about 15 minutes. Immediately transfer the cookies to a rack to cool. Just before serving, sprinkle the cookies with the confectioners' sugar.

—SALLY SCHNEIDER

PER COOKIE: CALORIES 55 kcal TOTAL FAT 4 gm SATURATED FAT .4 gm CARBOHYDRATE 4.6 gm PROTEIN .5 gm CHOLESTEROL .4 mg

COFFEE CRÈME CARAMEL

The soothing French classic crème caramel comes alive with a jolt of java. Using evaporated skim milk and a mixture of whole eggs and egg whites keeps the fat content under control. Topped with sparkling caramel sauce and garnished with shards of crisp caramel, the dessert is as lovely as it is low-fat.

4 SERVINGS

1	cup sugar
2	large eggs
3	large egg whites
1	12-ounce can evaporated skim milk
¼	cup coarse-ground coffee beans
¼	cup heavy cream
½	teaspoon vanilla extract

1. Heat the oven to 350°. Line a baking sheet with parchment paper.

2. In a small heavy saucepan, cook ⅔ cup of the sugar over moderately low heat, without stirring, until it melts and turns a rich tea-like brown, about 12 minutes. Immediately remove from the heat. Working quickly and carefully, pour about 1 tablespoon of the caramel into each of four 6-ounce ramekins. Drizzle the remaining caramel over the parchment and let stand at room temperature to harden.

3. In a large bowl, whisk together the eggs, the egg whites, and the remaining ⅓ cup sugar. In a small saucepan, warm the evaporated milk and coffee over moderate heat until steaming, about 3 minutes. Let sit for 1 minute. Whisk the hot milk into the egg mixture and then whisk in the cream and vanilla. Strain the custard into a measuring cup or pitcher and skim any foam from the surface.

4. Divide the custard among the ramekins and set them in a baking dish. Pour enough cold water into the dish to reach about three quarters of the way up the side of the ramekins. Transfer the dish to the lower third of the oven; bake until the custard is almost set but still shimmers when the ramekins are touched, about 35 minutes. Let cool in the water bath. The custards will be almost liquid in the center when removed but will continue to cook in the water bath. Refrigerate the crème caramels until cold, at least 2 hours.

5. To serve, dip the bottom of each ramekin in hot water. Run a knife around the side and unmold onto four serving plates. Break the reserved hardened caramel into large pieces and arrange around the custards.

—DIANA STURGIS

PER SERVING: CALORIES 373 kcal   TOTAL FAT 8.2 gm   SATURATED FAT 4.3 gm
CARBOHYDRATE 62 gm   PROTEIN 13 gm   CHOLESTEROL 130 mg

MOCHA MOUSSE

With its seductive chocolate and espresso flavor, this mousse makes an elegant dessert for company. Your guests won't believe that each serving has less than three grams of fat. Banana Madeleines, page 305, make an interesting accompaniment; the mousse is pictured with them on page 304.

8 SERVINGS

- ¼ cup plus 1 tablespoon unsweetened cocoa powder
- 1 tablespoon instant espresso powder
- 1 ¼-ounce envelope unflavored gelatin
- ½ cup plus 2 tablespoons sugar
- 1 cup 1-percent milk
- 2 large egg yolks
- ½ cup *fromage blanc** or nonfat ricotta cheese
- 1 teaspoon vanilla extract
- ¼ cup water
- 1 tablespoon light corn syrup
- 4 large egg whites, at room temperature
- ¼ teaspoon cream of tartar

*Available at specialty-food stores

1. In a small heavy saucepan, whisk the cocoa with the espresso powder, gelatin, and the 2 tablespoons sugar. Whisk in the milk and egg yolks until smooth. Cook over moderate heat, stirring, until the mixture starts to thicken, about 6 minutes. A candy thermometer should register 160°. Strain the chocolate base into a medium bowl set in a bowl of ice water. Whisk until cool and then whisk in the *fromage blanc* and vanilla. Remove from the ice-water bath and let sit, stirring occasionally.

2. Rinse out the saucepan and add the remaining ½ cup sugar, the water, and corn syrup. Bring to a boil, stirring to dissolve the sugar. Brush the inside of the pan with a pastry brush dipped in water to dissolve any sugar crystals and continue to boil, without stirring, until the sugar reaches the soft-ball stage. A candy thermometer should register 240°. Remove from the heat.

3. Meanwhile, in a large bowl, beat the egg whites at high speed with the cream of tartar until they hold soft peaks when the beaters are lifted. While beating, add the hot syrup in a thin, steady stream. Continue beating until cool, about 5 minutes.

4. Whisk the chocolate base until smooth. Stir in one third of the meringue until combined and gently fold in the remaining meringue. Spoon the mousse into four glasses and chill for at least 1 hour.

—ANN CHANTAL ALTMAN

PER SERVING: CALORIES 127 kcal TOTAL FAT 2 gm SATURATED FAT .9 gm
CARBOHYDRATE 22 gm PROTEIN 6.5 gm CHOLESTEROL 55 mg

INDEX

Page numbers in **boldface** indicate photographs.

F

FAT(S). *See also* **Low-fat cooking**
in game, 175
Fava-Bean Succotash with Crisp Phyllo
Rounds, **26**, 27
FENNEL
Roasted Fennel with Olives, **188**, 189
Shrimp and Fennel Risotto, **114**, 115-16
Fermented Black-Bean and Chili Sauce, 34
Feta cheese, variation using, 81
FIGS
Figs in Red-Wine Syrup, 253
Oatmeal Wedges with Winter-Fruit
Compote, 273
Fire-Roasted Corn with Spicy Red-Pepper
Puree, 186
Fireside Pinto-Bean and Chile Stew, 219-20
First courses, 27-35
Fish and seafood, 121-47. *See also specific
kinds*
Five-Lily Chowder, 41
French Toast, Caramelized-Apple, **230**, 231
Fresh-Fruit Cake, 290
Fresh Pears, Kiwis, and Oranges with
Rosemary Syrup, 250
Fresh Tomato Soup with Guacamole,
38, 39
Fried Rice with Asparagus, **208**, 209-10
Fried Rice with Peas and Sun-Dried
Tomatoes, 211-12
Fried Turkey Cutlets with Three-
Mushroom Gravy, 163
Fromage Blanc, 265, 309
Frozen Raspberry Yogurt with
Chocolate Meringues, **274**, 275
Fruit Soup with Champagne, 249
Fudgy Chocolate Brownies, 299

G

Game, fat in, 175
GARLIC
Baked Rice with Chickpeas, 213
Blanched-Garlic Puree, 67
Chicken with Chipotle Chutney and
Grilled Potatoes, **150**, 151-52
Chickpea and Red-Pepper Medley, 194
Fish in a Foil Packet, 125
Garlic Caesar Salad, 66-67
Garlic Mashed Potatoes, 206
Herbed Turkey-Sausage Patties, 232

Lemon-and-Garlic-Roasted Beets, 187
Lentils with Fragrant Rice, 222
Poached Cod with Tomatoes and
Fennel, 130
Potato and Red-Pepper Frittata,
234, 235
Quail and Skewered Vegetables with
Asian Preserved-Prune Sauce, 166-67
Roasted-Tomato Salsa, 17, **18**
Spinach Crostini, 25
Veal and Linguine alla Pizzaiola, 105
Wilted Winter Greens, 196
Gelatina di Frutta, 263
GINGER
Asparagus and Pepper Salad with
Ginger Dressing, **78**, 79
Cilantro Shrimp with Ginger Dipping
Sauce, 141
Fish Wrapped in Rice Paper, **120**,
121-22
Ginger and Honeydew Sorbet, 278
Ginger Cake, **288**, 289
Halibut with Spicy Vegetable
Sauce, 133
Lentils with Fragrant Rice, 222
Pineapple with Ginger Syrup, 255
Shrimp Escabèche with Ginger-
Grilled Pineapple, 31
Steamed Chicken with Chinese
Mushrooms, **156**, 157
Steamed Fish with Ginger and
Scallions, 124
Ginger-Beer Granita, 277
Gingerbread Loaf, 236
Glaze, Pork Medallions with Curry
Honey, 174
Gnocchi, Potato, with Tomato
Prosciutto Sauce, 106-7
Grains. *See specific kinds*
Grapefruit, Vietnamese Cabbage Slaw
with Chicken and, **84**, 85-86
Gravy, Three-Mushroom, 164
GREEN BEANS
Calypso-Bean Soup, **56**, 57-58
Lobster Américaine with Rice and
Haricots Verts, **138**, 139-40
New-Potato and Wax-Bean Salad, 83
GREENS
Swiss-Cheese Crisp with Mixed
Greens, 72
Warm Smoky Greens, 195
Wilted Winter Greens, 196
Grilled Chicken Breasts with
Caramelized-Onion Marmalade, 154
Grilled-Mushroom Salad, **70**, 71
Gritz Cheese Crackers, 14

GRUYÈRE CHEESE
Marie's Potato Gratin, **202**, 203
Swiss-Cheese Crisp with Mixed
Greens, 72
Guacamole, Fresh Tomato Soup with,
38, 39

H

HALIBUT. *See also* **Fish and seafood**
Caribbean Fish Stew with Green
Bananas, 136-37
Cod Steaks with Red-Pepper Sauce, 129
Halibut with Chile Mustard Sauce
and Cilantro Chutney, 134
Halibut with Spicy Vegetable Sauce,
132, 133
Hot-and-Sour Fish Stew, 135
HAM. *See also* **Prosciutto**
Herbed Turkey-Sausage Patties, 232
Potato and Red-Pepper Frittata,
234, 235
Warm Smoky Greens, 195
Hansen's mixed-greens juice, 33
Haricots Verts, Lobster Américaine
with Rice and, **138**, 139-40
HAZELNUTS
Hazelnut Wafers, 307
Pear and Honey Napoleons with
Hazelnuts, **264**, 265-66
Herb-Crusted Chicken with Toasted
Almonds, 159
Herbed Spaetzle, 224
Herbed Turkey-Sausage Patties, 232
HONEY
Citrus-Grilled Chicken with Mesquite
Honey, 153
Ginger Cake, **288**, 289
Honey Orange Cake, 291
Mashed Acorn Squash with Apples, 191
Orange Date Muffins, 238
Peach and Blackberry Crisp, 267
Pear and Honey Napoleons with
Hazelnuts, **264**, 265-66
Pork Medallions with Curry Honey
Glaze, 174
HONEYDEW
Ginger and Honeydew Sorbet, 278
Melon with Mint Lime Syrup and
Jalapeño, 251
Hors d' oeuvres, 13-25
Horseradish Dressing, Salmon and
Potato Salad with, 87
Hot-and-Sour Fish Stew, 135

CONTRIBUTORS

Jim Ackard is executive chef at Reebok Sports Club in New York City.

Jeffrey Alford and **Naomi Duguid**, Toronto-based food writers and photographers, are the authors of *Flatbreads & Flavors* (William Morrow).

Katherine Alford is a food writer and cooking teacher in New York and New Jersey.

Ann Chantal Altman is a chef and food writer. He teaches at Peter Kump's School of Culinary Arts in New York City.

Jean Anderson has written 20 cookbooks, including the award-winning *Food of Portugal* and *Doubleday Cookbook*. She most recently was a co-author of *The Nutrition Bible* (William Morrow).

John Ash is a cooking teacher, author, and culinary director at Fetzer Vineyards. His latest book, *From the Earth to the Table: John Ash's Wine Country Cuisine* (Dutton/Signet), was named cookbook of the year 1996 by the International Association of Culinary Professionals.

Julia Califano is a freelance writer in Hoboken, New Jersey.

Mary Carroll is a syndicated food columnist, recipe developer, and cookbook author. Her books include *The No Cholesterol (No Kidding!) Cookbook* (Rodale) and *The New Gourmet (CCA)*.

Bob Chambers is executive chef at Lâncome-L'Oréal in New York City.

Andrea Chesman is a food writer and cookbook author based in Vermont. She is currently working on *Salad Suppers* (Chapters), due out in the spring of 1997.

Annemarie Colbin is an author and the founder of The Natural Gourmet Cookery School in New York City.

Janet Hazen De Jesus is a California-based food writer and culinary instructor. Recent books include *Red, Hot, and Green* and *Turn It Up* (both from Chronicle).

Georgia Chan Downard, a cookbook author and cooking teacher, is culinary director of the TV Food Network in New York City.

Jean Galton is a cookbook author, food writer, and cooking teacher. Her most recent book is *365 Great Soups & Stews* (HarperCollins).

Sid Goldstein, a food writer and cookbook author, is vice president and director of marketing for Fetzer Vineyards and a co-author of *From the Earth to the Table: John Ash's Wine Country Cuisine* (Dutton/Signet).

Laurie Burrows Grad, a California-based food writer and cookbook author, is currently working on *Light and Easy Entertaining* (Simon & Schuster), due out in the fall of 1997.

Vincent Guerithault is chef/owner of Vincent Guerithault on Camelback in Phoenix, Arizona.

Joyce Jue is a food consultant, cooking teacher, and lecturer on Asian cuisine.

Hubert Keller is chef/owner of Fleur de Lys in San Francisco and author of *The Cuisine of Hubert Keller* (Ten Speed Press).

Matthew Kenney, chef/owner of Matthew's and owner of Mezze, both in New York City, is currently working on a cookbook featuring Mediterranean cuisine.

Marcia Kiesel is associate director of FOOD & WINE's test kitchen and a co-author of *Simple Art of Vietnamese Cooking* (Prentice Hall).

Bharti Kirchner is a cooking teacher and author whose most recent book is *Vegetarian Burgers* (Harper Perennial).

Deborah Krasner, a food writer and kitchen designer, is author of the forthcoming *Common Sense Kitchen Advisor* (HarperCollins).

Eileen Yin-Fei Lo is a cooking teacher and food writer whose most recent book is *The Chinese Way: Healthy Low-Fat Cooking From China's Regions* (Macmillan).

Stephanie Lyness, a food writer and recipe developer based in Guilford, Connecticut, is the author of *Cooking with Steam* (William Morrow).

Charlie Palmer is chef/owner of Aureole in New York City and the author of *Great American Food* (Random House).

Grace Parisi is a recipe tester and developer for FOOD & WINE and author of the upcoming book *Summer Winter Pasta* (Quill, an imprint of William Morrow).

Marge Poore is a cookbook author, cooking teacher, and culinary-tour leader. Her latest book is *The Best Steamer Cookbook Ever* (HarperCollins).

Hans Röckenwagner is chef/owner of Röckenwagner in Santa Monica, California.

Sally Sampson is the author of *Recipes from the Night Kitchen* (Fireside).

Sally Schneider, is a consulting editor for *Saveur* magazine. *The Art of Low-Calorie Cooking* (Stewart, Tabori, and Chang), her most recent book, won a James Beard award.

Michele Scicolone is a food writer, cooking teacher, and cookbook author whose latest book is *A Fresh Taste of Italy* (Broadway Books).

Martha Rose Shulman is a cookbook author, food writer, and cooking teacher. Her most recent book is *Mexican Light* (Bantam).

Diana Sturgis is FOOD & WINE's test-kitchen director.

Allen Susser is chef/owner of Chef Allen's in Miami and the author of *Allen Susser's New World Cuisine and Cookery* (Doubleday).

Marguerite Thomas, author of *Wineries of the Eastern States* and travel editor of *The Wine News*, writes the food and wine pairing column for *Santé* magazine.

Charles Wiley is executive chef of The Boulders and Carefree Resorts and teaches cooking classes in Phoenix.